The Literary Culture
of
France

The Literary Culture of France

Studies in the Essential Character

and Permanent Values

of French Literature

from the Earliest Times to the Present

collected, edited and annotated
by
J. E. G. DIXON

Published by New English Review Press
a subsidiary of World Encounter Institute
PO Box 158397
Nashville, Tennessee 37215
&
27 Old Gloucester Street
London, England, WC1N 3AX

Cover Design by Kendra Adams

ISBN: 978-0-9884778-1-0

First Edition

NEW ENGLISH REVIEW PRESS
newenglishreview.org

Acknowledgements

I owe my thanks of gratitude to a number of people who have helped me materially and in other important ways to realize this book.

First of all I am mindful of my many questioning students over the years who have expressed their appreciation of the insights they have gained into the varied values gleaned from their studies of French Literature, and from whose very questions I learnt much.

I thank Professor Elaine Limbrick, retired, of the University of Victoria, who probably no longer remembers the day when a retired professor from Winnipeg persuaded her to authorize him to convert a long typescript book onto machine-readable form, which he was subsequently able to edit on his newly acquired computer.

Carol J. Harvey, Senior Scholar of the University of Winnipeg, Guy Demerson of the University of Clermont-Ferrand, Hélène Cazes, professor at the University of Victoria, and Frédéric Delouche will, I hope, accept this testimony of my gratitude to them for their written endorsement of this work, in the forms of a Foreword and of reviews. It is too late to thank the late Robert Aulotte again. I recognize the debt I owe to my daughter Jacqueline in the prefatory words of the Index. And finally, but first and all the time, I offer my gratitude and lasting thanks to my beloved wife, Rika, who in this as in all my scholarly and literary and related endeavours, has never wavered in her support and encouragement and love.

France possesses a literature which forms an unbroken and vital unity, and which in its wholeness represents a personality of an incomparable kind.

   E.-R. Curtius

The most imperious duty of man is not to defend his ignorance, his separateness, his complacency—to put it bluntly, his selfishness. It is to fight against evil, and in order to fight against it he must know it. Confined to my study and library, and bound by the demands of my profession—you and me alike—how are we to educate ourselves in the miseries of life? How are we to break down the walls that separate us from our fellow-men? By literature; by the literature of realism.

   Gustave Rudler

When one considers the life of the great thinker and writer whom I call 'French literature', one is struck by the continuity of his effort, the good order of his experiments, the harmony of his history, and the logic of his development.

   And so, round about the year 1548, France resolved to undertake a great work and to devote hundreds of years to the doing of it. What is this work of a whole nation? What is this monument with which French literature is associated? I should answer at once, a portrait of Man.

   French literature has undertaken to depict man as he is, relentlessly: man individual, man social, the inner man and the outer man, man visible and man invisible, man subjective and man objective.

   Georges Duhamel

I consider that the mind would be perverted if it listened to, or were allowed to hear, only one of two voices of the dialogue—a dialogue not between a political right or left, but, much more vital and profound, between secular tradition, submission to recognized authorities, and free thought, the spirit of doubt and examination, which works towards the slow and progressive emancipation of the individual.

   André Gide

This work is dedicated, in the name of Truth and Justice, and of responsible Freedom of Expression, to all people—past, present and future, men, women and children—who with the pen and by their deeds, take up the cause of the never-ending crusade against tyranny, oppression, servitude, bigotry and outrageous coercion.

Contents

Foreword

I

ℐt has long been recognized that from the twelfth century to the present day the literature of France has been immensely rich and varied. Circulated broadly all over Western Europe in the Middle Ages, it is today a world literature of such vitality and prestige that it is virtually inseparable from Western culture as a whole. As Dr J. E. G. Dixon expresses so well, "Literature is the pre-eminent instrument of French culture, and French culture is one of the great pillars in the monument of European civilization." Once the cultural and intellectual centre of Europe, France was the source not only of literary movements, but also of new ideas and fresh attitudes towards life.

The French literature that flourished in the Middle Ages included secular and religious works in both prose and verse; it encompassed works of all genres—epic and lyric poetry, romances, saints' lives and drama. Among these early works, too, a variety of tones and registers is discernible. Alongside the courtly literature enjoyed by royal or aristocratic patrons, the growing urban audience demanded works that corresponded to their society and their ideas, and literary activity in a comic or satirical vein soon flourished. This literary activity that continued through the fifteenth century inspired an impressive critical tradition, opening up a space for debate, and for that free exchange of opinions which further strengthens the growth and development of writers. Criticism leads to a constant reassessment of form and theme, to innovation and renewal.

Such renewal is one hallmark of French literature. The great names of medieval France were followed by those of the Renaissance, men and women who sought a new aesthetic. Looking beyond the boundaries of time and place, all express new ideas and adopt new forms, thereby adding to France's literary inheritance.

However, their unbridled creativity as they introduced new genres into French literature and foreign words and structures into the language would lead to criticism in the following century. The Académie française, founded by Richelieu in 1634, has been arguably the single most important influence on the language of France and its literature. The language was stripped of the archaisms and regionalisms that characterized the Renaissance aesthetic, ensuring greater precision and clarity. Writers sought to express their ideas in a simpler, purer language, and literature was subjected to rules that ensured its coherence of plot in time and space.

For many eighteenth-century Enlightenment thinkers, literature was the servant of a radical scepticism, an important vehicle for attacking intolerance and absolutism, and the corruption of court and Church. The study and discussion of their works spread throughout Europe, introducing concepts and ideas that were to have a profound effect on the development of political thought. Some poets and essayists of the nineteenth century continued this tradition, and demonstrated a commitment to social and political action in their lives and their literature.

No era has known as great an explosion in literary production and criticism as the twentieth century and the first decade of the twenty-first, due in large measure to the development of modern communications. From Symbolism to Existentialism, from the New Novel to Post-Modernism, movement has succeeded movement, often provoking intense critical activity. Such criticism proves essential for correcting the more extreme aspects of a movement (Dadaism comes to mind), or for launching new modes of expression that may ultimately become established. Finally, with the advent of literary theory, a plurality of ways of reading and exploring texts has arisen.

Critics play a role in the growth and development of many facets of the human enterprise, and one cannot overestimate their importance for the vitality of cultural and intellectual renewal. Literary critics in particular are crucial for analysing a work and for detecting the values and ideas that constitute its specificity. In terms of French literature, for example, critics have taught us what is distinctive (seventeenth-century classicism), and what is part of a wider European movement (eighteenth-century romanticism). In short, they have contributed to defining the quintessential spirit of French literature.

The present work reflects Dr Dixon's lifelong interest in both the literature of France and its critical tradition. He is eminently qualified to undertake this work of synthesizing the critics' view of French literature through the ages. Educated at Oxford University and Stanford, he retired from the University of Winnipeg in 1991 after a career of teaching and research, with special interest in Christian humanism and the writings of Rabelais. The breadth of his scholarship is equalled by his intellectual curiosity, a commitment to accuracy and clarity (most evident in the quality of the essays he has translated from the French), and a well-honed ability to discern the values both of works of literature and critiques of those works.

—*Carol J. Harvey*

II

*I*n *The Literary Culture of France*, Dr Jack Dixon brings together seventeen texts about French literature and proposes a dynamic reflection with this anthology. As he states in his Introduction, "the writings have a unity which gives to the whole a special distinction, for their authors address themselves to the analysis of a seminal idea...they seek to answer such questions as: What is French Literature all about? Is there such a thing as an 'essential character' of French Literature?"

Thanks to the careful selection and arrangement of these studies, the book tells not about the history of French Literature, but of the specificity of the French conception of man and the world. In other words, they provide the reader with elements of answers given by French culture to the major questions of freedom, self-knowledge, commitment, politics etc. The project is, in itself, both ambitious and courageous: it relies on a philosophy of essentialism and examines permanent subterranean structures, themes, attitudes in French literature.

The selection of texts perfectly addresses the question formulated here and brings the reader, steadily and progressively, to the perception of the "French exception." As such, this book is a welcome complement to the bibliography: it proposes a bridge between Cultural Studies and Literary Studies. Moreover, thanks to his familiarity with French literature and to his expertise in the field, Dr Dixon manages to convey subtle and complex notions as if the material were simple and easy to grasp.

The six French texts he has translated for this work are lively and faithfully rendered. His notes, scarce, pointed and clear, are welcome for his English-speaking audience. The index is a model of its genre, rich, structured, relevant in all its entries.

One may disagree with the essentialist basis of this anthology but no one can dismiss it: the quality and number of important essays attest to the vitality of this philosophy in French writers, and show a stimulating debate between generations and centuries. This approach may not be trendy in our days of post-modern critique; nevertheless, it is an intellectually legitimate enterprise that Dr Dixon gives us.

This work is impressive, solid, sound, and reliable both in its contents and in its presentation. Last, but not least, I want to emphasize the need for this anthology: accessible to English-speaking students and to a larger audience, it demonstrates the diversity of literary and cultural approaches as well as reminds the modern reader of traditional and long-loved theories. Universalism has been demised only in recent decades and this collection of studies also underlines its former strength and grandeur. As a professor of French in an English-speaking University, I would be happy to use this book for studies in culture and civilization.

—*Hélène Cazès*

Carol J. Harvey is Professor Emerita of French at the University of Winnipeg, Canada. She has published books and articles on medieval French poetry, romance and drama, most recently *Medieval French Miracle Plays: Seven Falsely Accused Women* (2011). She has also written extensively on the francophone literature of Western Canada and edited the anthology *Paroles francophones de l'Ouest et du Nord canadiens* (2012).

Hélène Cazès is Professor of French at the University of Victoria, British Columbia. She specializes in Humanism and Cultural Legacies. Her latest publications include the direction of *Variétés bibliographiques* (Renaissance et Réforme, 34, 2), and of two collections of essays on humanism and friendship (*Bonaventura Vulcanius, Works and Networks*, Leiden, Brill, 2010).

Introduction

*T*his book is addressed not only to students and teachers of French literature, but to all English-speaking students and *amateurs* of French culture and civilization, irrespective of their degree of familiarity with the French language.

When studying any subject, it is helpful to get a bird's eye view of it, to gain an idea of its broad historical sweep, its nature, the principles that govern it, and the ends that direct it: to contemplate the pattern and design of a landscape in its wholeness, as well as to dwell on its topographical features.

It is one of the shortcomings of formal education that few attempts are made to explain the relationship between 'subjects' within the framework of human knowledge. The subjects of study of the humanities, and especially of literature, while not dependent on it, is furthered by an acquaintance with other fields of knowledge which throw light on the nature of man and the world in which he lives. And conversely, of course, the study of man in his fourfold relationship, with himself, with others, with Nature, and with his God, as depicted in literature, not only enriches other studies, but in itself affords a depth and a kind of experience which no other kind of writing can give.

Still less, it seems, do our schools and universities give training in that intellectual skill, the acquisition of which enables one to discern relationships between the diverse and apparently unrelated, "the power of perceiving analogies between things which appear to have nothing in common."

In the writings collected here—some of which have not before been available to the English reader, and of which others have been out

17

of print for many years—their authors have, from their attentive study of the whole visible field in space and time, the constellations, and all the major as well as many of the lesser luminaries in the galaxy of French literature, believed they have discerned certain qualities which they have in common and which characterize them as belonging to the literature of France and to the French mind, and to no other.

Man has need—a need intellectual, psychological, and moral—not only of the nation, but of the broader civilization of which it is at once a beneficiary and a benefactor. Literature is the pre-eminent instrument of French culture, and French culture is one of the great pillars in the monument of European civilization.

Reflection on these essays will give the reader a greater insight into the literature of France, and, it is hoped, stimulate in him the desire to go back again to the individual works. For it is the works themselves that count. And the aim of his reading—once he has outgrown the notion of literature as a 'subject'—is enjoyment and wisdom. Of the wisdom to be learned from literature we will not speak. Enjoyment, however will be enhanced, and indeed, perhaps, only fully achieved, when the works are seen in both their immediate and their universal cultural setting.

It has been found difficult to arrange these writings in a completely satisfactory order: probably there is none: with the sole exception of Louis Cazamian's, which forms a natural introduction to the book by virtue of his discussion of the origins of the French people and of the country that is France.

For the rest, it brings together seventeen of the most penetrating writings on French literature by renowned writers and critics of diverse provenance: French, Swiss, Spanish, German and American. Moreover, the writings have a unity which gives to the whole a special distinction, for their authors address themselves to the analysis of a seminal idea. In their essays they seek to answer such questions as: What is French Literature all about? Is there such a thing as an 'essential character' of French Literature? Can any unifying qualities or values be discerned in French Literature, from its beginnings to the present?

The writers believe that they do discern such values and qualities, such a character, in French Literature. Some see the same qualities; a few, different ones. But all have their distinctive contribution to make to this central critical question.

Many of our institutions of higher education tend today to centre on problems of *littérarité*, deconstruction, *intertextualité*, post-modernism, *écriture*, *sémiotisme*, metatextuality, etc. Useful as these methods and theories may be—albeit with strict reservations—they are in relation to literary criticism and philosophy of a piece with much contemporary historical writing, which refuses to see 'lessons to be learnt' from the study of history. The essays presented here deal, on the contrary, directly with what may be called the substance of French Literature. More than that: they go beyond the obvious and demonstrate what there is in French Literature that transcends its 'Frenchness'; what French Literature has contributed to European, indeed to world, culture and civilization; why, in a word, it is a pre-eminent instrument of education in its broadest and noblest sense, namely, what Man is and how he should live.

Of the twelve French writings included here, only six have been available before to the English language reader. Five of those essays I have translated myself; the sixth has been translated by a colleague and friend for this volume; and they appear here for the first time in English. Individually they are as relevant and as timely as on the day when they were first published. Collectively, seldom has the Comtean precept, "The whole is greater than the sum of its parts," been more revealingly appropriate.

*   *   *   *   *

It has been observed that the development of every great people and their nation is determined by the character of a crucial event which acts, as it were, as the midwife of that people's history. The story of the Greek people is often cited in illustration of that phenomenon, the Trojan War and its recounting by Homer being the seminal events which marked their indelible stamp, for good and ill, upon the Greeks.

If historical beginnings may be defined as the moment at which a people who later rise to greatness first awake to a consciousness of themselves as a distinctive people, this law of national evolution may be applied with equal cogency to France and the French.

If we look at the earliest moments of the historical awareness of the French and their literature, we find a comparable event. *The Chanson de Roland* may not enjoy the same exalted stature in world literature as the *Iliad*, but it and the battle at Roncesvalles as surely embody ideas, values, qualities and themes which have persisted throughout the course of French history, and which lie at the foundations of its civilization.

We will consider, first, the ideas and values which are incarnated in the leading actors of the heroic action, and then examine the principal literary qualities and themes which its unknown author enshrines in his work.

The action of the poem centres on the withdrawal of the French army into France from Spain, following an agreement between Charlemagne and the Saracen king; the appointing of the rearguard to protect the French army's withdrawal; the selection of the commander of the rearguard; the betrayal by the Saracen king through the treason of a Frenchman; the battle, and the heroic death of the rearguard and its leaders.

Today one hears frequently the glib phrase: Everything is relative. It was not the case at the dawn of French civilization. There was one absolute: it was God, and service to God. Close to it was service to the emperor or king, who was God's appointed secular ruler over men's affairs. Then came service to one's lord. This three-sided relationship determined one's place in the immutable hierarchy of things. Correspondingly, any betrayal of duty, any attempt to transgress the bonds that tied the individual to others, threatened the entire order and was visited with commensurate punishment. The individual was both weak and wilful, and needed the company of others, as well as firm external discipline, to direct his energies and to control excessive expressions of his selfness.

The treason of Ganelon the Frenchman is a far more heinous crime, and more severely judged, than the treachery of the Saracen king. First, treachery was expected of Saracens, who were not Christians. Second, Ganelon betrayed his own people, to whom he was tied by a sacred bond and solemn oath. This was also at a moment in history when Frenchmen were beginning to feel their distinctiveness and their nationhood. It is, and always has been, one of the most profoundly felt, because one of the most universal, human values in the human breast.

God, king, nation: all were more important than the individual. Yet individuality, selfhood, was a fact of human nature, a perverse fact, of course, and a force whose assertiveness caused no end of trouble.

In the *Chanson de Roland*, these two individuals, Ganelon and Roland, are singled out for special attention. They are depicted as equals. Yet Roland is favoured by Charlemagne. In the council of war, it is Ganelon who nominates Roland to be the commander of the rearguard. What only the listeners of this recited poem know is that the Saracens have bought Ganelon with a pouch of gold for this act, which is designed by the enemy as the means of getting rid of their most redoubtable foe, and of recovering lost territory.

Roland, for his part, when his rearguard army is attacked and he realises the betrayal and treachery, will not heed his friend's, Oliver's, exhortation to sound his horn and recall Charles's army. It would be the act of a coward, and quite unworthy of the chivalrous Roland, whose valorous exploits—in the service of Christianity and his emperor—have earned him universal renown.

In the example of these two individuals, who, in this one and only instance, put their own advantage or reputation above the common interest, we are meant to see the sometimes tragic and disastrous consequences which flow from them.

Ganelon is jealous of Roland, both because of his superior valour and of his being a favourite of the king's. It needs only a bag of gold, as an additional fillip, to tilt the balance.

Roland is guilty of the sin of pride. Despite Ganelon's treason, he could have saved himself, his friends, and his army if he had heeded Oliver's advice. But he brought about his own ruin, and with it that of thousands of good men. The *nemesis* attendant on *hubris* is, of course, a lesson straight out of the Greek tragic experience. And in the Christian experience, pride occupies the first place in the catalogue of mortal sins. From the Greeks, the lesson came down through the Romans and became a Christian precept, and penetrated the Middle Ages.

Not only does French literature become, at its very birth, a moral literature, and hence a powerful instrument of education; it is also a psychological literature. For in these two cases we see an attempt on the part of the poet to penetrate the mind of two of his characters and explain the motives which led them astray.

In all of this we see yet another dimension of the human experience, and which is to be one of the two main pillars of the edifice that became French civilization. It is freedom.

Man, as an intellectual and above all as a moral being, is a free agent. He is endowed with the rational power to distinguish between different possible courses of action, and the moral faculty to decide on the one as opposed to the others. But: "The paths of error are many, the path of right doing is one."

The often secret, inner life of men and women, and its visible manifestations in customs and in individual patterns or phenomena of behaviour, are permanent features of French literature. When they express themselves in sordid or base ways, they come to be known as 'realism', for which French literature was to become notorious—particularly, let us add, beyond France's own borders. This realism reached its culmination in the 19th century novel. But realism in French literature is nothing other than the unflinching honesty to see and to depict things as they are. It is particularly noteworthy to see what Gustave Rudler has to say on this topic.

It is strange that critics, especially foreign critics, should be so keen to pick up on this character of French writing, and fail to see its other, opposite, side.

We have seen it already, this other side, in the values and acts of Roland and his peers. It is called 'idealism'. No man can live a life worthy to be called human if he is not guided constantly by ideas and values that transcend his own individual significance. Whenever French writers portray the worst side of human behaviour, and the disastrous consequences which inevitably ensue—and the higher the sinner stands in the social order, the worse the disasters that befall the nation and people—they do not fail also to suggest its antidote, the values and conduct that will bring their boon to the common weal.

Don Fernand, in *Le Cid*, is a wise and virtuous ruler, like King Hamlet, and as a result his people prosper. Theseus is a derelict king—as is Claudius—and their people suffer for their sins and crimes.

French realism and idealism are, in fact, two facets of the truth about man's nature. There are few nobler callings than that of witness to truth, than the search for the truth about man.

Throughout the Middle Ages the Greek philosopher who was held up as an oracle was Aristotle. It was from Aristotle that this notion of man's nature came directly to them. They knew well enough that "Evil has many shapes, good but one."

It is in the representation of all the possible manifestations of good and evil that the philosopher, and the French writer, confront a paradox—a paradox which they do not sweep under the rug. It is that, in order to know good it is necessary to know evil—in order to resist it. This, surely, is the other moral justification of realism: one life is too short to encompass more than a small part of the spectrum of experience. In literature we experience the lives of others, and learn from them.

The question then arises: How does the author make his discoveries about man and his nature? The answer is, in simplified terms: He first creates them; he places a number of men and women together in a social setting; then he removes himself and observes them. That is the vision that Roland had of his God. He is a remote figure who does not, unlike the Greek gods, intervene to sway the action one way or the other. Man is on his own. The same is true of the reader of this poem. He sometimes wonders who, or where, the author is. But he is nowhere to be found. The author does not intrude himself into the actions. For if he did his creations would not be free agents.

This capacity of the author to detach himself from his creations is a remarkable intellectual and moral achievement, all the more since he is mightily interested in the outcome and sympathetic to the fate of his virtuous characters. Of course, he has his action mapped out in advance; but the temptation to interject an occasional opinion, to divert, albeit ever so slightly, the action of a personage out of his character, in a word, to influence the dénouement, is resisted even more strongly when his hero resists the temptation to sin.

Five hundred years later we meet these attributes united in one man. The poetry of François Villon, imbued as it is with Christian fervour, is a testament to the reality of good and evil. Like Roland, he is passionately concerned about his salvation. But whereas Roland is an aristocrat who 'fights the good fight' and is assured of salvation, Villon is a plebeian, he is a bad lad who has frequently been at odds with the authorities, and is far from assured of salvation. In his last known ballad, composed when he is in prison and awaiting execution in a few hours, he rises to the heroic height of standing outside himself and depicting himself as a cadaver swinging in the wind, with a few other felons, and, with his fellow men in mind, beseeches passers-by to have pity on them and *to avoid their fate.*

French literature aspires to the universal in man and in human experience. That is another way of saying that it seeks to discover the truth about all men, of all nations and all times. Hence the need for the objectivity acquired by detachment from his subject.

It often happens that the final years of a dying civilization produce a brilliant star. Villon was such a star. No doubt, at the time, he was indistinguishable from his surroundings. Only a century later his incandescent light shone like the evening star in the encompassing gloom, before being extinguished. When the light burned bright again, it was once more the light of the human spirit, but it shone with added rays.

Between *Roland* and Villon, France produced an immensely rich and varied literature. We cannot go into the beginnings of lyric poetry, but we must make special mention of a popular tradition of comic and satirical writing which was being created during this period. Apart from the psychological studies of oddities and foibles of human nature—a vein which was to prove inexhaustible—there was a deeper moral focus which discerned and took delight in exposing and ridiculing the pretensions of *authority*. The chief representatives of authority who became the butt of writers' wit were clerics, lawyers and doctors. Why should that be so? Because they promised much and delivered little. Because they waxed prosperous, often at the expense of the poor. Monks and doctors were generally lampooned good-naturedly. (But woe betide the monk or curé who seduced wives whose husbands were absent on Crusade.) Lawyers and usurers, on the other hand, were often savaged, for they set citizens against each other. Relatively benign and indulgent in the beginnings, this critical spirit became increasingly mordant and uncompromising with the centuries, as literature acquired an increasing prestige and writers earned an authority of their own. In some of their noblest works, French writers became the scourge of the entrenched, reactionary political and ecclesiastical authorities, who worked hand in hand, and the champion of the people, their victims.

This spirit was one of the brightest rays of the new light which was the Renaissance. But the critical spirit took upon itself a new target, and one that it would never have dared challenge before. That was *political authority*. We can almost pinpoint the precise moment at which French literature set itself the task of becoming the critic and the conscience of the ruler, and of acting as a beacon to wise statecraft. It was 1532-34, with the appearance of Rabelais's *Pantagruel* and *Gargantua*. Rabelais castigated the abuse of all power and authority, and created many scenes in which he expounded on, and portrayed in action, the difference between good rulers and bad. Indeed, the whole age is filled with treatises entitled *The Education of the Christian Prince* (Erasmus) or something similar. Why? Because they fell so far short of the ideal.

Two new elements in the French historical experience no doubt contributed to the birth of this critical spirit in literature, and to its perfection in Montaigne later in the century.

The first was war. For the first time in 200 years France sent an army beyond her national borders, when Charles VIII laid claim to the throne of Naples in 1494. These Italian wars were to preoccupy the French kings for 60 years. The second half of the century was filled with bloody civil wars. For the next 300 years, France was to unleash an unending series of aggressive wars of conquest and lust against her neighbours—that is, when her sons were not tearing out each others' throats. From this moment on, French writers have been unanimous in condemning war, and the political leadership which inflicts on its people the suffering it causes.

The second element was the discovery of man. The new generation of French thinkers and writers went to school with the Greeks—and with the Gospels. From the Greeks they absorbed the lesson that man was a rational being who lived in a rational world. Men liberated themselves from the stifling embrace of a Church which maintained its hold on its hostages' minds by false threats and falser promises. They began to discover that the mysteries of physical, biological and human phenomena obeyed natural laws, and that these laws revealed themselves readily to minds which had the courage to ask the right questions. This discovery gave them enormous confidence and power. It led to the greater discovery of man's capacity, and need, to think for himself. Pantagruel's advice to Panurge—"Do you not know your own mind? Everything hinges on that."—was revolutionary in its consequences, for good and ill.

The Gospels had been overlaid with the accumulated dross of the commentary of centuries until their teaching had been lost. The 'new men', schooled in Greek, went back to the original teachings of Christ and Paul and the Fathers, and insisted that men and women—and especially their rulers—live by their precepts.

Thus a new image of man was born, a picture very different from the one that had prevailed for many hundreds of years before. But the view of man that is to be discerned in French literature undergoes modification from age to age. Some ingredients of his make-up are constants; others are variables, and fit only their time.

The most persistent constant is man's wilful individuality, hence the need for authority and rules to keep his self-centredness in check. The excesses of the civil wars led to the imposition of rigorous controls by a state become absolutist, whose successive rulers claimed the title of kings ordained by divine right and endowed with the authority to rule by decree.

The literature of the 17th century accordingly avoided the most dangerous religious and political issues—except by oblique analogy, as in the tragedies of Racine—and cultivated the classical tradition in works whose authors, '*les anciens*', sought their inspiration in the models of ancient Greece and Rome, whilst others, '*les modernes*', sought and found rich material in contemporary social issues and individuals' foibles and vices. In so doing they jointly created a wonderfully rich psychological and moral literature. The old king, when he finally died, after having led his people in a series of disastrous wars, left a once great nation defeated, destitute and in despair. So fickle and biased is historical judgement that the reign of Louis XIV was once, and may still be, held up as the apogee of French civilization. What is civilization?

The following century could not have been more different, intellectually and morally, though politically and socially little changed. It became known as the age of reason, the Enlightenment. Its writers and thinkers questioned and challenged every institution, every theory, every principle that underlay the power of those who wielded, and abused, authority. In this regard, it may be seen as a resumption of the Renaissance spirit, following an unfortunate and long drawn-out interlude. It was the age which produced the towering monument of learning, wisdom, and philosophy, that imperishable landmark in the story of true progress, that clarion call of Humanity and the Spirit of Man, the *Encyclopædia*. Never before had people heard such things as were said about, and against: Torture, Tyranny, Slavery, War, Poverty, Despotism, Privilege, Papacy, Predestination. Never before had people heard of, let alone read about: Liberty, Happiness, Rights of Man, Democracy, Peace, Prosperity, Equality, Free Will.

It was heady stuff! No wonder the authorities took fright, and banned it. It was to be the precursor of the noble dissident writings produced during the savagery of leninism and stalinism in the Soviet Union.

But even the most promising and sunlit landscapes seem to suggest a dark cloud lurking beneath the horizon. This age fashioned a new vision of society and of civilization. They also fashioned a new model of man, who would be worthy of it. Their new man was a civilized version of 'the noble savage'—free, good and happy. Idealism is one thing, but it was not rooted in the observable facts of human nature. This was self-delusion.

Something went wrong. The authorities would not bend and France was wracked by revolution. In the aftermath of Napoleon and the final purging of the *ancien régime*, political factions were formed and everyone scrambled for power. The scrambling went on throughout the century and well beyond. At the same time, the common man began to assume a growing importance. His changing status is reflected in the new literature: the novel rose to dominance.

The portrait we have of the common man, bourgeois and worker alike, is not a pleasant one. He is depicted as being obsessively self-centred, and stopping at nothing to achieve his personal, narrow ends. Those ends are always material.

There is more. He is further depicted as being the product of two forces: heredity and, especially, environment. Most of the protagonists are brought to ruin. But whether victors or victims, they all owe their destiny to influences beyond their control. Men and women are no longer free agents.

This 'realist' literature reveals something even more disturbing: its early writers show little compensating moral sense. However, the writers of the second half of the century, whereas still depicting their protagonists as victims of their environment and, even more markedly now, of their upbringing or heredity, redeem their predecessors by restoring to literature an implicit moral judgement of the 'villains' who prosper. We count Flaubert, Maupassant and Zola particularly among these later realists.

The *mot* of Wilde, who himself had the keen moral sense of the humanitarian he was—"There is no such thing as a moral or an immoral book. Books are well written or badly written."—was a signpost to the future; as Zola's essay, *De la moralité dans la littérature*, written a few years earlier, in 1881, was, for the most part, a signpost to the past. (It is interesting to recall that, in that selfsame year, R.L. Stevenson published his essay, *The Morality of the Profession of Letters*.)

Perhaps it was felt necessary to iterate the moral dimension of literature because these critics saw signs of its rejection, or disregard. Perhaps they saw it also in society at large. If they were indeed detecting a change of current flowing in modern life, they could not have expected the cataclysm that was to engulf the whole of France in 1894-95 with the accusation, trial, conviction, degradation and imprisonment of an innocent Army officer for treason. Captain Alfred Dreyfus was a Jew, and a victim of the anti-semitism that was rife in France. Not since the Calas affair had there been such a flagrant case of injustice perpetrated in France. It is to the eternal credit, or even *gloire*, of a prominent French writer, Émile Zola, who took the lead in having the case judicially reopened, and the real criminal exposed, that Dreyfus was eventually, in 1906, exonerated and restored to his full civil and military status.

Zola had acted as the standard-bearer of the highest traditions of the French writer. French literature was not only a realist literature: it was a secular and critical literature as well. These qualities exerted an influence on the mind that led to its emancipation from error, prejudice, superstition and partisanship. It is the first article of the creed of the enlightened person that he stand aside and with the detachment that comes with conscious practice see things as they truly are.

In the last two decades of the century, the traditions that had nurtured the French mind begin to break down. Symptoms of a radical rupture with the past are most readily discerned in music and the fine arts. The cubist canvases of Picasso with their square, segmented bodies, their fractured figures, are universally known if not admired. Stories abounded of paintings being hung upside down and of sculptures being set up on any side except the 'right' one.

Music strikes the listener in strange and unexpected ways. A new composition ends at its première performance and there is a five-second delay before timid and hesitant applause is heard. A Canadian composer, informed by a casual acquaintance that he had been rediscovering *The Messiah*, inquired frostily if he were tone-deaf. When a music-lover, on hearing a very modern string quartet for the first time, complained of its being screechy and tuneless, and received the retort that in its structure it was impeccable, he observed that he had not gone to hear its structure.

When these new creative spirits were pressed to explain why they painted or composed like that, they were apt to reply that that was how the world was. Perhaps they would have been more accurate to have replied that that was how the world appeared to them, how they saw the world.

For there was no longer the disciplined endeavour to see things as they were. Detachment from one's subject was spurned. All that mattered was the expression of their private views, reactions and experience in their contacts with the external world. But it was not the 'personal' investigation of a Montaigne, who, while admittedly exploring the private world of his own mind, came to the discovery, to his surprise, of the universality of his 'human condition'. It was not the 'personal' art of the Romantic poets, who, while giving voice to their profoundest private feelings about life and its woes, attained to the expression of emotions common to all men and women. No: to the modern artist the only reality was subjective reality and only his or her personal view had significance.

Literature was, of course, equally afflicted with this modernism, whose hallmarks were a rejection of rigid forms and the licence to experiment with form, structure, matter and treatment. And experiment they did, even at the expense of alienating or disturbing readers. No longer were they constrained by the need to be understood or 'to please'.

For four centuries, such had indeed been the aim of writers. In the 16th century, the conscious and stated aim of writers was to combine "profit and delight." In the following century Molière wrote: "I sometimes wonder whether the first of all rules is not to entertain." Voltaire, in the 18th century, said much the same thing, in his own way: "All styles are good, except those that bore"—in order, above all, to instruct. This literary philosophy came straight from Horace: "The writer who has managed to blend profit and delight wins everyone's approbation, for he gives his reader pleasure at the same time as he instructs him."

Henceforth, however, the reader would not necessarily be entertained or instructed. He would not necessarily even be able to make out the author's 'meaning'. Criticism was no longer an exercise in appreciation, it became an effort of interpretation. "*Le monde est bleu comme une orange,*" wrote a poet. One reader's interpretation is as good as another's. And all may be 'right'.

Of course, not all writing was hermetic. It may even be fair to say that it was poetry that lent itself most readily to experimentation and novelty. The play-goer and novel-reader would not long put up with writing which constantly demanded prolonged mental wrestling to make something out of it. Perhaps writers made more demands on their readers than they had traditionally; but that was to be no deterrent. Age-old traditions could not be swept away so easily. French literature, a *humanist* literature in the best sense of the term, will always have man and his nature, human society and its destiny, for its focus, no matter what forms it may take. And many writers were as lucid and compelling in their thought and expression as any who had preceded them.

1
The Background

by

Louis Cazamian

From: L. Cazamian: *A History of French Literature* (Oxford: Clarendon Press, 1955), Part I, Chapter 1, "The Background." Reprinted with permission of Oxford University Press.

I. The Elements of French Nationality

*T*he national personality that was to express itself through French literature awoke by degrees and stirred dimly before it grew to full consciousness... An attempt to define the question in terms of race could not be more ill advised. The decisive element in the birth of the French people seems rather, when all is considered, to have been of a psychological nature; it lay in a sense of community that emerged among various groups and an instinctive will to live under one law. In the country that was to be France history shows us a mixture of different stocks. What proportion of the earliest recognizable one—the dark-haired, round-headed type that still crops up in large areas, especially of the centre, the south-east, and south-west—survived under the tidal wave of the Celtic invasions; what relation the Gauls themselves bore to these, to the Belgians, and the Germanic tribes along the Rhine, and whether the Gauls were to any extent permeated and modified, in more than their language and culture, by the Roman conquest, with its implanted colonies, its network of administrators and magistrates; what was exactly the outcome of the Frankish invasions, and how far in their turn, before a fusion was accomplished, the Franks superimposed more than a thin layer of military and political rulers; these, and sundry other issues—like the settling of Burgundians in the east and north and Wisigoths in the south; of Scandinavians not only in Normandy but over the northern half of the country; of Greeks in the south-east, British immigrants in Brittany, Saracens and Moors in the south, Basques in the southwest—are not to be easily and lightly dismissed. The problems remain, even if the main body of contemporary opinion has come round to agree that among all these strains the contribution of the Gauls themselves remained by far the most substantial. But what the Gauls were ethnically, and how related to this or that stock, is still a moot point. A single assurance persists in the mind of the layman: the French as a race are the creation of historical ages; and by the purity of the French blood nothing can be meant but a synthesis, a composite temperament evolved through the centuries of a civilization that found and elaborated itself continuously.

Another physical factor, however, entered largely into the relative unity of that civilization. Deeper even than racial determinations is the influence that no race can long resist, and which is probably the chief origin of race itself: the land. In it lay the genuine substratum of French nationality. Of many conflicting elements it did most to shape the French spirit, and through that French thought and literature. By its slow but unceasing action widely different trends were brought to converge. Nature had laid the cradle of a nation in the gently hollowed-out basin whose centre is Paris. She had not made her wish quite obvious, had not given what was to be France the all-round individuality of island Britain; but two high mountain walls, the Alps and the Pyrenees, and three ocean seaboards did plainly mark five sides of a hexagonal figure, of which only the sixth, to the north-east, rested on a conventional and a disputed basis.

Within this regular, almost geometrical frame the genius of the earth and sky helped a mind to evolve that was also clear and logical. With its situation, its main aspects, and its nicely balanced physical configuration, the land is neither strongly northern nor overwhelmingly southern; it keeps in a temperate, intermediate zone. A sense of measure seems to emanate from the just distribution of the high and low grounds, from the symmetrical courses of the four big rivers through the plains spreading from the central uplands. The French landscape has its regions of ruggedness; it can be excessive and, as it were, arbitrary; but it is mainly characterized by its moderation, its humanity, the environment having been adapted to man as man was to the environment; by the smoothing away of irregular features, and the natural grouping of perspectives into wholes, sobered and unified beneath the patina of time. Above all it is privileged in the quality of its light. This is rarely blinding, rarely quite obscured by fogs, but for the most part spreads a gentle brilliance, and seems to sink of itself into the deeper strata of the mind, making clarity of thought a pleasure and a need. Clouds will often darken the day in the west and north, the strong sun of the south will burn at times with African fierceness; but the luminous sky of France normally has some of that purity and transparency which were to the Greeks a familiar experience and a suggestion of the joy of living.

The mind that grew in intimate and constant association with this setting developed a peculiar quality, of which some traces can be descried from the first; it evolved with a kind of dimly conscious persistence, and incorporated the adverse influences that the events of history brought to bear upon it. The human elements that had been longest in contact with the soil—the pre-Celtic and Celtic tribes remained the core of French nationality; and the character given to them all, under the common name of Gauls, by ancient writers shows a distinct analogy to the temper of the modern French. With a continuity that persisted in spite of all accidents France emerged among the formations of early medieval Europe and her civilization began to shine with a lustre of its own. Through violent struggles, periods of expansion and retraction, she managed to survive, whilst the French monarchy, after the breakdown of Charlemagne's empire, was rising steadily above the great barons of the realm. Fresh provinces, again and again added to the monarchy's possessions, gradually followed the same lines of development; they may have momentarily altered the balance of the kingdom, but they never upset for good the tenor of the national personality. The law of its being was already too definite; and the French mind had entered, with a sureness which seems almost to reveal some groping knowledge and concurrence, upon the course of its destiny.

Still, however unified the genius of France may have been from the beginning of its conscious life, its very wealth of tendencies implied the presence of diverse strains, and seeds of a positive duality were deeply implanted in it. Literary history seems to support these views. The temper of French poetry during the last 150 years, for instance, has undergone a change which cannot be entirely explained in terms of previous tradition. That romanticism should have struck such roots in the land which had identified itself with the classical ideal would tend to show that the roots of romanticism pre-existed, even if they had long seemed abortive. An irresistible inference is that what may be called the 'Latin' or 'Romance' elements in French culture did take the lead, and were preeminently active in moulding and shaping the personality of France; but that other elements, not completely fused with the former, remained present and obscurely effective in the progress of that personality, making themselves felt at intervals, and asserting themselves more strongly after the great intellectual change of the late eighteenth century. The thought, inspiration, and feeling which welled up in Rousseau and have more or less influenced the work of most great French writers ever since must be connected with virtualities of the French mind itself which had mostly lain dormant, although they can be traced or divined not a few times during the previous 800 years.

How should these other elements be identified and named? Bearing in mind the arbitrariness and fragility of all racial labels, one is driven to admit that the least misleading epithet that can be applied is a purely geographical one—let us say 'northern'. Just as the original genius of the English people and English literature grew from a mixture of races and a cultural graft that mingled Mediterranean influences with the predominant Teutonic stock, the no less original spirit of French literature derived from a similar fusion, in which the proportions of the components are reversed. It cannot be forgotten or ignored that however rapidly the Franks, Belgians, and Burgundians may have been assimilated by the Christian religion and the superior civilization of the romanized Gauls, they brought with them energies and instincts that made and kept them different through all the cross-breeding of the national life. This distinction between the south and the north of France, with all that it has implied and still implies socially, morally, and artistically, must never be lost sight of when the political or literary history of the people is interpreted. A stronger proportion of the various post-Celtic and northern invaders settled in the north and east, where they preserved rather more of their ethnical individuality. The fact, even after so many centuries, is still visible in the features of these provinces. Besides, when all is said, the 'Celtic genius' is itself rich, with a wide range of faculties and powers. From that decisive complexity all attempts to interpret the variegated course of the intellectual evolution of France must draw some of the main data on which their conclusions can be based.

The light of these remarks may perhaps be turned with some profit on the broader periods and changes in the development of French literature. But any effort to associate the characteristics of this or that individual writer with the several influences of this and that strain is bound to be adventurous and unsafe. The facts of collective psychology, in so far as they may be acknowledged at all, must intervene only, and then with the utmost caution, in the discussion of general movements. With this proviso it can be pointed out that the feudal system had its roots very largely in the habits and manners of the northern invaders; so that the *chansons de geste*, steeped as they are in the ideals and feelings of the feudal age, and however essentially French they may be in their spirit, were none the less originally related to the Germanic elements of the nationality in the making. This leaves the *Chanson de Roland* as it was and should remain, the focus of the moral and the literary personalities of early France.

Still, we must return to the point from which we started. If, wishing to study the literature of France, one tries to reach the accessible elements of her national originality, they are to be looked for in the world not of blood but of mind. The data in the former are merely conjectural; in the latter, though elusive they are concrete and open to direct observation. French writers from the first can be regarded as falling approximately into two main intellectual groups, seldom found in their exclusive wholeness but clearly defined and easily deduced from literary facts. The individuals themselves belong in varying degrees to both groups; a perfect singleness of allegiance to one, a perfect union and balance of the two, are not unexampled, though very rare. The spiritual history of France in far the longer part of her past shows the greater frequency and normality of a temper which is primarily intellectual, with the imagination and feeling under control; able to wield logical argument, and finding pleasure in its effectiveness; fond of the rational ordering of ideas and things. The writers of this type will aim preferably at clearness of expression, neatness of form, and coherence of structure; at a hierarchy of qualities in which emotion itself and the imagination will be checked and subjected to measure. It need hardly be said that this is the inner reality from which the instinctive addiction of French literature to the classical ideal grew and was long confirmed. That another temperament, however, from the first existed among the French, in which the main tendency was reversed, with a subjection of intelligence to imagination and feeling; that for long it asserted itself in occasional and erratic ways; that it was eventually liberated, when it revelled and rioted in its freedom and assumed superiority and command—all these facts coalesce into a psychological rendering of the outstanding events in the history of French literature. In the intermittent ascendancy of this complementary temper some of the substance of the periods from the origins to the later eighteenth century, and in its growing supremacy much more of all that followed can be interpreted, if not actually explained. Explanations, properly so called, are of course not conceivable in such a field; our generalizations do not lend themselves to deductive use. They serve rather to illumine the course of literary history and should be kept in the background; a potential aid to interpretation.

Yet emphasis should be laid here on the fact that the importance of the Celtic strand in the early growth of France is not so lightly dismissed today as it used to be; and that the Celtic spirit itself, though distinct and different from that of the other northern invaders, and despite the persistent obscurity of the whole problem, bears after all more affinity to the northern than to the southern element. This may add weight to the view of a modern critic,[1] who considers that the symbolist movement owed more, in its deeper inspiration, to Celtic than to English or German influences.

---

1 John Charpentier, *Le Symbolisme*, 1927.

II. The Language

The first extant monuments of the language and the literature of France are to be viewed against the background of this organic growth and must be interpreted in terms of it, for they are themselves among its most significant tokens.

The development of the French language shows no such dramatic incident and disturbing influence as the Norman Conquest, with its linguistic consequences, did in the history of English. The popular Latin that the Romans implanted in Gaul did not mix with the native stock. It underwent a process of spontaneous evolution and change which obeyed only phonetic forces; and the number of Celtic or Germanic words that found their way into the vocabulary being relatively small, their presence did not tell on the very structure of what remained thoroughly a Romance language. The process of transformation was slow enough to evince some measure of regularity and to bear the imprint of those mental needs which from an early date had characterized the growing nation. The undoubted confusion of what may be called 'middle French' in the fourteenth and fifteenth centuries is hardly comparable with the chaotic features of the corresponding period in the evolution of English.

There was, however, from the first a duality in the spontaneous development of the French language which might have proved an awkward hindrance to its organic growth. In the southern provinces—a generous epithet here, which includes a large part of the centre, and reaches as far north as the River Loire—the Latin stock gave birth to dialects with a more marked rhythm; and this family, called *langue d'oc* or, from the name of one of its branches, *provençal*, though *limousin* would be historically more accurate, produced a literature that for more than a century appeared to be the main expression of French culture. But various historical influences, and an inner decay, for which an explanation must be found in collective psychology, caused a gradual blight to settle on the promises of the south and the focus of French civilization to shift decisively to the north. When, about the fifteenth century, the French of Paris spread finally over the southern provinces, the defeat of the *langue d'oc* had been for some time a foregone conclusion; political ascendancy, and the self-consciousness of the national mind, had concurred in making the northern limb the trunk of the tree.

The dialects of the north (*francien, bourguignon, lorrain, champenois, picard, wallon, normand*, etc.) were rather less musical; but from the first they evinced a distinct and vigorous tendency to make speech a convenient means for the communication of thought. A major impulse was pretty uniformly at work, serving an instinctive need for clearness and simplification. The syntax moved away from the synthetic genius of Latin towards a more and more analytic form. Just as French words dropped their endings, to the advantage of the originally accented sylla-ble, even the reduced declension which had only two cases disappeared in the generalized use of prepositions. The various dialects gradually yielded precedence to that of the 'Ile de France' or 'français' (*francien*) properly so called, which, centring round the Paris region, shared natu-rally in the advance of the unifying authority of the kings.

What the qualities of the instrument were the future was to show. But the progress of the language down to the seventeenth century, what-ever it may have owed in the Renaissance period to writers, grammar-ians, and critics, was largely the work of the people itself, seeking a form of expression that satisfied its craving for directness. The diseases of af-fection, mannerism, or exuberance which again and again interrupted this growth had their seeds in the misguided zeal of theorists and cote-ries; the masses possessed from the first an intuitive sense of the sobriety which was the final achievement of the classical age. The fight waged by Malherbe and his successors was won because it was backed by the silent preference of a whole nation. On the plain but logical texture that was being fabricated by the anonymous centuries the great artists could superimpose the beauty of individual style.

The starting-point of this long development, the first text in early French known to us, is the *Serment de Strasbourg* (842, but transmit-ted by a later manuscript). It still looks very close to Latin, perhaps un-avoidably so, as it is a pure document, rather stiff, with little promise of the light ease that French was to pursue, and gradually achieve, as its supreme value. No wonder that eight centuries were needed to shape this extremely rough tool into a fine and polished means of literary ex-pression...But it is no illusion to perceive some slight advance as early as the end of the ninth century, in the *Cantilène de Sainte Eulalie*; and a sense of beauty is clearly active in the *Chanson de Saint Alexis* (probably from the latter part of the eleventh century), with the ascetic fervour that raises and animates its softly sounding lines.

The common literary language of the French had to win its ascen-dancy over the rival dialects; but another and a harder struggle was tak-ing place all through this transitional age: the newfangled tongue was to assert itself, to establish its right and conquer its heritage, against a formidable enemy in possession of the whole vantage ground—the Latin of the Church. For several centuries, while the unceasing progress of French can be observed and measured, Latin was so secure in its many strongholds that it did not seem to lose what its young competitor was gaining. Not only the clerics but most of the lay writers, who had been trained on the ancient language, gave it almost as a matter of course their most earnest work and most serious thought. Besides theology, ethics, philosophy, law, rhetoric, grammar, the chronicles of the past, and the rudiments of the sciences, many literary subjects as well were treated in Latin. Latin poems were written in verse that was not built on the classical prosody but on the new syllabic rhythm, with the addition of rhyme. This school of humanist expression, which lived and throve through the Renaissance and lingered into the seventeenth century, produced during the medieval period a very large body of literature in which the incipient traits of the French intellectual temper can be plainly traced, and which was often translated into the vernacular, sometimes by the authors themselves. If this abundant treasure were taken into account the Middle Ages would have an even better claim to be regarded as what they were, a highly creative period in the history of letters.

III. Early Flowering

It is indeed a characteristic trait of French literature that it should have begun to flower at a relatively early stage in the development of the nationality that nourished it and the language in which it was expressed. Neither Italy nor Spain can show quite so forward a growth; in both countries the influence of the French *chansons de geste* contributed to foster the development of a native poetry. If the test of conscious artistic quality is granted its due importance, Europe had nothing by the beginning of the twelfth century, outside the field of such classical works as survived, that could compare with the *Chanson de Roland*. In England, the first two writings in which an artistic intent is brilliantly active, *The Owl and the Pussycat* and *The Pearl* belong one to the thirteenth, the other to the fourteenth century; but with the latter we reach the age of Chaucer, when in several domains a glorious compensation was reaped for the delay.

In what concerns England delay was, of course, due to the dramatic fate that disrupted her natural growth, and with the Norman Conquest implanted a usurping culture and tongue in her soil. France at that period had long outlived her own invasions, and evolved her original civilization out of equally mixed materials. All through the era of the Crusades she was an expanding force, the strongest among the fresh-born nations of medieval Europe, diffusing her genius and spirit over the neighbouring lands and peoples. The smoother course of her history during those centuries cannot by itself, however, account for her more rapid progress towards clear, orderly, and artistic self-expression. It cannot be simply, on the other hand, that she belongs rather to the Mediterranean area, and that the south in almost everything grows more quickly than the north, since Italy and Spain, although more southern, did not outrun her. This factor is probably of some importance, but the main cause must be sought elsewhere.

One falls back upon the deeply rooted individualism of the French mind; an attitude in which the clear consciousness of one's distinct being and of one's faculties is implied; with this self-consciousness, again, the activity of the mental powers is more or less bound up. These features have been from the first its proper attributes, and together form that unique complex, a national character, something almost as definite as that of the individual being. Precociousness, prompt impressions, vivacious reactions were part and parcel of the earliest temper of France, both physical and intellectual, and were to remain so through her long history. The trait links up with the eagerness of judgement, feeling, and action which has so often been noticed and is itself responsible for some of the best, and some of the worst, French qualities—the impatience and fiery lack of control, for instance, that drove the scornful knights of Philippe and Jean against the unbreakable wall of English archers at more than one momentous fight, and that still make the political life of their descendants unstable and eventful.

Such facts of elementary folk-psychology are well known. It is impossible not to trace their influence in the literary leadership which France so distinctly assumed among the slower cultures of western and central Europe from the eleventh to the fourteenth century. For the better part of 300 years she was in a position of brilliance and authority more undisputed in the field of civilization than anything she may have known later. The seeds were there; nature had sown them and they grew more rapidly than in human groups where the possibilities were no less rich but the corresponding development was more tardy. A biologist might suggest that with the *sera juventas* (youthful seed) of the northern stocks—Scandinavian, Teutonic, or English—the promise of a deeper-rooted and more lasting creativeness was involved. But the implied criticism so far has not proved valid; groups may not be ruled by the same laws as individuals; and the French genius, after ten centuries, does not seem to be threatened with exhaustion.

Whatever the future may hold for that genius, an outstanding fact of its past is that the season of its flowering was early and luxuriant, an intellectual and artistic expansion in which all western Europe shared, indeed, but the example and encouragement of which had their focal point in France. Some allowance must be made, of course, for the favouring circumstance that the kings of the 'Capétien' dynasty, from Louis VI to Philippe le Bel, were efficient agents of the cause of national aggrandisement, which they served with a persistent will, and most of them, no doubt, with self-interested ambition. But it can still be maintained without illusion that French culture itself, in close touch with the process which moulded French political unity, was reaching a high degree of intensity and variety. The medieval system as a whole knew an organic integrity and a well-rounded definiteness of outline during the twelfth and thirteenth centuries; and although our social as well as our ethical sense today will be shocked by not a few of its crude or revolting features we must grant that in many respects it *was* a system, while thought and art did hallow it with the sanctions of genuine spirituality. Paris had the second-oldest university in Europe and attracted thousands of students and scholars from abroad; the Romanesque and later the Gothic style of religious architecture covered the soil of France with shrines whose beauty has not been surpassed; the *roman breton* soothed the imaginative craving for adventure and wonder; the 'Mystères' gave its first expression to the awakening dramatic instinct; the intoxication of refined intellectual love sustained the upsurge of lyrical poetry; the allegory flourished in vast and bold structures; while the philosophy of the schools and the eagerness of clerical or lay thinkers made the period what has often been called an earlier Renaissance. This fire did not burn selfishly within the as yet narrow bounds of one nationality; other flames were emulating and reflecting it beyond frontiers which were less fixed and solid at that time than they were to become; and all western Europe was involved in the glow and enthusiasm of a cosmopolitan age whose common Christian faith was the deepest principle of its moral harmony.

2
Literature and Intellectual Life in France

by

Ernst - Robert Curtius

From: Ernst-Robert Curtius: *The Civilization of France* (New York: Random House, Vintage Books, 1962), Chapter IV, "Literature and Intellectual Life". Edited by J. E. G. Dixon. All attempts to locate the copyright holder failed.

*L*iterature plays a far larger part in the cultural and national consciousness of France than it does in that of any other nation. In France, and in France alone, can literature be regarded as the nation's most representative form of expression...France cannot be understood politically, socially, or even from the purely human point of view if literature is left out of account, if we fail to grasp the central, uniting part it plays in every sphere of the life of the nation. Further, unless we read the French classics, and read them in the way the French read them, we cannot possibly understand France. All the national ideals of France are coloured and shaped by literary form. In France if a man wishes to be regarded as a politician he must be able to express himself in some form of literature. If he desires to exert influence as a speaker he must have a thorough knowledge of the collective literary treasure of the nation. No man who is not master of the spoken or of the written word can exert any influence in public life. In France the thorough knowledge of the specialist can never atone for a lack of literary culture. It is only in France that we find the type of political writing of which Barrès and Maurras are the representatives at the present day:[1] that type of book which attracts the literary person by its style and the politically-minded person by its formulas. Such books may contain polemics, analyses, doctrine—but one thing they may never be: purely specialist literature. In France politicians may write novels and novelists may compose political books without losing the right to be "taken seriously." Chateaubriand was a cabinet minister and the inventor of a new type of prose at one and the same time. Claudel is one of the great French poets of the present day: at the same time he is an ambassador of the Republic. Some of the most brilliant books of most recent French literature have been written in the Ministry of Foreign Affairs on the Quai d'Orsay.

In France the close connection between literature and the State dates from the seventeenth century. Richelieu and Louis XIV deliberately established this connection. In the eighteenth century literature was used for the purposes of social criticism and political reform. The Revolution of 1789 was steeped in literature, as were the Revolutions of 1830 and 1848. The Second Republic placed Lamartine at the head of the State; the Third Republic made Victor Hugo a senator and the patron saint of their *laique* religion. His funeral was transformed into a national celebration. Anatole France, similarly, was buried with all the official honours of the Republic. From Victor Hugo comes the saying, "Literature is civilization." Of France, at least, this is true.

---

1 Written in 1930. Ed.

In France literature fulfils the function which among us[2] is divided between philosophy, science, poetry and music. Why have these forms of intellectual and artistic expression no representative value in France? Let us briefly survey their position in the civilization of France. We will begin with philosophy.

Philosophy in France has become a concern of the educated only when it has appeared not as pure philosophy, but as a wisdom distilled from the experience of life and from knowledge of the world, as a lever for political emancipation, as the intellectual forerunner of new social forms, or as the ally of natural science. Scarcely ever, however, has it dominated the minds of the educated classes by the power of metaphysical speculation. The metaphysical passion of the East, of the Greeks, and of the Germans is alien to the French spirit. In Germany intellectual culture may be philosophical, in France it can be only literary. The great French metaphysicians—Malebranche, Maine de Biran, Hamelin, to name only a few—lived in great seclusion and never came into contact with the intellectual movements of their time. Even Comte only became known to a wider circle a generation after his death. In the realm of philosophy the French have absorbed chiefly the intellectual achievements of the sceptics, of the thinkers of the school of the Enlightenment, of moralists and social philosophers; this selection is typical of the values of French civilization.

It is, however, an undoubted fact that Descartes is the most important factor in the intellectual history of France. Why? There are several reasons. The *Discours de la Méthode* is written in a style which the Frenchman requires in the literary classics. Neither in range nor in intelligibility does Descartes overstep the bounds of that which the cultivated Frenchman, with his literary tastes, can assimilate. The work of Descartes established and made legitimate the conception that even the philosopher must adapt the expression of his ideas to the habits of thought and speech of the *honnête homme*.

Bergson declares that "*la philosophie française s'est toujours réglée sur le principe suivant: il n'y a pas d'idée philosophique, si profonde ou si subtile soit-elle, qui ne puisse et ne doive s'exprimer dans la langue de tout le monde.*"[3] Bergson considers that this is a particular virtue of French philosophy. But surely this simply means that philosophy has to submit

---

2 Curtius was German. Ed.

3 "French philosophy has always followed the principle that there is no philosophical idea, no matter how profound or subtle, that cannot, and must not, be expressed in the language of the man in the street."

to the dominion of the literary conventions and to the tyranny of ordinary human understanding. This process, however, has a bad effect on philosophy. Cramped within the limits of certain forms of speech and expression not of its own making, philosophy loses much of its force; for all its efforts at independent criticism are checked by an artificial barrier. The final result of this subordination to the literary conception is this: that which was conceived as philosophy is consumed purely as literature. Cartesianism also has had to go through this process.

But the literary form of the *Discours de la Méthode* only partly explains its influence. There are other reasons. Rightly or wrongly, Cartesianism may be reduced to a formula—to the simplest which can be imagined, and one which throws a great deal of light on the national temper. It is regarded as the philosophy of reason, of reason pure and simple. Every Frenchman has feeling for the *clare et distincte percipere*. It is possible to believe that the Cartesian conception of Reason includes all those tendencies toward *bon sens*, logic, order, clarity, which are so deeply rooted in the French character; once this has been granted these very tendencies are explained and justified from the philosophical point of view. Thus an absolute legend has been formed around Descartes and Cartesianism. The difficult and complex philosophy of this great thinker has been forcibly simplified and toned down until it is represented as a mere catchword, which ultimately does not mean much more than the *clarté française* of which we hear so much. Descartes as the law-giver of Reason and the liberator from faith in authority—this is one of the clichés which constantly recur in the intellectual conventions of France. In popular presentations of the subject the genius of Descartes is extolled because ultimately he is said to represent the development of that sane human reason which every French peasant possesses. Writers of this kind even claim that the most splendid incarnation of the Cartesian spirit at the present time is that of Marshal Foch—which leads to the natural conclusion that it was the Cartesian method which secured victory to France in the World War.[4] In ways like these the figure of Descartes has been misrepresented and his teaching has been obscured; indeed, we may say quite definitely that this popular Cartesianism has become the greatest hindrance to the development of the true philosophical spirit in France. Both abroad and at home it has spread the idea that the French mind is purely rational—an idea which everyone who penetrates into the genuine and deep nature of France at once perceives

---

4 This is not an invention of my own. I found it in Chevalier's *Descartes*.

to be false. For this reason today all serious thinkers in France are giving their whole attention to the endeavour to reveal afresh the philosophy of Descartes in its pure form, to remove it from the sphere of popular philosophy, and to incorporate it organically into the whole realm of the great achievements of French thought which are so little known. This, however, does not alter the fact that even today French philosophy is still the concern of specialists and of a small group.

There is still another reason why philosophy in France could never form the central point of its intellectual life. It has wrongly allowed itself to be dominated by literary form and average intelligence; it has also surrendered to natural science. When Bergson declares, "*La philosophie n'est que le prolongement de la science,*" (Philosophy is a mere extension of science) he is in the line of ancient tradition. The philosophical spirit of France hesitates to formulate a system. It does not feel the necessity to articulate and construct afresh the whole range of being from the idea of the Logos. The philosophical spirit of France accepts "Reality" without reflection, and so orders its ideal synthesis that the usually valid existence of things is respected, so that one can still use the individual materials of the philosophical structure, even when one does not accept the conception as a whole: "*Les morceaux en sont toujours bon,*" as Bergson says ... French philosophy centres on "physics," using this word in its ancient comprehensive sense. In Descartes geometry and metaphysics are so closely connected that it is impossible to decide which is foremost. French philosophy was primarily occupied with "the abstract and concrete sciences of inorganic matter" (as Bergson expresses it), that is, with mathematics, mechanics, astronomy, physics and chemistry; then it analysed social life; then, through Comte, quite logically it produced a classification of the sciences which begins with mathematics and ends in sociology. Taine and Renan continued this line of development. Bergson himself does not, or does not primarily, make the Dionysiac affirmation of the universe, nor is he a rebel against the fetters of the understanding as he is generally considered amongst us, but a careful thinker, who tries, upon the basis of experience and natural science, to outline a positive metaphysic.

Thus French philosophy easily loses the possibility of moving the spirit in its ultimate depths, because it pays tribute to powers outside philosophy and preserves their "inherited rights": speech, literature, natural science, reasonableness, and, finally, the national habit of mind. It realizes exactly as many philosophical ways of thinking as are possible to unite with the stable forces of civilization. The "philosophical spirit" can be considered an attribute of France only so far as it limits itself to the need for logic and the general conceptual approach to all problems. In this sense Bergson was able to say: "*Le besoin de philosopher est universel: il tend à porter toute discussion, même d'affaires, sur le terrain des idées et des principes. Il traduit probablement l'aspiration la plus profonde de l'âme française qui va tout droit à ce qui est général, et par là, à ce qui est généreux. En ce sens, l'esprit français ne fait qu'un avec l'esprit philosophique.*"[5]

Both the excellences and the defects of French philosophy are the result of the sense of reality, the desire for stability, and of the anthropocentric order upon which the French conception of Civilization is based. Its conservative humanism could not endure either the pantheism of a world-intoxicated ecstasy, the transcendental idealism of the creative spirit, the knowledge of salvation which desires redemption and depreciates the value of the world, or the moral criticism of a heroic will to power. A Hegel, a Schopenhauer, a Nietzsche are unthinkable in France. They would destroy the garden of civilization and the realm of humanity. The sense of infinity cannot live freely within French philosophy. But philosophy can only be supreme where it can roam freely through unexplored spaces without hindrance. This is why philosophy can only play a secondary part in the intellectual life of France....

Science also must yield pride of place to Literature. Humanistic studies above all do not have the position in France which they occupy among us. In France they lack the stimulus which they received in Germany from Humanism and from Protestantism. In Germany, indeed, the union of both these forces prepared the way for the florescence of our humanistic studies. In France humanism has expressed itself rather in literary (Ronsard), or philosophical (Montaigne), or in political (Montesquieu) form than in the historical-philological form. But the event which was of far greater influence was the suppression of Protestantism. Amongst ourselves its tendency toward independent private judgment and independent criticism of the great questions of the destiny of individuals and of nations has been to the advantage of the development of the humanistic studies. In France there never has been anything of this kind. A Dr. Faust would be as impossible here as a Herder or a Hegel. Thus it comes to pass that in France the humanistic

---

5 "Philosophizing is a universal need: it tends to direct all discussion to the realm of ideas and principles, even talk about business. In all probability it expresses the profoundest need of the French mind, which seeks out the general, and hence what is generous. In this sense, the French mind and the philosophical bent are as one."

studies, compared with our development, have flowed partly into the broad streams of literature and of politics, partly into the limited area of specialized research, while some have been diverted by the lure of natural-science methods or have been transformed into psychology or sociology. Naturally these are only the broad features of the development, and many exceptions could be mentioned; but they *are* exceptions, and for the most part (think of Renan, for instance) they can be traced back to the fertilizing example of German science. To the above we must add another consideration: the sphere of the intellect, if we may use simplified expressions, is static to the Frenchman, while to us it is dynamic. In research the French expend their energy on Nature rather than on the intellect. To them "Science" means initially and essentially natural science. Hence in France it is highly honoured, because it serves the cause of the domination of Nature by man, the emancipation of man from the elements, and the liberation of the intellect from the authority of dogma, society, and custom. In France, therefore, the most popular form of science is medicine. We need only recall the pride of the "enlightened" apothecary Homais in *Madame Bovary*! This, of course, was a caricature, but it has a basis in reality. The medical man is *le curé du républicain*. A chemist and doctor like Raspail (1794-1878) was able to play the part of a political "Patriarch of Radicalism," and to prove the truth of this claim by many years of imprisonment gallantly endured. A Positivist like Littré (1801-1881), who was both a doctor and a philologist, was regarded by the Republicans as a "Sage", who placed the results of his thought at the service of the politicians. From 1900 onward Pasteur and Curie have been the symbolic figures in whom the genius of science is incarnate. During the last ten or twenty years there has been a great deal of discussion in France about the "value of science." The whole idea was that of the mechanistic natural science which was both the factor of progress and the opponent of the Church. In France the exponent of the national spirit is not the philosopher, nor the musician, nor the scholar, but the man of letters.

The counterpart of the person known amongst us as a *gebildeter Mensch* (educated person) is in France the *lettré*. The *lettré* is the man or woman who is versed in literature. He knows his classics, or pretends to know and admire them. He knows how to produce apt quotations from the great national writers. Once I accompanied a *lettré* to a great government building of several storeys. We had to pass through many passages and ascend many stairs. As we walked along he remarked, *Nourri dans le sérail, j'en connais les détours.*[6] We were supposed to know that these lines came from Racine's *Bajazet*.[7] At the present time in France there are many complaints about the decline in literary and humanistic culture. The French may be pessimistic if they choose. From our point of view France is still the land of the humanist tradition.

There is a classic description of this tradition in Sainte-Beuve's Inaugural Lecture given at the École Normale in the year 1858. Anyone who desires to understand French literature should study these pages: *De la Tradition en littérature, et dans quel sens il la faut entendre.*[8] Sainte-Beuve compares the humanist literary tradition with the great Roman roads which spanned the whole Empire and led to the Eternal City, and are still visible at the present day...

Sainte-Beuve's conception of tradition has already become historic. It still preserves the unity of style of the late Classicism of the eighteenth century and of the Empire. But the heart of his contention is still valid at the present day. The problem of tradition is expressed differently in present-day France, but it is still a vital element in the national life. When France collected herself after the War she began to recall her Graeco-Latin tradition. The *Collection Guillaume Budé*—a new edition of ancient authors with translations—was founded, and in a few years it has achieved a great success.

French classicism and humanism are indissolubly connected. In France, quite as much as in Italy, Virgil is one of the ineradicable and fundamental elements of culture. French humanism passes through Rome to Athens, whereas ours[9] usually leaves Rome out of the picture. Classical and classicist France has generally regarded Hellas with a certain mistrust. It is the mistrust of the Romans toward the Graeculi. Rome stands for law and order, Greece for plays, sophistry or myths. Plato is too near to the Mysteries. It is true that there has been a Platonist tendency in France, but it did not form part of the main stream. Among the French classic writers it is easy to distinguish the "Romans" from the "Greeks". The Romans are Corneille, Bossuet, Montesquieu; the Greeks are Racine, La Fontaine, Fénelon. There has always been a French Hellenism, but it is mostly a psychological and rationalistic Hellenism, to

---

6 "Reared in a seraglio, I know all its secret places."

7 We would be less unimpressed if the quotation were slightly less irrelevant—unless the writer's friend were really brought up in a harem! More to the point might have been: *"Je sais de ce palais tous les détours obscurs."* (Andromaque, III, i.) Ed.

8 See Contents and page 63. Ed.

9 See note 2 above.

which Pindar and Aeschylus are more remote than Euripides and Aristotle. We [Germans] seek in Greece the mysteries of Orphism; France seeks the symmetry of the Parthenon, the moderation of the Greeks, and the wisdom of Athena. Even the French who see in Greece the highest revelation of the intellect cannot sacrifice to it the Latin idea. When Charles Maurras asserts that "the Valois and the Parisis were like Attica in its purest form," he also blames those who deny the service which Rome has rendered to the world. Rome has perpetuated Hellenism—but unfortunately also Semitism and the poison of Asia.

To be a Hellenist and despise the Romans is an exceptional, not a contradictory, attitude. Today it appears now and again among scholars whose political views lean toward the Left, who see in the Roman idea the support of the idea of authority in Church and State, whereas to them Greece (Archimedes!) means an asylum for free research and independent thought. A popular reconciliation formula has been given by Victor Hugo with his brilliant simplicity: *La France est de la même qualité de peuple que la Gréce et l'Italie. Elle est athénienne par le beau et romaine par le grand. En outre elle est bonne."*[10]

Sociologically the esteem in which literature is held is expressed very clearly. The significance of the French Academy is perhaps the most impressive example of this fact. To be received among the forty immortals is the highest honour which can fall to the lot of a Frenchman. Cabinet Ministers, generals, ecclesiastical dignitaries, strive to attain this honour. The Académie is the national representative of literature. Through it France has made intellect a national institution. "*L'Académie,*" says Renan (*Essais de morale et de critique*), "*comptait à peine quelques années d'existence, et un immense résultat était atteint, l'ennoblissement de l'esprit. Jusque-là, mendiant, parasite ou pédagogue, l'esprit n'avait point eu de forteresse, et avait cherché son asile à l'ombre de l'église et du château féodal. Désormais c'est l'homme d'esprit qui accorde aux gentilshommes le titre de confrère."*[11]

Since the day when it was founded it is true that the Académie has often had to endure attacks of Gallic mockery, and to incur the reproach

---

10 "France is of the same calibre of people as Greece and Italy. She is Athenian by the cult of Beauty, and Roman by dint of Grandeur. She is virtuous to boot."

11 "The Academy," says Renan (*Essais de morale and de critique*) "had hardly existed for a few years before it bore impressive fruit—the elevation of the mind. Until then, whether beggar, parasite or pedagogue, it had sought its patron in the shadow of church or feudal castle. From that day forward it has been the man of intellect who has conferred upon the local squires the accolade of *confrère.*"

of rigidity and stagnation, but it still preserves its prestige, and by the election of men of the highest intellectual rank it can always renew its strength. This prestige, to the extent that it feels itself bound up with the French idea of civilization, is greater abroad than it is in France itself. It is greater in the provinces than it is in Paris, where gossip and detraction form part of the necessary stimulus of the literary life. But it still has power today to stir the ambition of the best intellects. Reception into the Académie secures to the fortunate immortal an increase in power and independence, which is of great value. The Academician is courted by all those who have been announced as candidates for the Académie and by the still larger group of those who hope one day to enter this eminent body. Further, the Académie has an annual sum of 200,000 francs to administer in literary prizes. And this gives it a far-reaching influence. Finally, the Academician is an *homme arrivé*. He need take no more notice of anyone. During the period of his candidature he has to exercise a most careful silence to avoid offending anyone. Once he is elected he regains his freedom of opinion and of speech, "The Roman slave," says Fernand Vandérem,[12] "knew such joys only on the day of the Saturnalia. The Academician . . . knows this joy every day of his life." Material advantages also accrue from the fact of election. As soon as an author can add the magic words *de l'Académie française* to his name, his royalties and the editions of his books increase greatly.

As we know, the Académie was the creation of the absolute Monarchy, and the Classical epoch of French literature coincided with the period of Louis XIV. French classicism reflects the consciousness of sovereignty possessed by the French Monarchy. But it was able to outlive it, and for the past two and a half centuries it has been the most important interpreter of the value of the French mind to the world. The Classical literature of France grew out of the intellectual movement of the Italian Renaissance. Corneille, Racine, La Fontaine would have been, it is true, great poets apart from this, but they would not have become classics, if by a classical literature we mean one which has been formed on a great model and upon a system of aesthetic reason. The French classics were intended to be rational imitations of the ancients. This idea came to them from Italy. Italian humanism had elaborated a theory taking as its base the Poetics of Aristotle, in the course of a most active and stimulating controversy, between 1527 and 1613. But whereas in Italy the poetical production of the Renaissance arose quite independently of these theo-

---

12 *La Littérature*, Hachette, 1927.

ries, the rationalistic intellect of France watched over the poetic genius carefully and gave it its laws. From Ronsard to Malherbe and Boileau we see a close connection between the method and practice of poetry. The French classics were developed through a historical process which lasted for more than a century.[13] Ronsard and his school (about 1550) had laid down the principle of the imitation of antiquity. In a second cycle, about 1630, the rules of this imitation were constructed into a body of doctrine; the classical doctrine was finally complete. The development was then crowned by the generation of great Classical writers of 1660. These three phases were so detached from each other that each rejected the preceding one because it had reached a higher standpoint. Thus the great classicism of the third phase overcame the doctrinaire spirit of the second, and replaced it by the taste which we call the *grand goût classique*. The mechanism of work done according to rule had become an organic instinct. The double dependence—on ancient literature and on Italian poetry—had been overcome by the mature independent sense of form of the national genius. The great works of this period are not artificial imitations; they are natural achievements. In them the period of Louis XIV created a style which is entirely French, which by means of the theory of imitation has developed into a complete originality. There is now no longer any trace of the humanism of the Italian *Cinquecento*. The Renaissance has been replaced by a new world style of classic stamp which France created, and which she evolved at the moment when the classical genius of Italy succumbed to the Baroque. It is characteristic that Bernini's plans for the completion of the Louvre in Paris were not approved. The Colonnade of Perrault was in greater harmony with the taste of the period, and at the present day it still gives a very impressive testimony to the ideals of order, symmetry and moderation which France evolved at that time. Whoever has grasped the significance of the form of the Hotel Biron in Paris (now the Rodin Museum) will also understand the same achievement of proportion in the Classical literature.

That the French classics created a world style, in contra-distinction to all other literature, was due above all to the happy accident that this development took place at the same time as the highest point in the power of the French Monarchy and the prestige of the French State. The King himself took a great personal interest in the whole matter. He took Molière under his wing and protected him against his enemies. He

---

13 Cf. René Bray, *La Formation de la doctrine classique en France* (1927).

called Racine to his court, made Bossuet tutor to the Dauphin, and Fénelon tutor to the Duke of Burgundy. *Esther* and *Athalie* were written for the pupils of St. Cyr, the *Discours sur l'histoire universelle* and *Télémaque* for the royal princes. It seemed to be a repetition of the Augustan age: the monarch of a world empire gathering around him a group of eminent men whose brilliance shed a reflected glory upon his person and upon the system of the State. This comparison occurred forcibly to the people of that day, and was the reason for the "*Querelle des Anciens et des Modernes*." The fact that there was a strong desire to imitate the great models of antiquity led finally to the production of a literature of similar value. French Classical literature had attained its majority. The cultural consciousness of the period claimed that its own value ought to be recognized and that it possessed a glory of its own. Until the end of the *ancien régime* the political predominance of France smoothed the way for the expansion of the classical style in Europe. It was this actual element of power which carried the poetry of Boileau, the tragedy of Racine, Le Nôtre's art of landscape gardening, the architectural ideas of Versailles, the court ceremonial and the dictionary of the Académie into foreign lands. The greatness of the Classical school consists precisely in that it is more than, and different from, a French royal style. Racine, Molière, Boileau, La Rochefoucauld, La Bruyère, Madame de La Fayette, and the other founders of literature surpassed Lulli and Le Brun. The spirit of the literary art of the epoch survived the forms in which it was then expressed, and its style of decoration. As early as the eighteenth century the connection between the classical spirit of literature and the Catholic state religion—a connection which had previously been rather loose—was severed. The connection with the authority of the Monarchy and the State was severed also. Voltaire was to achieve this separation. Classical literature could now develop the sceptical and free-thinking elements of rationalism of which *frondeurs* like Saint-Evremont, or Cartesians like Fontenelle, had been unofficial representatives in the preceding era. It was now able to combine itself with the English philosophy of the Enlightenment and with the criticism of the day. It was able to prepare the way for the Revolution, and thus enabled Taine to submit the thesis that the *raison oratoire* of the Classical school had been the intellectual agent of the upheaval. It is, of course, true that this classicism of the eighteenth century differed entirely from the classicism of the seventeenth century. But it still preserved the earlier formal traditions. Voltaire's *Mérope* is constructed on the pattern of the tragedies of Racine.

This pseudo-classicism was destroyed by the literary movement of the nineteenth century. But for that very reason the real greatness of the Classical school again became apparent. In France when a literary movement, or an individual author, has reached artistic maturity, his work almost always reveals an aesthetic kinship with the artistic instincts of that period. No French author can ever forget that the Classical school is behind him, and even when he is unconscious of it the fact of this tradition will help to shape his style. The indefinable essence of the classical spirit arises ever anew on the soil of France. In Valéry and Gide the Symbolist school of 1890 attained the clarity of form and the closeness of texture of the Classical school; even in Dadaism its most talented supporters developed along these lines. The persistence of this classical instinct is, naturally, a result of conscious cultivation and tradition. Every Frenchman has passed through the school of this classical literature. The schoolboys of the Third Republic receive the basic elements of language, of artistic and psychological culture from works which were ripened in the sunshine of the Monarchy. This classical literature is not the private preserve of the intellectual élite; it has become a national possession. This was possible because it was not connected with any particular view of the world, and also because both in language and in artistic feeling it is definite, lucid and pleasing.

Since France, as a country, occupies a central position, her literature too may be described as a literature which stands midway between two extremes. It is not characterized by supreme inspiration, nor by depth of feeling for life, but by the harmonious balance of intellectual moderation...The values of French literature do not lie in the absolute greatness of individual personalities, but in the elevation of the collective level and in the inward continuity of the intellectual tradition. It is characteristic that to the question: "Who was the greatest Frenchman?" no one can find an answer. France has produced no Dante, no Shakespeare, no Cervantes, no Goethe. Instead, however, she possesses a literature which forms an unbroken and vital unity, and which in its wholeness represents a personality of an incomparable kind.

In our [German] intellectual system of values the idea of genius is supreme. We expect genius to renew for us the face of the world or to create a spiritual world of its own. The French mind has different values. It rates balance higher than force, and perfection higher than originality. France has produced great poets, but the greatness of its literature is not based upon poetry but upon prose. Rivarol, the most profound and most brilliant spirit of old France in its decline, once said, "*C'est la*

prose qui donne l'empire à une langue; la poésie n'est qu'un objet de luxe."[14]
This is a political point of view; it is, however, only the political aspect
of a fundamental intellectual attitude. The wonderful verse of Racine is
as near to prose as poetry can be without giving up the attempt to be
poetry. In France it is impossible to imagine a purely lyrical poet being
admitted to the narrow select circle of eminent names in which the nation contemplates the highest elements in its intellectual wealth. "*Le lyrisme est un accident chez nous,*" says G. Lanson, "*la création en a été tar-
dive et laborieuse; la source du lyrisme s'ouvre, en somme, assez rarement
dans l'âme française.*"[15] Flaubert wrote in 1852: "*Il faut déguiser la poésie
en France, on la déteste*"[16] (December 16, 1852, to Louise Colet). And
Baudelaire: "*La France éprouve une horreur congénitale de la poésie.*"[17]
And earlier still André Chénier: "*De toutes les nations de l'Europe, les
Français sont ceux qui aiment le moins la poésie et qui s'y connaissent le
moins.*"[18]

The fact which impresses critics most of all is the non-lyrical character of the literature of France. There was, indeed, once on French soil
a flowering of lyrical poetry in which the tenderest poetical flame burnt
steadily: the Provençal poetry of the twelfth and thirteenth centuries.
The Northern French lyrics of the Middle Ages were formed on that
model, although they did not attain to the same heights of magic and
primitive charm. But the art of the troubadours was only able to flourish
in the midst of that Southern French culture which was destroyed by the
Albigensian Crusade, the Inquisition, and the reforming activity of the
Dominicans. This destruction is one of the sacrifices which France has
made for the sake of her political and intellectual unity.

The French tendency to scepticism and mockery, to that view of
reality which is free from all illusions, has always been a hindrance to
the development of the poetical faculty. To mistake well-turned verse for
poetry is a danger which lies in the very character of French literature.
The historical reason for this lies in the system of French classicism. The
aesthetic doctrine of the Classical school dealt only with poetry, that is,
with the mode of literature for which the ancients used verse. So it came

---

14 "It is prose that gives a language its dominance; poetry is a mere luxury."

15 "Lyricism is an accident with us; it came about late and with difficulty. To be blunt,
the source of the lyric muse springs but rarely in the French soul."

16 "In France, poetry needs to be disguised; it is detested."

17 "In France we have a congenital hatred of poetry."

18 "Of all the countries of Europe, the French like poetry the least and appreciate it the
least."

to pass that in France the idea of poetry became an artistic conception which was purely formal and defined, and based entirely upon the classical model. This explains the fact that rhymed speech is frequently mistaken for poetry. For all ages this mistake was sanctioned by Boileau. Boileau belongs to the impeccable French tradition, and his position is equally impregnable.

Several times youthful rebels ventured to try to shake his authority, but they almost always ended by making an apology. Sainte-Beuve is a typical example of this change of front. Boileau is always "saved," however artificial the method of rescue may be. Prosaic correctness is covered by his name. By many who swear by him he is less read than praised, but he remains a symbol of excellent craftsmanship and artistic proportion. Flaubert, when he was growing old and when the young naturalistic school sought to annex him, used to refresh his mind with Boileau. A Romantic like Delacroix could write: "*Boileau est un homme qu'il faut avoir sous son chevet, il délecte et purifie; il fait aimer le beau et l'honnêteté, tandis que nos modernes n'exhalent que d'âcres parfums, mortels le plus souvent pour l'âme, et faussent l'imagination par des spectacles de fantaisie.*"[19]

Boileau's greatest opponent was Victor Hugo. But if Boileau kills poetry by his "reasonable smoothness" (Rémy de Gourmont), Hugo endangers it by his swollen rhetoric. André Gide once gave this reply to the question of who is the greatest French poet. "*Victor Hugo, hélas!*" Victor Hugo certainly stands alone by virtue of his forceful speech, the wealth of his images, his sparkling antitheses, and the furious force and eloquence of his language. He intoxicates and captivates. But this language, which flows along so majestically, is speech, not song. No literature can produce poems which can compare with this for rhetorical effect. The peculiar quality of Hugo and his greatness—the element which secures him an immortal place in the heart of his nation—is his brilliant capacity for expressing the feelings of the people as a whole. He is the "*écho sonore*" of the masses, giving audible expression to the spirit of the people in its political and social agitation. His verses vibrate with the beat of drums and the sound of trumpets. He is the singer of the people. He is at his happiest when he exalts Paris, sings the epic of the Revolution and of the Empire, or the social visions of the future of the nation and

---

19 "Boileau is your perfect bedside book. He delights and refines; and teaches you to love all that is beautiful and honest; whereas our modern writers give off acrid fumes, deadly to the soul for the most part, and who pervert the imagination with their extravagant productions." Eugène Delacroix, *Oeuvres littéraires*, i, 96.

of humanity. There is no detraction from his fame in the statement that the purely lyrical quality which distinguishes the language of Goethe or Keats is almost entirely absent from the poetry of Victor Hugo.

Purely lyrical poetry in the great style is very rare in France before Baudelaire. The appearance of the *Fleurs du Mal* (1857) was therefore one of the greatest and most remarkable events in the literature of France. Baudelaire was scarcely understood by his contemporaries. It was only the Symbolist movement which began to do honour to Baudelaire. For many years, in the criticism of the Académie, he was considered only a writer of the second rank. It is only today that this opposition seems to have been broken down. Baudelaire's poetry has captivated the literary public in even wider circles. Today the main question is, as Léon Daudet has recently expressed it: "Victor Hugo or Baudelaire?" This question represents a revision of aesthetic values which is of great importance for a true estimate of French literature.

The case of Baudelaire has a still more far-reaching significance. Since Baudelaire there has been a modernist movement in French literature. In France, Classicism, Romanticism and Naturalism all have this in common: they are all immediately accessible to the normal consciousness of the enlightened European. One can enter these literary regions on the ordinary level. It is possible to define them and to explain them exhaustively.

With Baudelaire the situation was altered. Here we enter a world which can no longer be grasped by reason. It is only possible to understand it at all if one has a feeling for the mystery of poetry, a sense which the average man may lack just as much as the feeling for music or the capacity for mystical experience. After Baudelaire came Mallarmé and Valéry, Rimbaud and Claudel, and the younger and most recent poets who have broken down the firm structure of the rational theory of the universe. Quite recently there have been great discussions in France about the conception of *poésie pure*. Henri Brémond, that sensitive psychologist and historian of French mysticism whom the Académie claimed as one of its own elect some years ago, has made a brilliant plea for "pure poetry." But the very fact that he makes this plea shows how new and unusual the view of pure poetry is to the French mind.

This whole development means a far-reaching change in the literature of France. There are two literatures running parallel to each other in France today, and one above the other: the traditional one which is accessible to every educated reader, and that of "modernism" in which a new form of consciousness is foreshadowed. The latter is the laughing stock of popular journalists, who feel that they are the official representatives of the French *bon sens*. Probably both forms of literature will continue to exist.

In France, literature of the rationalistic kind will never cease to call forth the admiration of the best intellects. For it possesses aesthetic values which will outlast changes in forms of consciousness. Perhaps only a Frenchman can appreciate them fully. A passage from a letter of Flaubert will make this clear: "*Nous nous étonnons des bonshommes du siècle de Louis XIV, mais ils n'étaient pas des hommes d'énorme génie; on n'a aucun de ces ébahissements, en les lisant, qui vous fassent croire en eux à une nature plus qu'humaine, comme à la lecture d'Homére, de Rabelais, de Shakespeare surtout; non! mais quelle conscience! Comme ils se sont efforcés de trouver pour leurs pensées des expressions justes! Quel travail! Quelles ratures! Comme ils se consultaient les uns les autres, comme ils savaient le latin! Comme ils lisaient lentement! Aussi toute leur idée y est, la forme est pleine, bourrée et garnie de choses jusqu'à la faire craquer. Or il n'y a pas de degrés: ce qui est bon vaut ce qui est bon. La Fontaine vivra autant que le Dante, et Boileau que Bossuet ou même Hugo.*" (1853)[20]. Those who are not French would feel it impossible to place La Fontaine alongside of Dante. But Flaubert's way of thinking will always remain a living opinion in France. Gide, in his African diary (1927), makes the following entry: "*Achevé la lecture complète des Fables de La Fontaine. Aucune littérature a-t-elle offert jamais rien de plus exquis, de plus sage, de plus parfait?*"[21]

In the intellectual as well as in the social sphere France is both the land of daring innovations and of tenacious conservatism. In France an artist who discovers a new world of beauty will easily find a small group of admirers and disciples, but only very late in life will he gain admittance to the pantheon of taste in which the generally recognized possessions of the national intellectual wealth are preserved. So long

---

20 "Those worthies of Louis XIV's time constantly amaze us, but they were not men of stupendous genius. We experience in their presence none of those gasps of astonishment that lead us to think them possessed of a super-human nature, as we do notably when reading Homer, Rabelais, and Shakespeare. No, to be sure! But what conscientiousness! What labour! What self-correcting! What pains they took to find the exact expression to fit their thoughts! How studiously they conferred with each other! How well they knew their Latin; and how meticulously they read! Hence it is that their thought is complete in its fullness, its form is filled, and stuffed full to bursting with substance. It allows of no degrees: what is good is simply good."

21 "Read all of LaFontaine's Fables at one go. Has any other literature anything more exquisite, wise and perfect to offer?"

as he does not possess the official sanction which is conferred by the salons, by criticism, and by the Academy, he will never be considered complete. Stendhal, Balzac, Flaubert, Mallarmé, the Impressionists—all went through this process. This is the reason why so many French artists and poets have first of all found sympathy and understanding in foreign lands, whereas at home their claim to fame was acknowledged only very hesitatingly. The final judgment on the worth of an author is delivered in France fifty years after his death. Official taste tends to be still more reserved when foreign countries are lavish in their praise. The protectors of the French tradition usually arise and stigmatize the new tendency in arts as "non-French." This means that the aesthetic controversy is carried out into the political arena. Because artistic taste in France is regarded as a national possession, it must be preserved from becoming falsified or foreign in its form. When the national tradition in taste is based upon the standard of the Classical school, naturally everything which is non-Classical is an alien importation, poisonous and harmful. At the present time several critics still argue heatedly about these questions: Can we say that Rousseau, or the Romantic movement, or the Symbolist movement were good? Can they be regarded as French? From the sixteenth century onward the influence of foreign literature has made itself felt again and again, at certain periods, in France. But just as regularly reaction has followed, a "nationalizing" of taste, a defensive reaction, whether it was directed against Spain, Italy, England, Germany or Russia. The assimilation of a foreign intellectual world is never carried through completely. Controversy still rages around Shakespeare and Goethe. In France there will always be critics who will express loudly their distaste for the tiresome foreigner, like the old Sarcey when he exclaimed: "*Assez de Shakespeare, assez d'Ibsen, assez de Tolstoi, assez de Maeterlinck. Rentrons en France, que diable!*"[22]

The greatest creations of the literature of France, classical tragedy and the modern novel, have this in common (which, further, is a specific peculiarity of the French intellect): both are an analysis of the passions. While German literature tends to become metaphysical, that of France is psychological. From Montaigne to Racine, from Balzac to Proust, this quality is revealed with an ever-renewed delicacy. French literature is an inexhaustible discourse upon man. It is a course of instruction in the knowledge of humanity.

French literature has no myths; in this it resembles the literature

---

22 'Enough of Shakespeare! Enough of Ibsen! Enough of Tolstoy and Maeterlinck! What the devil, let's get back to France!"

of Rome which has no epic of gods or heroes. The Greek Olympus is interpreted in France in an allegorical or psychological sense. In general, mythology is not missed. The Classical genius of France can say with Martial:

> quid te vana iuvant miserae ludibria chartae?
> hoc lege, quod possit dicere vita "Meum est".
> non hic Centauros, non Gorgonas Harpyiasque
> invenies: hominem pagina nostra sapit.[23]

Indeed, all aspects of French literature reveal man, express that of which life can say: *Meum est*. The feeling for the reality of the human heart, the revelation of its tragic or grotesque secrets constitutes its greatness. What are the conflicts which move humanity? Thus ask Corneille, Racine, Pascal. What is hidden in the remote corners of the soul? So ask Montaigne, La Rochefouchauld, La Bruyère. Desire for power, ambition, physical passions—French Classicism subjected this play of forces to an analysis which will always remain valid. Its psychology is a realism free from all illusions. French literature has in its memoirs, collections of letters, maxims and aphorisms, a characteristic mass of material with which other literatures have nothing to compare. It is inexhaustible. It will always exercise the greatest attraction for those whose lives are concerned mainly with love or politics, for those who have more to do with people than with dead things, for those who influence men and who must learn to know men. The French psychologists from Montaigne to Proust are men of the world who know it through and through. They do not present love as a myth nor do they enter into metaphysical speculation about it; but they ask: How does love arise, how does it find its realization, why does it pass away, how does it drift into error? Is there anywhere else save in France a psychology of love like that which we find in *Adolphe*, in the *Chartreuse de Parme*, in the *Éducation sentimentale*? This could only arise in a country in which love is regarded as the obvious and chief concern of humanity, in which the language has created such untranslatable expressions as *faire l'amour* or—if we go into a higher sphere—as *aimer d'amour*. It is only in French society that psychology and the life of love are woven into an almost indissoluble unity. Only a type of humanity which is preoccupied with the desires and the

---

23 "Why do the false ravings of worthless writings give you pleasure? Read this, which Life can say is truth itself. Here you will find no Centaurs, Gorgons or Harpies: in my pages you will understand Man." (Epigrams, X, iv, 7-10.) Ed.

results of love could produce such a psychological literature. The love proclaimed by Dante can lift us to the stars; *Romeo and Juliet* can flood us with poetry; but with Racine we say: "That is exactly right."

In our literature there is a great deal of theology, whether it be that of Lessing, Herder, Goethe, or of Hölderlin. In France theology is, and remains, the province of the Church alone. A free religiosity, a personal synthesis of religious and secular experience, can scarcely flourish there at all. It is of course true that theology, that the deepest and most intimate experience of Christianity, that the most spiritual form of mysticism, can be expressed in literary form. Pascal, Bossuet, Fénelon, to name only three, prove this completely. But theology, like all other forms of the intellect and of science, will only become part of the intellectual possession of the educated of France by way of literature. This, again, is a characteristic feature of French literature. Science penetrates into the consciousness of the educated people only after it has declared itself in an exemplary literary form. One function of French literature is the popularization of knowledge, or to put it differently, the despecialization of science. In France great thinkers and research workers have often been great writers as well: Descartes, Montesquieu, Buffon, Michelet, Taine, Renan, Bergson. Philosophers who wrote badly, like Comte, had to wait half a century for official recognition. Characteristic of France also is the type of writer who himself is not a creative scholar but who can interpret for the literary public the results of a certain science. Thus in the period of Louis XIV, Fontenelle made astronomy accessible to the Court, and Voltaire made a survey of world history for Madame du Châtelet. The Frenchman will allow himself to be instructed in all forms of knowledge if the literary form is good. In France, in the ranks of the intellectual types, the writer ranks higher than the scholar. For the intellectual life of France the literary circles mean far more than the universities. Everything can be said, and if well said it will find a hearing. And what has once been well said will live on imperishably in the memory of the nation.

The intellectual tradition of France is incarnate in the whole body and series of its classical works. Only he who accepts this tradition, assimilates it, and comes to terms with it, can hope for his part to represent the spirit of his nation. In France anyone who wishes to educate in matters literary and intellectual, who desires to have readers, listeners, and disciples, must complete this whole process. He must know how to value and balance the Classical and the Romantic schools, scepticism and spirituality, the heroic sentiment and the pert mockery, the profane and the sublime. ln France's tradition, Charles du Bos said once: "*Il existe un grand dialogue dont il nous faut souhaiter qu'il dure aussi longtemps que notre race, car il s'en dégage la musique la plus compréhensive et la plus solennelle que le génie français ait fait rendre à l'instrument qui lui est propre: le dialogue Montaigne - Pascal. Un Français est profond dans la mesure où, à son rang, il sait maintenir ce dialogue vivant en lui.*[24]

The German would decide either for Montaigne or for Pascal. The Frenchman will feel that he cannot sacrifice one for the other. In the entire company of great authors he sees reflected the wholeness of the worlds of intellect and spirit. He comes to regard literature with a respect bordering on reverence. In France alone is there a *religion des Lettres*: the surrender of the whole intellectual existence and of all the powers of faith to literature to its tradition, its cultivation, and its admiration. Only a French poet, Mallarmé, could write: "*Tout existe pour aboutir à un livre.*" In France as Thibaudet has said, there exists a "mysticism of books"; and in this minds which are otherwise separated by all the conflicts of politics, aesthetics and general outlook on life can meet and make friends. It is, of course, true that every day these conflicts—in every French newspaper—break into the sphere of literature. But it is still true that in France—and nowhere to the same extent as in France—there is a superior sphere which rises above these conflicts. This is the sphere of "pure criticism"—this phrase is used in the same sense as the expression *poésie pure*. In pure criticism, discussion is replaced by dialogue; it will never wholly refrain from pronouncing an opinion, but it does not condemn, and it does not argue. It contemplates in the mirror of the written word the complicated course of human affairs. It has become a final form of wisdom. It is one of the purest expressions of the French mind.

---

24 "There has existed in France a grand dialogue which we must strive to keep alive for as long as our race, for it is the source of the most universal and solemn music which the French genius has produced from the one instrument unique to our people: the Montaigne-Pascal dialogue. A Frenchman is profound according as he is able, depending on his station in life, to sustain the dialogue within him." See Charles DuBos page 113.

3
On Tradition in Literature

by

C. A. Sainte-Beuve

From: Charles-Augustin Sainte-Beuve, *De la Tradition en littéra-ture, et dans quel sens il la faut entendre*, the Inaugural lecture delivered by Sainte-Beuve before the Ecole Normale on April 12, 1858. Published in *Causeries du lundi*, t. 15. English translation by A.J. Butler in Selected Essays of Sainte-Beuve (London: Edward Arnold, n.d. [1894]).

$\mathscr{I}$f, as I have been more than once informed, you are good enough to wish to see me open this course of lectures, for my own part, believe me, I was no less eager to find myself among you, fulfilling the honourable and highly-prized duty entrusted to me; to which I henceforth devote myself unreservedly. But, anxious as I am to attack the detailed study of our literature, and to undertake with you a review of the principal literary works of our most brilliant century, I ought to say a few words to you by way of introduction, relating both to the spirit which I mean to bring to that examination, and to that in which I have to ask that you will be kind enough to hear me. I have written a good deal in the last thirty years—that is, I have scattered myself about a good deal; so that before starting upon a course of instruction in the proper sense, and laying down certain rules and principles which will at least indicate the general direction of my thought, I need to gather myself together, in order that there may be no misunderstanding between us, and that, as a consequence, my words may come before you with all the more freedom and confidence. You are the persons who will hereafter have as your special office and ministry to watch over the tradition, the transmission of classical and humane letters, to interpret them continually to each fresh generation of young persons; I, for my part, see myself charged, with a kindness which does me honour,...with the duty of preparing you for these worthy and important functions. I find myself naturally led to discuss what especially strikes me in that career which we shall henceforth share, and that which it most concerns us to make quite sure of.

There is such a thing as tradition. In what sense must we understand it—in what sense is it our duty to maintain it?

There is a tradition; who would deny it? For us it exists all traced out. It is visible like those immense, magnificent avenues or roads which used to traverse the empire, ending at what was called preeminently the City. Descendants as we are of the Romans, or, at any rate, adopted children of the Latin race—that race which was itself initiated by the Greeks into the cult of the beautiful—we have to embrace, to understand, never to desert the inheritance received from those illustrious masters and fathers, an inheritance which, from Homer down to the latest classic of yesterday (if there be a classic of yesterday[1]), forms the brightest and most solid portion of our intellectual capital. This tradition consists not solely in the collection of memorable works which we bring together in our libraries, and which we study—a large part of it has passed into our

---

1 And why not? For us the last of the classics was Chateaubriand.

laws, into our institutions, into our manners, into the education which we unconsciously inherit, into our habits, and into all our fundamental conceptions. It consists in a certain principle of good sense and culture which, in the course of ages, has penetrated so as to modify it into the very character of our Gaulish nation, and which entered long ago into the very composition of our wits.

All that it concerns us on no account to lose, all that we must never allow anyone to damage, at least without making it known, and giving the alarm as in a common peril, is there.

I am not going to establish any comparison between two classes of things profoundly distinct and wholly unlike, but I am going to make my thought more obvious by means of a comparison.

M. de Chateaubriand, recalling some fine chapters of the *Esprit des Lois*, ended his *Génie du Christianisme* by setting himself this question: "What would be the state of society today if Christianity had never appeared on the earth?" As may readily be supposed, answers crowded under his pen, and sprang forth from all sides.

A learned English author, Colonel Mure, in his *History of Greek Literature*, for his part sets himself this question: "If the Greek nation had never existed, or if the works of its genius had been destroyed by the grandeur and predominance of Rome, would the races which now stand at the head of Europe have raised themselves higher in the scale of literary culture than did the other nations of antiquity before they had been touched by the breath of Hellas?" It is a grand and beautiful question, one of those which most set us thinking and musing.

I have often mused, I have often asked myself, under all sorts of forms, and taking many special instances, putting myself at every point of view, what would have been the destiny of modern literature (to consider that point only) if the battle of Marathon had been lost, and Greece brought into subjection and slavery, crushed out of life before the age of Pericles; even at a date when she would have retained in her distant past the broad and incomparable beauty of her first great Ionian poets, but without the reflecting focus of Athens?

Let us never forget that Rome, by dint of her own energy and ability, had, when the second Punic war came to an end, already arrived at the most widely extended political power, and at the ripeness of a great state, without so far possessing anything like a literature properly so called or worthy of that name; she had to conquer Greece in order to be taken captive, in the person of her generals and her famous chiefs, in order to be touched with that noble fire which was to redouble and to perpetuate her glory. How many nations and races, if we except that first Hellenic race so privileged above all others, so singularly endowed, are or have been in this respect more like the Romans—that is to say, have of themselves possessed in regard to poetry or literature nothing more than a primary, rudimentary, rustic development, in no way exceeding a first wild growth? That was sufficient for nomad peoples who had in front of them the green forest or the steppe with its spring blooms—something short, simple (or coarse), invented on the spur of the moment, formless and vague, quite close to the earth, or too near the clouds.

I hear them coming, it is true, I hear the Northern nations growing and forming themselves with their warlike or festive songs, their mythology, their legends; I do not deny that there is a poetical faculty up to a certain point universal in humanity. All the nations which have successively gone forth from the central point, the heart of Asia, are recognised today as brothers and sisters of the same family, and of a family which has an air of nobility stamped on its brow; but, in all this numerous family, one brow was chosen among all, one elected maiden, upon whom incomparable grace was poured forth, who received from her cradle the gift of song, of harmony, of measure, of perfection—Nausicaa, Helen, Antigone, Electra, Iphigenia, Venus in all her noble forms; and if we suppose this enchanting child of genius, this muse of a noble house, cut down and sacrificed before her time, is it not true that all mankind might have said, like a family when it has lost the daughter who was its joy and its honour, 'the crown is fallen from our head'? If one could, with difficulty, collect all the wild crops, would they be worth one of her garlands? Would all the scattered plunder, all the small change of the others piled and heaped together, be equal in worth and weight to a single one of her golden talents?

I do not fix to one spot, I do not isolate that primary Hellenic beauty, and for that very reason I am not afraid to ascribe so much to it. You know as well as I that Rome, by herself, and if she had not been touched by the golden wand at the very moment when she was breaking it, was in danger of remaining for ever a mere power, lying with crushing weight on the world, whether as senate, camp, or legion. It was the buoyant soul of Greece which, passing into her, and mingling with the firm and judicious good sense of those politicians, those conquerors, produced in the second or third generation that assemblage of genius, of talents, of accomplishments, which makes up the fine Augustan age. Whether directly, or thenceforth by means of the Romans, that buoyant soul, that spark (for a spark is all that is wanted), that fiery or subtle germ of civilization, has never ceased to act at decisive epochs, to give life and be the signal for unexpected bursts of flower, for Renaissances. The very literature of chivalry which we see breaking forth, for the first time, in its precocious and brilliant development in the south of our own France, beside the Mediterranean, seems to have been brushed and caressed by some distant breath from ancient shores, which may have brought with it some invisible seed. Christian antiquity, imperfect from a literary point of view, but morally in a high position, had not in those ages ceased to be at once an active vehicle and a fund of wealth. Would Dante have had the idea and the power to compose his monumental poem, belonging so completely to the Middle Ages, if he had not perceived what tradition, incomplete as it was, had transmitted to him, in the way of memories, reminiscences, or fertile illusions, and if he had not literally had Virgil for his guide, support, and half-fabulous patron? However that may be, Beatrice, and the inspiration whence she issued, were surely a new sentiment in the world, for our tradition is neither locked up nor exclusive; we are glad to recognise that delicate sentiment of love and courtesy which belongs to chivalry, to see in it yet another ornament added to mankind's crown, side by side with atticism and urbanity. But let us never separate ourselves from atticism, from urbanity, from the principle of good sense and good reason, which in it is combined with grace. What we must never lose sight of is the feeling of a certain standard of beauty suited to our race, to our education, to our civilization. Not to have the feeling for letters, meant to the ancients the same thing as not having the feeling of virtue, of glory, of grace, of beauty—in one word, of all that which is really divine upon earth; let that be still our watchword. There is no question here of distinguishing between the Greeks and the Latins. For us, their legacy and their benefactions are merged together. Doubtless *Graecia capta ferum*[2] is at the bottom of everything, that is the starting-point. But the Roman force, the Roman arm, the Roman speech and practice, also pervade everywhere. That has been the great instrument to propagate and cultivate. No doubt Isocrates, in his famous panegyric, said, quite rightly at his own date, just before Alexander: "Our city has left the rest of mankind so far behind it in thought and in eloquence, that its pupils have become the masters of others; she has done her business so well, that the name

---

2 "Greece taken took her fierce captor captive and bore her arts to Latium's farms." (Horace, Epistles II, i, 156). Note: Although Rome had conquered and now controlled Greece, the older country's art and literature exercised a powerful sway over the tastes and aspirations of the Roman Intelligentsia. Tr. and Note by Jacob Fuchs. Ed.

of Greek seems to be no longer the designation of a single race, but that of intelligence itself, and that we call people Greeks who share rather in our culture than in our nature." With even more authority, Pericles said the same thing in that admirable panegyric of Athens which he introduced so magnificently into his funeral eulogy of the warriors who had died for their country. Never has there been a better description of that happy city where no chagrins, no jealousies, no rigid austerities offended the eye or mortified your neighbour's pleasure; where it was a joy merely to live, to breathe, to walk abroad, and where the mere beauty of buildings and public edifices, the beauty of daylight and a certain air of festivity, drove sadness far from the mind, where it was possible to love beauty with simplicity of life and philosophy without being effeminate; where wealth was used for a practical purpose and not for ostentation; where courage was not blind like that of the furious Mars, but enlightened and knowing its own reasons as befits the city of Minerva, the true Athens after the ideal of Pericles, his creation and his work, the school of Greece (*'Ellαδos 'Ellαs 'AΦnvαi*),[3] such as he had made it during the long years of his personal supremacy and potent persuasion; for we have in Pericles the most noble and brilliant type of the popular chief, the man who becomes dictator of a democracy by reason, eloquence, talent, and continual persuasion. In another very memorable discourse which Thucydides puts in his mouth, doubtless not without good cause, Pericles handles the Athenians as in later days he would have handled the Romans; he makes every effort to sustain and fortify them against the double trial of the war and the terrible plague; he lays himself out to breathe into those citizens of a great city, brought up in ways and sentiments worthy of it, the courage to make head against the greatest disasters. Speaking to them even then as to a people that were kings, proving to them that from the moment they had once been such they could not recoil, but were condemned to remain so always or to exist no longer, no longer even to expect, if they should fall, the usual conditions of subject-cities, he enunciates for their use the most decided public and political maxims: "To be hated, to be odious at the present time, such has been the lot of all those who have aspired to empire over others; but whoever incurs this odium for great causes takes the right side, and has no occasion to repent." And in truth, if one could always hear the Pericles of Thucydides, that Demosthenes not in word only but in action, one would no longer allow the Romans to boast as they have done that they

---

3 The author apparently intends to refer to the τῆς *Ellάdos παίδευσιν* of Thucydides, II, 41. (Translator's note.)

had added solidity to the delightful genius of the Greeks.

But the Athenians were only able to accomplish half his wish, and of this work which Pericles dreamed and more than dreamed, put before them, the work of constancy, of lasting energy, and of world-wide political empire, it was the Romans who undertook the accomplishment in proportions of far other breadth, and not only by sea but by land.

While the Greeks, fallen, cut off from exercising public virtues, became with few exceptions more frivolous, more voluble, more sophistical, more sycophantic, more romancing than they had ever been, the conquerors seized that precious divine element—a portion of the Promethean fire—and animated with it their practical vigour and their solid good sense in a temperament which united vivacity and consistence. It matters little that it was only the picked men among the Romans who possessed that refinement and that delicacy, not the whole people as at Athens; posterity only knows the picked men. I shall, however, never admit that Rome, even that Rome of the people which we have since seen to be possessed of so fine and so keen powers of raillery, had not, from the moment when she had leisure and opportunity, acute wits simultaneously with the gift of agreeable and dulcet language.

This must have become established pretty nearly in the time of Cicero, both the word and the thing: *Favorem et urbanum*, says Quintilian, Cicero *nova credit*.[4] By that time, accordingly, we get the other City, preeminently so-called, that in whose light Cicero wished that he might always live, so as to be the more sure of never growing rusty—the Rome of Catullus and Horace and onward to that of the younger Pliny. Such are our fatherlands.

After Trajan's days, when the hour of Roman decadence definitely struck, ecclesiastical literature, which was about to be born, did not enter as quickly or as directly into the inheritance of literary beauty as Rome had done in its first contact with Greece. The torch was not passed from hand to hand. In Greece alone, by a singular good fortune, and a remnant of its birthright privilege, that sacred literature, in the mouth of a Basil and a Chrysostom, recovered, without effort, copiousness and harmony, and almost the accents of Plato.

But at Rome and in Africa the Latin of the early fathers was harsh, far-fetched, and laboured, even while the thought was original, excellent, and often sublime. Christian writers started from a principle too different, too contrary to external beauty, to be able to greet it at first

---

4 "Cicero regards *favor* and *urbanus* as [words] but newly introduced into the language." (Quintilian VIII, iii, 34.) Tr. H.E. Butler. Ed.

sight, or when they met it to refrain from shocking it. But as ages went on, after revolutions and cycles laboriously accomplished, the stars came into conjunction again, and became favourable, harmony and supreme beauty were rediscovered; this blazes out and glows in the world of the Arts, in that kindly Rome of Raphael and Leo X; in a less brilliant, but perhaps more estimable style, in the style of morality and of eloquent language, of sincere and convinced poetry, it reappeared in France in the reign of Louis XIV. There was a day when Biblical grandeur and Hellenic beauty met and were fused and mingled in spirit and in form with a lofty simplicity; and when we speak today of tradition, and of that which would have failed if it had been lacking, of what would have been missing in the most charming stories, in the most noble pictures of human memory, we have the right to say, in each case, by an equally incontestable title, there would have been no Homer or Xenophon, there would have been no Virgil, there would have been no Athalie.

But you will say that great men of letters have been produced entirely outside of this tradition. Name them. I know one only, and he is great enough, no doubt —Shakespeare. And in his case, are you quite sure that he is entirely outside? Had he not read Montaigne and Plutarch—those copious repertories, nay, rather those reserve hives of antiquity in which so much honey is stored? An admirable poet, and no doubt the most natural since Homer, though in such a different line, of him it has been written with perfect truth that he had so creative an imagination and that he paints so well and with such conspicuous energy all his characters—from heroes and kings, down to innkeepers and peasants—"that if human nature had been destroyed, and that if there remained no other monument of it than his works alone, other beings might know from his writings what man had been." It is not to you I need say that this man, of all men so human, was not a savage nor a man of irregular life; that we must not confound him, because he has sometimes carried energy or subtlety to excess, or because he has given in either to the coarseness or the refinements of his own time, with eccentrics and madmen full of themselves, intoxicated with their own nature and their own works, "drunk with their own wine." If we could see him appear suddenly and walk in person, I imagine him to myself (as an ingenious critic has shown us[5]) noble and human of countenance, having nothing about him of the bull, the boar, or even the lion; bearing in his physiognomy, like Molière, the most noble features of the species— those which speak most of the soul and the intellect; moderate, sensible

---

5 Tieck.

in talk, and most often, whether through pity or indulgence, smiling and kind; for he has also created beings who ravish us with purity and kindness, and he dwells at the centre of human nature. Is it not to him that we must go to find the very most expressive word for rendering kindness—"the milk of human kindness"? a quality which it always seems to me essential that energetic talents should mingle with their force if they are not to fall into sternness or into insulting brutality; just as in the case of fine talents inclined to be too kindly I should require, to save them from insipidity, that there should be added a little of what Pliny and Lucian call pungency[6]—the salt of strength. Thus it is that talents become complete; and Shakespeare, in his own way, saving the faults of his time, was complete. You may reassure yourselves; great men in every line, and above all, I will say, in the intellectual order, have never been crazy or barbarous. If any writer appears to us in his conduct and in his whole personality to be violent, unreasonable, given to shocking good sense or the most natural proprieties, he may have talent, for talent, even great talent, is compatible with many perversities; but be sure he is not a writer of the first quality and of the highest mark among mankind. Homer sometimes nods, Corneille in conversation is heavy and nods, La Fontaine nods; they have their moments of absence, of forgetfulness; but the greater men are never permanently extravagant, ridiculous, grotesque, ostentatious, boastful, cynical, or unseemly. For my own part, however large the allowance I may make for natural varieties and singularities, I shall never fancy to myself the revered choir of the five or six great men of letters and of creative genius of whom humanity can boast, and who after all can only be the five or six leaders among the honourable folk of the universe, as a band or pack of crazy maniacs rushing each with his head down after their prey, on the chance of catching it. No, tradition tells us; and, as the consciousness of our own civilized nature tells us still more plainly, reason always must have, and definitely has, the first place even among these favourites, these elect of the imaginative power; or if she does not constantly keep the first place, but allows an access of high spirits to run its course, she is never far off, as she stands by smiling, awaiting an hour which is at hand—the moment of recovery. This is the literary religion to which we belong, even though surrounded by the most lively audacities, and to this we would always belong.

As a critic, I may perhaps be allowed to invoke the example of the greatest of critics, Goethe—of whom we may say that he is not only tradition but that he is all traditions united. Which, from a literary point of

6 The *amaritudo* of the Latin author, δριμύτης of the Greek.

view, predominates in him? The classical element. In him I can see the Greek temple even on the shores of Tauris. He wrote Werther, but it is Werther written by one who carries his Homer into the fields, and who will find him again even when his hero has lost him. It is thus that he has preserved his lordly serenity; no one dwells in the clouds less than he; he enlarges Parnassus, he makes stages in it, he peoples it at every station, at every summit, at every angle of its rocks; he makes it like, perhaps even too like, that pinnacled rather than rounded hill, Montserrat in Catalonia, but he does not destroy it. Without that taste for Greece which chastens and tethers his universal indifference, or, if you prefer, his universal curiosity, Goethe might have lost himself in the indefinite, the indeterminate. So many summits are familiar to him that if Olympus were not his summit by predilection, where would he go? or rather, where would he not go? he, the most open-minded of men, and the most advanced in the direction of the East? His transformations, his pilgrimages in the pursuit of the various forms of beauty, would have had no end, but he came back, he settled down, he knew the point of view from which to contemplate the universe that it might appear in its most beautiful light. As for himself, whenever we wish to form an image of the critical spirit at its highest pitch of intelligence, and of considered understanding, we figure him to ourselves as an attentive and watchful spectator, curious from afar off, on the look-out for every discovery, for all that goes by, for every sail on the horizon—but from the heights of his Sunium.

He it was, the author of Werther and of Faust, one who knew what he was talking about, who so justly said: "By classic I understand sound, and by romantic, sickly." But as the classic, and even the romantic, form part of tradition, if we are to consider it in its entire series, and in the full extent of the past, I must pause at this saying of Goethe's, and I should like to try to explain it to myself.

Well, then, the classic, in its most general character and in its widest definition, comprises all literatures in a healthy and happily-flourishing condition, literatures in full accord and in harmony with their period, with their social surroundings, with the principles and powers which direct society, satisfied with themselves. Let us be quite clear, I mean satisfied to belong to their nation, to their age, to the government under which they come to birth and flourish (joy of intellect, it has been said, is the mark of strength of intellect; that is no less true for individuals), those literatures which are and feel themselves to be at home, in their proper road, not out of their proper class, not agitating, not having for their principle discomfort, which has never been a principle of beauty. I am not the person to speak ill of romantic literatures, I keep within the terms of Goethe and of historical explanation. People are not born when they wish to be, they cannot choose their moment for hatching out, they cannot, especially in youth, avoid the general currents which are passing in the air, and which blow dryness or moisture, fever or health; and there are similar currents for the soul. That feeling of fundamental contentment, in which there is, before all things, hope, into which discouragement does not enter, where you may say that there is a period before you which will outlast you, which is stronger than you, a period which will protect and judge, where you have a fine field for a career, for an honourable and glorious development in the full light of day—that is what gives the first foundation, upon which afterwards arise, like palaces and temples in regular order, harmoniously constructed and regular works.

When you live in a perpetual instability of public affairs, when you see society change often before your eyes, you are tempted to disbelieve in literary immortality, and consequently to grant yourself every licence. Now it falls to nobody's lot to give himself this feeling of security and of a steady and durable period, one must breathe it in with the air in the hours of youth. Romantic literatures, which are above all things matters of sudden assault and of adventure, have their merits, their exploits, their brilliantly played parts, but outside of established rules. They perch themselves astride of two or three periods, never getting fairly into the saddle on a single one, uneasy, inquiring, eccentric by nature, either much in advance or much in arrear, in other respects wilful and wandering.

Classical literature never complains, never groans, never feels ennui. Sometimes, in company with sorrow, and by way of sorrow, one may outstrip it, but beauty is more tranquil.

The classic, I repeat, possesses among its other characteristics that of loving its own country, its own times, of seeing nothing more desirable or more beautiful. It is legitimately for and of these. Its motto should be 'Activity with tranquillity.' That is true of the age of Pericles, of the age of Augustus, no less than of the reign of Louis XIV. Let us hear the great poets and the orators of those periods speak under their fair sky, as it were under their dome of blue, their hymns of praise still resound in our ears: they carried the art of applause very far.

Romanticism, like Hamlet, has home-sickness, it seeks for what it has not, seeks it even beyond the clouds; it dreams, it sees in visions. In the nineteenth century it adores the Middle Ages; in the eighteenth, it

73

was already revolutionary with Rousseau. In Goethe's sense of the word, there are romanticists of various times. Chrysostom's young friend Stagirius, or Augustine in his youth, were of this kind, Renés before their time; sick men, but they were sick men who might be healed, and Christianity healed them by exorcising the demon. Hamlet, Werther, Childe Harold, the true Renés, are sick men of the kind who sing and suffer, who enjoy their malady—romantics more or less in a dilettante way; they are sick for sickness' sake.

Oh! if one day in our fair fatherland, in our capital which grows daily in magnificence, which is for us so fine a representative of the country, we felt ourselves happy, honestly happy of belonging to it; if, above all, young souls, touched by a kind inspiration, caught by that praiseworthy and salutary contentment which does not engender a childish pride, but only adds emulation to life, could feel themselves happy to live in an age, under a social system, which allows or favours all the finer developments of humanity; if they would not from the outset put themselves in an attitude of revolt, of opposition or faultfinding, of bitterness, of regrets or of hopes too late or premature; if they would consent to spread out and to direct all their powers in the wide field open before them, then the balance would be restored between talent and its surroundings, between men of parts and the social system; we should find ourselves again in unison, strife and moral sickness would cease, and literature would again of itself become classical, both in grandeur of line and in what is essential, its fundamental basis. It is not that people would have more talent or more knowledge, but more order, more harmony, more proportion, a noble aim, and simpler means and more courage to arrive at it; we should perhaps begin again to have works that would last.

It is here no mission, no claim of ours to produce such; we have above all to preserve them. What is the best and surest manner of maintaining tradition? In the first place it is to possess it complete, not to concentrate and crowd it upon certain points too close together, not to exaggerate it here and overlook it there. There is no need to tell you these things, since the models are familiar and present to you, from the first beginnings, and in different literatures, and your minds are furnished with true standards of comparison in every kind. Others have set up the pillars on the foundation of yourselves, you have the patterns of true beauty. He who can see Plato, Sophocles, Demosthenes, face to face, is under no temptation to grant too much, even to the most illustrious of the moderns. That is the weak point of those who only possess one language and one literature. Frederick the Great granted everything to

Voltaire, even to Voltaire as a poet, and adjudged to him all the crowns, merely because he had no sufficient standard of comparison. Through over-narrowing of tradition, through making it too cut and dried, many of those who at the beginning of this century claimed the exclusive title of classics, were, in the strife of that time, those who could least do so.

As each age renews itself, portions of recent tradition which are believed well-based crumble into ruin after a certain fashion, and the only result is, that the indestructible marble rock appears all the more in its true solidity.

In order to maintain tradition, it is not always sufficient to attach it firmly to its most lofty and most august monuments, it is necessary to verify it and to check it incessantly at the points nearest to us, even to rejuvenate it, and to keep it in perpetual relation with what is living. Here we touch a somewhat delicate question. It is no business of mine to introduce into the curriculum too recent names, to go out of my way to judge the works of the present day, to confuse functions and parts. A professor is not a critic. The critic, if he does his duty (and where are such critics at the present day?) is a sentinel always awake, always on the look-out; but he does not only cry 'Who goes there?' he gives help; far from resembling a pirate, or delighting in shipwrecks, he sometimes, like the coasting-pilot, goes to the help of those whom the tempest overtakes as they enter or leave port. The professor's obligations are smaller—or, I should say, different. He is bound to more reserve and more dignity. He must not go far from the sacred places which it is his part to show and to tend. Still, he cannot entirely escape all knowledge of novelties, of arrivals and approaches, announced with all pomp, of sails which are signalled from time to time on the horizon as those of invincible armadas. He must know them, at least the chief of them. He must have his opinion. In a word, he must keep his eye on the neighbouring shore, and never go to sleep.

To go to sleep on tradition is a danger with which we are little threatened. We are no longer in the days when, if you were born in a capital, you never left it. We have seen classics who have grown feeble in the second generation, who have become sedentary and home-keeping. They have acted like the son of Charles V, of all emperors the most travelled, that Philip II who never stirred from his Escurial. Nobody nowadays has any right to rest so quiet, even in the best established admirations. One thing or another is constantly moving as we watch it, and there open, as in our old cities, long, new vistas which change the most familiar views. Instruction is bound, whether it will or not, to take fresh bearings, to reconsider in these things. There are ways also in which it can renew itself, in which it can modify the manner in which it does service to taste, and defends tradition. I will take our seventeenth century for example.

Criticism and erudition are guided by the historical spirit, have devoted themselves for some years past to a great work which has its value, and the importance and undoubted utility of which I should be far from depreciating. There has come a taste for original sources. People have wished to make a closer acquaintance with everything by the aid of papers and documents at first hand, and, as far as possible, unpublished. In this way they have succeeded in penetrating the secret of many things and the most private opinions of many persons, to know in almost daily detail the grounds of their admiration for Henry IV, for Richelieu, for Louis XIV, to count up the hidden springs of their administration, and to follow all the movements of their foreign policy. Thanks to this publication of diplomatic documents, what formerly was possessed by only a few learned men, the private domain of Foncemagne or of Père Griffet, has been put at the disposal of everybody. State secrets of the past have ceased to exist. Nor have people limited themselves to the historical figures properly so called; they have chosen to go into the inner court, to the private fireside of men most eloquent either by pen or by word. Their papers have been examined, their autograph letters, the first editions of their works, the evidence of their surroundings, the journals of the secretaries, who knew them best, and in this way notions have been formed to them somewhat different, and certainly more precise than could be obtained from the mere reading of their published works. People of taste in former times in their literary judgement of works were a little too indolent, too delicate, too much people of the world; they stopped at researches of the least difficulty, and shrank back as from thorns. Even the critics by profession, elegant as they might be, did not sufficiently inform themselves beforehand of everything which might give to their judgement perfect guarantees for exactitude and truth. We know a good deal more today than they did about many points in the subjects on which they touched. We have at hand all the resources that we can desire; without speaking of biography, bibliography, that entirely new branch once held to be not repaying, that science of books of which it has been said that it too often dispenses people from reading them, and which our genuine men of letters used formerly to leave to the Dutch critics, has become Parisian and fashionable, almost agreeable and certainly easy. The most humble beginner, if he will only devote two or three mornings to it, can with little trouble know all that concerns the material part of the books and the personality of the author upon whom he is for the moment engaged. Those are the advantages, the benefit of it; but, on the other hand, the inconveniences of these new methods at a period when there is too little of the higher criticism to act the part of watcher and judge, have not been slow in showing themselves, and if I am not mistaken, we have them on every side full in our eyes.

Not a day passes without someone announcing a discovery; everyone wishes to make it his own, everyone boasts of it, and puffs his wares unchecked. Disproportionate importance and literary value are attributed to works hitherto unknown. People are proud of 'finds', merely curious (when they are that), which cost no thought, no effort of the mind, but merely the trouble of going and picking them up. One would say that the era of the scholiasts and commentators was reopening and beginning anew; a man gets no less honour and consideration for this, nay, more, than if he had attempted a fine novel, a fine poem, or tried the ways of true invention, the lofty roads of thought. There has been a change in the level of public approbation, while at the same time the writer's own point of honour has been displaced, and his ambition has been perceptibly lowered. It is a very general and very pronounced misunderstanding which has mixed itself up with a useful thing. As for works which, having been produced conscientiously and modestly—we could quote examples of them—invite esteem, I see the moment at hand when there will no longer be crowns enough for them.

Let us maintain the degrees of art, the stages of intelligence. Let us encourage all industrious research, but let us in everything leave the master's place to talent, to careful thought, to judgement, to reason, to taste. For example, I esteem highly those dissertations which we see produced every year on special subjects, in which the author often seeks to excavate somewhat further than had already been done, to add something to what people knew already. I draw instruction from them, you will write some yourselves before long, good ones I hope, even new ones. But must I admit that, when I see the titles which are far too complacently affixed to them, the promises, the public pledges of discovery, 'So-and-so from unpublished documents', I a little distrust the taste and the perfect accuracy of the conclusions. I shall not advise you to do it, but I should be just as glad if people would put, on the title-page once for all, 'So-and-so according to judicious ideas and views', even were they ancient.

You must quite understand the extent of my hesitation. Far be it from me, I say again, to wish to diminish the esteem due to a fashion of research which has become general, and which under the slightly confused and dusty appearance of a big inventory is tending to renew, perhaps to freshen, in future days the surface of literary history, although I suspect that literature has less to gain from it than history may have. If time, the great devourer, makes the memory of many facts disappear and annihilates the true explanations of them with their witnesses, it is also in many respects the great revealer. It raises from underground other unexpected witnesses, and discloses many secrets that could not have been hoped for. But having said this, and notwithstanding these supplementary inquiries which are always being opened, let us, if possible, preserve the light touch, the delicate and prompt impression of good taste; in presence of living works of the mind, let us dare to keep our judgement clear and alive also, sharply defined, unhampered, sure of itself even without documents to support it.

I am not afraid to vary my examples, my comparisons, and to choose those which will bring you most into touch with my thought. As you know, Thucydides collected notes to the composition of his fine, his severely simple, history for twenty years long. He must have written some sort of memoranda or detailed journals about all the events which he watched from the retirement of exile. Artist and historian, when he had once set to work he used them freely, taking or rejecting as it suited his plan or not, and then destroyed them or never thought of them again. I do not say that it would not be extremely interesting today to have those notes—if by chance they had been preserved—but I do say that in the system which would tend to prevail, which already does prevail, people would come to prefer them decidedly to the composition itself, to that history of the Peloponnesian war that is so perfect, so epic, or rather dramatic, and in which there is such an austere unity of action. People would come on the whole to prefer the materials to the work, the scaffolding to the monument. Thucydides' note-books rather than the statue of bronze which Thucydides raised! You who are going to Athens, who go there day by day, you will resist to the best of your power this upsetting of the points of view, even in what belongs to modern times, and if, in regard to these, truth at any price (or what is taken for it), if curiosity decidedly wins the day over art, you will at least take care that the old method, and what has sprung from it, shall remain in honour, an object of worship and of study, present to the memory and to the meditation of those faithful intellects which can still be touched by the idea of beauty.

But although this disposition is admitted and recognised between us, although while we profit as best we may by the occasionally some-what cumbrous instruments of modern criticism, we shall retain some of the customs, even some of the principles of the old criticism, as-signing the first place in our admiration and our esteem to invention, composition, the art of writing; sensitive above all to the charm of wit, to lofty or subtle talent, you will not conclude from this that we shall necessarily, in regard to celebrated books and their writers, fall into a monotonous and universal frame of laudation. The best way not only of appreciating but of getting others to appreciate fine works is to have no predilection, to give one's self full liberty every time one reads them or speaks them, to forget, if possible, that one has possessed them for a long time, and to begin upon them again as if one had only today made their acquaintance. Thus steeped again in its source, one's opinion, even if it may sometimes remain inferior to what one had previously formed, at any rate recovers life and freshness. The man of taste even though he be not destined to teach and have his full leisure, ought for his own sake, it seems to me, to return every four or five years upon the best of his old admirations, to verify them, to put them to the question again as though they were new—that is to say, to reawaken and refresh them even at the risk of seeing them now and then somewhat deranged; the important point is that they should be living. But have no anxiety about the result. All of those admirations which are well founded, if the reader himself in his inmost soul has not become in the interval less worthy to admire beauty, will all or nearly all gain and increase by this honest review; as we advance in life really beautiful things appear more and more beauti-ful proportionately to our greater opportunities of comparison.

We will try, then, not to admire more than we should, or otherwise than we should, not to give everything to one century, even to a great century, not to stake everything at once on a few great writers. In speak-ing of them we will try to concentrate our praise upon their principal merit; for even in the case of great authors there is one principal merit. It is only our contemporaries who have every merit, the most contradic-tory at the same time; with the ancients, and with the classics we shall be more sober, and this sobriety will itself be homage.

And in this matter I am cautioned to be circumspect when I re-member how reserved in eulogy are all the greatest minds, the steadiest and loftiest intellects in different lines—Laplace, Lagrange, Napoleon—but also how they let their eulogies apply accurately to the principal point of a man's merits or talents. Then it needs but one word to stamp him for ever; that word is fixed and engraved. I know that lower down, when one belongs to the mere majority of mankind, there is less need to count one's words or to be cautious in admiration; but even so one should know how to direct one's praises, and not let them go up like a rocket. Let us leave it to others to excite themselves with exaggerated imaginations which go to the head, and are near akin to a gentle intoxication. I know no more divine pleasure than a clear, distinct, and felt admiration.

In the case of an author I am not going to praise the art where the chief features are force and grandeur. If I praise the art in the *Provinciales* I shall, in the same Pascal, praise only the force and moral energy of the *Pensées*; I shall bow down before the grand, mighty, sublime language of Bossuet, certainly the most impetuous, the most copious, which has burst forth in the French tongue; but if it is a question of elegance and grace I shall keep the palm for Fénelon. When I come to speak of Boileau I shall only moderately praise the poetry or the thought of his satires, the thought even of his epistles. Still we shall very clearly see his rare poetry in some epistles and in the *Lutrin*. But above all I shall display him to you as full of sense, of judgement, of honesty, of sound and piercing words spoken to the purpose, often with courage—a character armed with reason, and clad with honour, and for this reason, as much as for his talent, deserving all the authority which he exercised even within two paces of Louis XIV.

It may sometimes happen that in this number of successive appreciations and judgements into which I shall put my best care our measures may differ a little, that there may be some cases in which you will find me less keen than you reckoned, and where you will admire more than I do certain qualities of our writers. I shall be happy in this as in other things to be outstripped by you. We shall have to make certain reciprocal concessions to each other. I have often remarked that when two good intellects pass totally different judgements on the same author we may safely wager that it is because they are not, in fact, fixing their thoughts, for the moment, on the same object, on the same works of the author in question, on the same passages of his works; that it is because they have not the whole of him before their eyes, that they are not, for the moment, taking him in entirely. A closer attention, a wider knowledge, will bring together differing judgements and restore them to harmony. But even in the regular graduated circle of lawful admiration a certain latitude must be allowed to the diversity of tastes, minds, and ages. But I am forgetting. We shall have plenty of opportunities of together applying and verifying, in assiduous practice, the various observations which I am here laying before you, without overmuch order and method; the *Ars poetica* of our master, Horace, having long ago given us authority for this fashion of free discursiveness upon matters of taste. Be sure that if on this first occasion I have brought under your notice so many recommendations, so many critical remarks, if I have appeared to be giving you many pieces of advice which others have already given you much better, it has not been without addressing much of it to myself first. You will do me a service in the first place, by recalling them to me; and still further, by daily offering me, from your knots of thoughtful and eager young men, the best and most living answer to what is too often the final word, the last barren result, of a life spent in isolation and too self-centred thought.

As time goes on you will make me believe that I can, for my part, be of some good to you, and with the generosity of your age you will repay me, in this feeling alone, far more than I shall be able to give you in intellectual direction, or in literary insight. If in one sense I bestow on you some of my experience, you will requite me, and in a more profitable manner, by the sight of your ardour for what is noble; you will accustom me to turn oftener and more willingly towards the future in your company; you will teach me again to hope.

4
The Essential Character of French Literature

by

Ferdinand Brunetière

From: Ferdinand Brunetière: "Sur le caractère essentiel de la littérature française", in *Etudes critiques sur l'histoire de la Littérature française*, Vème série (Paris: Hachette, 1896). English translation by J. E. G. Dixon.©

$\mathscr{I}$t is to be sure a bold and imprudent undertaking to attempt to express or to sum up in a word the essential character of so vast, so rich and above all so diverse a literature as French literature. What connection in effect could be found between a story of the Round Table like the *Chevalier au lion* by Chrétien de Troyes, for example, and the *Maître de Forges*, or some vaudeville by Eugène Labiche? Everything about them is different, including the language; and still more the authors themselves, to say nothing of their times and their places. But, by way of defining its essential character, if we begin by thus eliminating from the history of the literature all that has diversified it, what does there remain? What literary or even historical elements remain, and what shall we have done other than to reduce to the point of evaporation, so to speak, the material we have taken it upon ourselves to consider? This objection is easy to answer. If it is not absolutely true that a great literature is the adequate expression of the genius of a race, and that its history is the faithful summary of that of a whole civilization, the contrary is undoubtedly even less true; and whatever difference a period of six or seven hundred years might have effected between a troubadour of the 12th century and a vaudevillist of the Third Republic there must necessarily be some relationship between them. Is it not permissible to add that in a Europe where for a thousand years so many races have mingled and merged, it is perhaps more markedly in their literatures that the great historical nationalities have become conscious of themselves? What resolves the issue and what in the long term justifies the attempt to define the essential character of the literature, are the factual consequences which seem to result from it: it is the light that this character, once defined, throws in some way on the innermost history of a literature; it is what it tells us of the cumulative formation of the national souls. Suppose for example that the essential character of Italian literature is that it is what might be called an artistic literature. This characteristic alone immediately distinguishes and separates it from all other great modern literatures, from French as from German, and from English as from Spanish—in which, undoubtedly, works of art are very numerous, but in which you will find very few which are principally this by conscious design and intent, the sole aim of the author in creating them being, as with Ariosto or Tasso, to follow a poetic caprice or to realize a dream of beauty... By that very fact is explained the prestige which this same literature exercised over the minds of men of the time of the Renaissance. Frenchmen contemporary with François I and Henry II, Englishmen of the time of Henry VIII and Elizabeth, were afforded their first feelings for art by the Italians; and if the idea of the innate and intrinsic power of form is not the whole of the Renaissance, would it not perhaps be the most far-reaching part?...

Let us take another example and say that the essential character of Spanish literature is that it is a chevaleresque literature. Is it not true that the whole of her literary history is illuminated by it as by a beam of light? Epic songs of the *Romancero,* novels of adventure, the drama of Calderon and of Lope de Vega, mystical treatises and picaresque novels—we grasp the bond which forms a connection between these very different works: their family resemblance, the hereditary feature which bears witness to their common origin, that Castilian *pundonor* whose exaggeration, in turns sublime and grotesque, is worn almost indifferently, as we see it in the history of the *Knight of the Mournful Countenance* at the extremes of dedication or of madness. In our modern Europe, political and industrial, utilitarian and positivist, if we have not entirely lost the feeling for the chevaleresque it is because of Spanish literature; and of the spirit of the Middle Ages it is that which has preserved for us all that has deserved to survive...

The essential character of French literature is more difficult to determine. Not that our national literature is in itself more original than any other, nor richer in great works and in great men: nothing would be more impertinent than to make such a claim. And if the Spanish have no Molière or the English no Voltaire, we for our part have no Cervantes and no Shakespeare. But French literature is without doubt the most abundant and the most prolific, not to say the most fertile, of all modern literatures, for the fact is that it is the most ancient; and, without vanity, we can recall that neither Dante in Italy nor Chaucer in England have dissimulated what they owed, the first to our troubadours, and the second to the anonymous authors of our old *fabliaux.* Is it not also the most purposeful and pains-taking? Or, if you wish, the most gracious—that which in all times has been the most receptive of foreign literatures, which has largely taken its inspiration from them, and which has scrupled least to convert them to itself in form and substance? Ronsard is almost an Italian poet, and Corneille, with elements of the Norman in him, is almost a Spanish tragic poet who, when he is not finding his inspiration in Calderon or Lope de Vega, finds it in Seneca or Lucan, both of whom were from Cordova. We also have prose-writers like Diderot who have been the centre of discussion for more than two hundred years as to whether they are the most German or the most English of our Champenois. And soon, if we do not take care, only the Russian novelists Goncharov or Shchedrin will be read in Paris. Let us add that, being international or cosmopolitan in this sense, French literature is even more so in the sense that no other literature takes pride in having attracted to it more foreigners: Italians from Brunetto Latini, the master of Dante, to Galiani, the friend of our Encyclopaedists, Englishmen like Hamilton and Chesterfield, and especially Germans like Leibnitz and Frederick the Great. That it is which has made French literature so diverse, and which makes it so difficult to characterize in a word.

II

If, however, we were to say that before anything else— and before being defined by those qualities of order and clarity, of logic and precision, of elegance and politesse, the enumeration of which has become almost banal—our literature is essentially sociable or social, this would not perhaps be expressing the whole truth, but if I am not mistaken it would not be far from it. Prose writers and even poets from Chrétien de Troyes to François Coppée, from Froissart or Commynes to the author of the *Esprit des lois* and the author of *Essai sur les Moeurs*, hardly anyone in France has written without having society in mind, without ever separating the expression of his thought from regard for the public whom he was addressing, nor consequently the art of writing from that of pleasing, persuading and convincing. "The very poets of Greece," Bossuet has said somewhere, "who were in the hands of the whole people, instructed them even more than they entertained them. The most illustrious of all conquerors considered Homer as a master who taught him to rule well. That great poet was not less effective in teaching how to obey and how to be a good citizen. He and so many other poets whose works are not less grave than they are agreeable, extol only the arts useful to human life, are imbued only with the common weal, the motherland, society, and that admirable *civilité* which we have explained." In so defining the essential character of Greek literature, Bossuet was at the same time, and unknown to himself, defining his own literary ideal. But in any event what he says there of Aeschylus or Sophocles is not less true of Corneille or of Voltaire—of the latter of whom it must be said that this concern to extol the arts useful to human life impaired his theatre. And if there were any doubt that this preoccupation were the heart and soul of our literature, the number and diversity of the facts which it explains in the history of our national literature would suffice to convince me.

So it is first of all, that all the qualities that we have mentioned—order and clarity, logic and precision, rigour of composition and urbanity of style—all are dependent on it as so many effects of one and the same cause. If what is not clear is not French, it is not in the original character of the language or in some unknown secret virtue that the reason for it must be sought. Our vocabulary or our syntax, reduced to their essential elements and considered in themselves, have nothing which differentiate them from the syntax or vocabulary of Spanish and Italian. They have the same origin and in more than one respect the same evolution. But whereas in Spain or in Italy the writers, and especially the poets, pre-occupied with making their language more sensual, more harmonious and more beautiful, were not even deterred from the extremes of Gongorism or Marinism, in France on the other hand the whole aim of our writers in general and of our prose writers in particular has been to be better understood, and to that end in their successive works to tend toward greater simplicity, clarity, and lucidity.

Rivarol makes a perceptive and profound remark in this connection in his famous *Discours sur l'universalité de la langue française*: "Study the writings of the ancient authors that have bean translated into the modern languages. Thanks to the facility with which almost all other languages model themselves on or adapt themselves to Latin or Greek, they render the originals faithfully, including even the obscurities. A French translation on the other hand is always an explication." It could not be better stated; and I shall reproach him only for having sought in the character of our language a reason which seems to me rather implied in the conception of their art formed by our writers. It is out of respect for the reader, and, as Bossuet said, out of *civilité*—if their aim is to make themselves accessible to all, not only to their compatriots but to foreigners too—that our writers of the 17th century have purged the French sentence of those learned and Greek and Latin mannerisms which still weighed it down and encumbered it. Similarly, in the following century, if the brisker, more agile, unadorned phrase of Voltaire came to replace the ampler, richer, more organic phrase of Pascal and Bossuet, it is again out of *civilité*, since it was intended to reach new strata of less educated readers and to enlighten them. Similarly again, in our own times, if the Romantics have demanded the right, in prose as in verse, to use a less dignified and less select vocabulary, and consequently a more popular vocabulary than that of the classics, where is the reason for it to be found if not in that *civilité* which they have appeared at times to violate for the sake of making themselves better understood in their turn by a less select and a less dignified public, and therefore a more numerous public, than that of Voltaire and Pascal?

The first and principal aim of our great writers has therefore been to be read. It is not the universality of the French language which has effected the universality of the literature; rather is it the universality of the literature which has made the French language universal. Civilized Europe did not read Rabelais and Montaigne, Voltaire and Rousseau, because they were French: they studied French in order to be able to read the *Essais* of Montaigne and the *Contrat social* of Rousseau. The consequence is quite clear. If the French language has become clearer and more logical, more precise and more polished than any other, it was not so originally and it had no reason in itself for becoming so. The whole honour belongs to our great writers. It is they who have made it such, and if they have done so it has been for the purpose of making it more fitting for the role or the social function which they have all assigned to literature since the earliest times.

It is that fact also that explains the superiority of our literature in the genres which might be called popular: I mean those which exist only with the complicity of the public. There is no orator without an audience, no drama without a theatre, no correspondence where there are not at least two people, and no moralists[1] without salons.

Consider the eloquence of the pulpit in this connection. If there has never been in any language a more eloquent preacher than Bossuet or a more vigorous preacher than Bourdaloue, it is because independently of their personal qualities none have understood or developed better than they in their *Sermons* the political and social virtues of Christianity. In a very different order of ideas, among our dramatic writers, I see hardly any save Racine and Regnard who have not prided themselves on being correctors or directors of morals; all others on the other hand—Corneille and Molière, Voltaire and Marivaux, Beaumarchais and Diderot, Dumas and Hugo—have had that as their aim. Look at the masterpieces of the French novel from the *Astrée* of Honoré d'Urfé, not to go back farther, to Zola's *Germinal*. In these there is no analysis of states of soul as in the novels of Richardson or George Eliot. The French authors depict the morals of the society of their times. The good French novels—with the exception of *Adolphe* or *René*, which are not novels—are all social

---

1 The French word *moraliste* does not mean what is meant in English by moralist. It applies to a writer whose principal concern is with the moral and psychological problems facing man and society in his time. The fact that these change so little accounts for the timelessness and perennial appeal of French literature. See also Duhamel, *The Church of French Literature*, page 118.

portraits. And what shall I say of our great letter writers: Mme de Sévigné, Mme de Maintenon, Mme du Deffand, Voltaire? What preoccupation with the world and consequently with others! What care is taken to entertain, to instruct and to please! This is carried so far that a truly private correspondence like that of Mlle. de Lespinasse, in which the writer thinks only of what is related to her dominant passion, astonishes us and sounds a jarring note in the history of our epistolary literature. But for society, but for the curiosity which they have always had about society, but for the obvious pleasure which they have always found in studying its slightest customs, where would our moralists be—La Rochefoucauld and La Bruyère, Vauvenargues and Duclos, Chamfort and Rivarol, Stendhal and Joubert? If ever writers could say that all they did was to "render unto the public what they had lent them", it is undoubtedly they; and in that very fact resides the reason for their superiority over all those who, in other literatures, have tried in vain to compete with them.

Another result of this way of understanding and of treating literature has been that the properly literary qualities have in French gradually extended to subjects which seemed by their very nature to be least suited to them. By the very fact that our great writers have never divorced the idea of their art from that of the interest, the profit and the pleasure of the reader, it has come about that anything that can entertain or instruct has in France found its way into the domain of literature. So it is that the most abstract subject-matters, and by definition the most remote from common experience, have in French become the source of masterpieces which we are justified in placing side by side with the tragedies of Racine or the fables of La Fontaine. Do I need to give examples? The *Provinciales* is but a collection of theological pamphlets. The *Entretiens sur la pluralité des mondes* is a treatise on Cartesian astronomy. The *Esprit des lois* is a compilation of universal and comparative jurisprudence. *Émile* is no more than a pedagogical novel. I shall say nothing of the *Histoire naturelle* or of the *Contrat social*. Yet what tragedies of Corneille or Hugo, what novels of Lesage or Prévost, what odes or elegies, have done more or as much for the diffusion of literature and the renown of the French name? In truth, Buffon said nothing so ridiculous, as some appear at times to believe, when he advised the writer "to name things only by the most general terms"; and those who still make fun of the precept and of the master have not understood him. Buffon meant that so long as the geometers and the natural philosophers, the theologians and the jurisconsults, the scholars and the philologists—in brief, so long as all the specialists used only the technical language of their science, so long would they be denied that intelligent curiosity, that interest, and that general sympathy which are so necessary to them. In other words, he was advising them to be men before embryogenists or Hebrew scholars. His advice may entail certain disadvantages, but who will deny its general merit?

Here it is that we encounter the overriding reasons for the universality of French language and literature. Twice at least in the course of their long history, French literature and the French language itself have exercised over the whole of Europe a profound influence which other languages, such as Italian, which is perhaps more harmonious, and other literatures, such as English, which is in certain respects more original, have however never possessed. It is in a purely French form that our *chansons de geste*, our *romans de la Table Ronde*, and our fabliaux, whatever their origin might have been, won over, seduced and charmed the imaginations of the Middle Ages from one end of Europe to the other. Much later, in a Europe where classicism held sway, from the beginning of the 17th century to the end of the 18th century, for 150 years French literature enjoyed a sovereign reign, in Italy and in Spain, in England and in Germany. Is it necessary to recall that if Lessing prevailed over Voltaire it was with the concurrence of Diderot; and if Rivarol wrote his *Discours sur l'universalité de la langue française* it was not his national vanity that was behind it, since he was himself half Italian, and the subject having been proposed by the Academy of Berlin?

All kinds of reasons have been given for this universality of French literature; but the real reason is to be found in the eminently social character of the literature. If, then, our great writers are understood and appreciated by everyone, it is because they write for everyone, or better still, it is because they speak to everyone about matters which are of concern to everyone. They are enticed neither by the exceptions nor by idiosyncrasies. Their sole concern is to treat of man in general, whose milieu is the common paths of the society of the human race; and their very success is a proof that this universal man, whose existence has so often been contested, continues to be and to live, and, in the process of change, to preserve his familiar appearance.

Let me give a few examples. Why has Guillen de Castro's *Cid* not had the same Europe-wide success as Corneille's, which lacks some of its qualities? The answer is that Guillen de Castro, as a true Spaniard, has seen only the heroic side of his subject. He has not seen what Corneille for his part has so effectively brought out: the conflict of Rodrigue between his passion and the social law. He has exhausted the pictur-esque interest, but the properly human interest has escaped him. Again, how did Racine in his *Phèdre* transform the matter of the Greek Hip-polytus? What did Voltaire, in adapting and distorting Shakespeare's *Othello*, hope to add to his *Zaïre*? Also a social conflict, as in Corneille the conflict between love and religion—the eminently human drama of the hesitations, perplexities and torments of Zaïre, who is torn between what on the one hand she owes to her birth, and what on the other hand she cannot help conceding to her passion.

There, indeed, is the reason for the reception which they have ev-erywhere received. In the questions they raise the essential interests of *civilité* or of humanity itself are at issue. Since all there is that is most admirable in the world is to be found in the social institution, all their thoughts dwell on it; and so their expression could not be a matter of in-difference to anyone. Who indeed would not be interested to know how far the rights of one's country extend over its citizens, or the rights of the father over his children, or those of the husband over his wife's; how so many conflicts which arise every day between our various duties are resolved; by what expedient the needs of the individual and the rights of society are reconciled, or according to what higher principle they are united and become merged, instead of being set in opposition and con-tradiction to each other? It is not for having been reduced but for having been dedicated in its entirety to the examination of these questions that French literature has gained its universal stature. Other reasons may well have contributed to it, but this remains the principal one.

I do not deny that the character of the language has also played a part in it, as I have already said. It may also be held that the popula-tion of France, which in the 17th century formed one-fifth of the total population of civilized Europe; the privileged situation of France in the centre of the Europe of that time, and, as it were, at the confluence of the literatures of the North and the South; the good fortune enjoyed by the French language under Louis XIV, and even under Louis XV, to serve in all ways as a model to the Court of Charles II of England or the Court of Catherine of Russia—all of these have played a part in promoting the diffusion of ideas and of French literature. But those are essentially secondary or derivative reasons, which would not have been decisive in themselves: none of them would have assured the universality of French literature, since it is clear that none of them in former times assured the universality of Spanish or of German literature... To seek in the politi-cal action of France the reasons for the universality of her literature is tantamount to looking for the reasons for Voltaire's popularity in his unbelief, or the reasons for Hugo's fame in his political opinions. But that would lead us to the same conclusion, since it would still lead us to the eminently practical or pragmatic, and consequently social, character of their prose or verse.

Can it not also be said that this same characteristic which explains the finest qualities of French literature accounts also for its defects and shortcomings? The long inferiority of our lyrical poetry is undoubtedly an eloquent example. If the *Pléiade* failed in its lofty enterprise; if Ronsard and his friends left behind them an equivocal reputation from the literary point of view; if over a period of 250 or 300 years there has been nothing more vapid than the French ode or elegy, there is no reason to accuse Boileau or Malherbe, but solely the force of circumstances. The truth is that when it is the task of literature to fulfil a social function, and the duty of the poet to adapt his ways of thinking and feeling to the common ways of thinking and feeling, when he is denied the right to intrude himself or even to let his individuality appear in his work, then the living wellsprings of lyricism are dried up or dammed up. French literature has thus paid for its superiority in the popular genres by its too obvious inferiority in the genres which might be called personal. In order to make itself accessible to everyone it has had to eradicate all expression of personal feelings as a matter of principle. It has similarly denied itself all that is most intimate and individual in the expression of noble sentiments that might be imparted by local detail or a particular inflexion, lest it admit into its descriptions or analyses any elements which were not the same in all times and in all places. The predominance of this social character, by subordinating all others to it, has reduced the manifestation of the author's personality to what is implied by the *proprie communia dicere*[2] of the Latin poet...

Is that the reason why French literature has sometimes been accused of lacking depth and originality? I believe that our great writers have assumed a worldly or courtly coquettishness for the purpose of dissimulating or, better still, of disguising that profundity which certain Germans—of the school of Hegel, for example, or of the famous Jean-Paul—tell us readily they have tried to introduce into their works.

---

2 *Difficile est proprie communia dicere* (Horace, *Ars Poetica*, 128). The author clearly understands this to mean that French writers are constrained "to deal with general matters in an individual (original) way." This is probably the correct interpretation, though others are possible; for example, '*communia*' has been taken to be 'topics not treated before.' Ed.

Those who write in French pride themselves on expressing clearly things that are sometimes profound, but it seems that too many who write in German have made it a point of honour to formulate obscurely things that are clear. Is Kant really more profound than Pascal, or Fichte than Rousseau? Fichte or Kant, absorbed as they are in the slow elaboration and admiring contemplation of their own thought, leave to their readers the trouble of sorting it out, whereas Pascal or Rousseau spare them that trouble. It is in any event the effect of the same cause. The French writer would consider that he had failed in his task if it were necessary to struggle to understand him. He much prefers to be considered superficial rather than obscure. It seems fitting to add that in an eminently social literature like French literature, in which the issues debated are by definition the interests of humanity itself, the occasions for being profound in the philosophical sense of the word are naturally less frequent than in a literature like German, in which the great pretention of the writer is to arrive at noumenal concepts of everything...

I would answer in similar terms the charge that French literature lacks originality: I do not deny it either. I explain it by, and again refer it to, that same social character. It is possible to live outside and as it were on the margin of the society of other men, although it is rather difficult. And one can, if one wishes, boldly refuse to conform to common customs and received opinions. But if one wishes to live in society and for society one must necessarily begin by submitting to its customs and opinions since this is the only way that one has of changing them. Men are not persuaded against their prejudices. Just as, then, if we would learn the mastery of nature we must begin by submitting to her laws, the knowledge of which affords us the means of circumventing them, so with greater reason we shall find how to triumph over prejudices only to the extent that we have begun by sharing them. In this sense an eminently social literature will always be less original than a literature whose ideal tends, as formerly the ideal of Italian literature tended, only toward the realization of pure beauty, or, as English literature does today, toward the free manifestation of individual energies. There, if you wish, is the weakness or the defect of classical French literature. At least it would be if, as I have tried to show, this weakness had not been in effect one of the conditions of its strength.

III

I should now like to show what a revealing light this definition of its essential character throws on the obscure episodes of the history of French literature. The discredit and final oblivion into which the victims of Boileau have fallen, for example—to which might be added, I think, the majority of Voltaire's victims; the contradictory judgments which are so often passed, and which are still passed, on precious society; the quarrel of the ancients and the moderns, the importance of which has strangely enough been misunderstood for so long; the nature of the revolution brought about in the literature of his time by the author of *la Nouvelle Héloïse* and the *Confessions*; the true point of the debate during the early years of the present century between the Classics and Romantics; all of these become clear, interrelated, and all fall into place when related to the essential character of French literature. If the names of the Théophiles and the Saint-Amants are today almost forgotten, it is because they insisted on writing personal literature in an age when, the tendency of minds being eminently social, they did not have on their side that complicity of opinion without which no one in France has ever been able to succeed at anything. Similarly, what the Romantics have demanded is the right to be themselves, to free themselves from the constraints that they felt weighing upon them when they recalled the masterpieces of an impersonal literature; and, what is very strange but also very significant, hardly had they won that right than they renounced it... But all these questions are of little interest except to the historians of literature. That is why, having pointed them out, I prefer, in order the better to bring out the essential character of French literature, to contrast it with the essential character of English literature.

In comparison with French literature, defined and characterized by its spirit of sociability, English literature is an individualistic literature. Setting aside the generation of the Congreves and Wycherleys, and perhaps also the generation of Pope and Addison, to which we must not forget Swift also belonged, it seems that the English write only to afford themselves the external sensation of their individuality. Whence that humour which might be defined as the expression of the pleasure which they feel in sharing a likemindedness. Whence the abundance, wealth, and plenitude of the lyric vein which we find in them—if individualism is, in effect, the source of it, and if an ode or an elegy is as it were the involuntary afflux and the brimming over of the most intimate, secret and personal aspects of the poet's soul. Whence also the eccentricity of their great writers in comparison with the rest of the nation, as if in fact they became most completely themselves only when standing out against everyone, including even those who believe they resemble them most...

It is good that there should be such diversity and difference between our national temperaments and literatures. For five or six hundred years it is this that has contributed to the greatness not only of European literature but of western civilization itself: namely, the qualities that all peoples have poured into the common treasure-house of the human spirit after having slowly developed them in national isolation. To one we owe the sense of mystery and, so to speak, the revelation of the beauties to be found in the obscure and the elusive. To another we owe the feeling for art and what might be called the comprehension of the power of form. A third has transmitted to us all that was most heroic in the conception of chevaleresque honour. To yet another we owe our knowledge of all that is most ferocious and most noble, most beneficent and most fearful, in human pride. As for us French, however, our role has been to weld, to merge together, and as it were to unify within the idea of the general society of the human race, what contradictory or hostile elements may be contained in that notion. All Europe had borrowed from us our innovations and ideas in order to adapt them to the genius of her diverse races. When taking them up again in our turn, and adopting them in their transformed shape, we have asked only that they should promote the progress of reason and humanity. Where they have been obscure we have clarified them; we have rectified what corrupting power they have had; what was parochial in them we have generalized; and we have humanized them when guilty of excesses. Have we not also at times diminished their greatness or debased their purity? If Corneille assuredly made Guillen de Castro's somewhat barbarous heroes a little more like us, La Fontaine when imitating the author of the *Decameron* made him more indecent than he is in his own language. And if the Italians cannot reproach Molière for what he has borrowed from them, the English have the right to complain that Voltaire had little understanding of Shakespeare. But it is not less true that in winnowing out from the individual man of the North and the South that idea of the universal man for which we have so often been reproached, if any literature among modern literatures has as a whole been the very spirit of the common good and *civilité* it is French literature. And it follows of necessity that this ideal has not been so vain as it has often been claimed, since, as I have tried to show, from Lisbon to Stockholm and from Archangel to Naples, it is precisely the manifestations of this ideal that foreigners have been delighted to come back to again and again in the masterpieces, or rather in the whole uninterrupted panorama, of the history of our literature.

5

The Wisdom of France

by

Fortunat Strowski

From: Fortunat Strowski: *La Sagesse Française* (Paris: Librairie Plon, 1925), Chapter 1, "La Sagesse française". English translation by J. E. G. Dixon.©

*T*he new methods being applied so successfully today to literary history[1] show us only one thing: how each age is produced and in turn produces the next. These methods enable us to see the influences at work from hour to hour, and so enable us to explain, after a fashion, the genesis of masterpieces. But such methods, far from revealing the durable and lasting values of these works, merely give us the notion that literature is like running water, like a river which flows and passes on, so that the only unity they have is time and succession in time.

When a great literature is surveyed from a little farther off and from a broader point of view, another, more important, unity is perceived. There is no truly national literature which does not retain its character from age to age, and which does not form a whole—or rather which has not its own personality.

The personality of French literature is one of the most complex there is, while not ceasing to be one. It is made up of numerous elements, which combine in a succession of conflicts and compromises, of interruptions and resumptions, to culminate in those moments of balance and perfect harmony which are the triumphs of the great centuries and the great geniuses. Knowing those elements is not less necessary than tracing the evolution of their times.

There is one among those elements which seems to prevail over all others. Apart from the time of the Pléiade and the Romantic period, that element has always appeared with a remarkable note of stability and permanence. It is like a national instinct, the irresistible tendency of the French genius. It consists in the habit of psychological observation, in an aptitude for moral[2] questions, in a propensity for understanding

---

1 Written in 1925. The new methods Strowski refers to were those being applied to the writing of history itself, and were directly inspired by positivism. They sought to achieve the exactness of the history of facts, and relied preponderantly on primary sources, unpublished documents, and the sources used by the authors under study. Exponents of this method were, for example, Abel Lefranc and Gustave Lanson. The reader interested in pursuing this question should turn to Irving Babbitt, *Modern French Criticism*, pp. 383-387.

2 Strowski uses both the words *moral* and *moraliste*, and the words *psychologue* and *psychologique*. However, the French word *moral* can itself mean either 'moral' or 'psychological'. Psychology, as an objective discipline concerned with the phenomena of human behaviour and their causes, does not make judgements of value. Ethics, of course, is concerned with right and wrong, good and evil, and distinguishes necessarily between ends and means. As for the French word: "the word *moral* is one of those which show that the French language, fond as it is of the reputation for clarity and precision that it has acquired, can if need be make provision for ambiguity." Preface

man. French literature is a literature of moralists. Here are some proofs and examples.

II

Towards the end of the sixteenth century a magistrate, a gentleman of a wealthy, recently ennobled family, and influential through his connections, lays down his offices, abandons his ambitions, says farewell to city and court, and retires to his château not far from the Dordogne. Idleness weighs on him. Something of a writer by nature, fond of *belles-lettres*, an indefatigable reader, he turns to books to relieve his boredom and is absorbed by them. He then resolves to write, or, as he puts it, to dictate his musings. What will his musings be about?—ideas?—philosophical systems? Has he not after all translated a great semi-metaphysical work entitled *Natural Theology*, by a fourteenth century monk? He will be neither theologian nor philosopher. Even less will he resort to fictional romances. What he will compose is the *Essays*: the most detailed, precise, and penetrating study of human nature, replete with wise thoughts and advice about how to live. As you have realised, we are talking about Michel de Montaigne, who, following his inclination, becomes a moralist to the core, because he always was one, just as he was a Gascon and a Frenchman.

Another gentleman—but this one a great lord from one of the noblest families of the realm—has been through all kinds of adventures. Love and politics have taken the flower of his years. He seeks repose at last, and takes stock. He is an epicure; he is pampered by a lady-friend, who is one of the finest female minds of the century: in a word, Pascal's friend. He too finds diversion in writing—as a great nobleman, to be sure, and so as to indulge his whims without restraint. The book he writes is as succinct, as brief, and as pointed as Montaigne's was nuanced, varied, and protean. But as to the contents of the book, it is still, and unfailingly, about human nature, with rules for the regulation of human nature. For such is the subject-matter of the *Maxims* of La Rouchefoucauld.

A scholar, a very great scholar, one of those powerful minds which reduce the awesome chaos of the external world to rational order and harmony, was converted to Jansenism when he was about thirty, yet

by Samuel Sylvestre de Sacy to his edition of Descartes, *Les passions de l'âme* (Paris, Gallimard, Collection "Idées", 1969), p.11. It has therefore been translated as 'moral' or 'psychological' according to the requirement of the context. Ed.

without losing the scholar's cast of mind. He threw himself passionately into the theological disputes of his faction, in writing, speech, and action. He became involved in a hundred intrigues and quarrels of a kind which quickly caused frayed tempers. Finally, ill and exhausted, he renounced these bitter and debilitating squabbles in order to work thereafter for his and others' salvation. He drafts an apology of the Christian religion. Being delicate in health, and in constant pain which inhibits prolonged periods of work, he is unable to complete the Apology he had begun; all he leaves behind are fragments and preparatory notes. He was thirty-nine when he died. What are the contents of those notes and fragments of a mathematician-physicist whose brief existence was taken up so much by studies, polemics, and passions? Little in the way of mathematics, abstract ideas or metaphysical discussion, but the real and factual study of men as they are. In his *Pensées* Pascal depicts the human condition. Pascal was a moral writer.

A final example. This time a man of learning, somewhat pedantic, a man of strange temperament; he knows the classics, some modern languages, history, geography, genealogy, etc. He takes on the education of the grandson of the Great Condé, an unenviable task which occupies much of his time and brings him nothing but vexation and fatigue. However he finds the leisure to write for his own diversion. This work, his solace and closest confidant, his favourite and the most filling pastime, is the *Characters, or the Manners of this Century*. The title suggests the contents.

La Bruyère is also a moralist.

Montaigne's *Essays* first appeared in 1580, the *Characters* in 1688. A century sufficed to produce Montaigne, Pascal, La Rochefoucauld, and La Bruyère, who may be called, without in the least detracting from the most self-esteemed foreign literatures, the world's greatest moralists.

After the above we will have other moralists, who, despite their having been deprived of the best in the field, will still find something wherewith to enrich our knowledge of man: Duclos, Vauvenargues, Chamfort, then Joubert, and still others! They will necessarily be reduced to being gleaners. But the poor gleaners, the late-comers, will none the less themselves be moralists of note. And there will be no lack of them until the French spirit ceases to dominate French literature.

It might be objected, in a certain sense, that this procession of moralists fails to prove our assertion; that it only demonstrates that our literature had the fortune to produce a wealth of observers preoccupied with man and the conduct of life; and that those successful writers, being born at the right time and with the right gifts, created a trend which did not itself however correspond to a deep-seated propensity. But here we have corroboration which strengthens our remarks and serve to give them general application.

Even when it is in no wise a question of their acting as moralists, even when they have no desire to act as moralists, our great writers are as it were condemned to being moralists. Descartes was France's greatest deductive genius. He maintained he could derive knowledge of everything there is under the sun from a few clear and self-evident principles. He was a mathematician; he carried his intoxication with science to the nth degree, almost to the point of absurdity. He claimed that science would give him possession of the secrets of nature, would reveal God and the soul by an infallible method. He promised he would deduce the means of extending life for centuries: a hundred years was not enough for him! Even so, this conceited savant found himself constrained to say how one must regulate one's life and live with others. At this philosophical juncture he dropped his arrogance and ceased his reasoning and deduction. He was now far from being confident and assertive. He consulted Montaigne and commented on Seneca; he observed the common run of men and women, his fellow-beings. As much in his *Discourse on Method* as in his *Letters to Princess Elizabeth* he is a moralist pure and simple—a moral philosopher, if you like, or an amateur moralist, but still a moralist.

To complete this demonstration by example I wish to add another unintentional moralist, in complete contrast to Descartes, and still more distant from the vocation of moralist than from that of geometer. I mean La Fontaine. La Fontaine was a born poet, and purely a poet. Absent-minded and unconcerned, he bestirs himself only when it comes to composing exquisite verse. His poetry is music. He is an elegiac poet above all. When he seeks a change from elegy, he finds diversion in racy and sensual narrative, as befits an elegist. His tales are not of his invention, and he writes solely for his own pleasure. In a word, he is the opposite of Montaigne, La Rochefoucauld, La Bruyère, not to speak of Pascal. One day the fancy takes him to compose rhyming fables—animal adventures to serve as object-lessons for children. His early fables are racy tales; then he warms to the game. The animals he portrays take on distinctive characters and complex feelings. Beneath their colourful masks La Fontaine depicts all of human nature: the characteristics of men with their vices, faults, and absurdities, and complete with gestures. His fables will prove to be a marvellous treasure-house for moralists.

And that is what the French genius does.

I shall not pursue this inquiry indefinitely—to show, for example, how the best preachers become moralists when they mount the pulpit— St. François de Sales, Bourdaloue, Massillon, not to mention Bossuet and Fénelon. I shall not dwell, beyond the seventeenth century, beyond Molière, Racine and their disciples, on the eighteenth century which is also a century of moralists, be it in the theatre with Marivaux or the novel with the boldest novelists. If Italian literature is the school of art, imagination and passion; English literature the school of sensibility and poetry; and German literature the school of fantasy and metaphysics; French literature—with the exception of the periods of the Pléiade and Romanticism—had always retained its preoccupation with the study of men: to know and depict them, to explain the inner springs of their actions, to penetrate the secret of their "conditions and humours," and to teach them how to live. French literature is the school of Wisdom.

III

The above examples would suffice to make clear what is to be understood by the moral vocation of the French genius, and what is meant by the expression "philosophy of man" as applied to our literature; but our ideas can be made still more explicit.

This concern with learning about men and the art of living with them is to be found occasionally among other nations. Such problems are impossible to disregard: every literature, from time to time, discovers in them a source of appeal or beauty, and touches on them. But other literatures, even if we discount the fact that they only treat of them sporadically, do not turn them to the same account as our moralists. The English novel of fifty years ago paraded a huge cast of human beings, and studied and analysed them down to the minutest detail. What it sets out before our eyes is their daily existence. We come to know the quality of their souls, and, if I may put it thus, the fine points of their individuality. However, the authors of those novels are not moralists. They enchant us, they beguile us, they move us; but they do not give us a general idea of what men are and how one should behave with them. They do not depart from the individual; there is too much humour in them.

Our moral writers have the gift of suggesting the universal form of the human condition that lies behind the individual. And yet they never overlook reality, and they are never puffed up by pride into attempting to construct the idea of man out of nothing. They do not take an abstraction about man as their starting-point; nor do they aim for a general definition of man. They endeavour to ground their philosophy in a factual and empirical knowledge of the individual, analysed in real life and observed in the details of his daily existence. Heinrich Heine, in a famous epigram, shows us a professor of philosophy who has made a construct of the world and rounded it into a perfect sphere. There remains a hole. To fill it he stuffs his dressing-gown into it.

The French moralist accumulates observations, arranges them, and draws a conclusion from them if he can; but he respects reality. Montaigne said that we get to know a man better when we can see him in his daily life than when he is stirred by violent emotions or rises above himself.[3] With those of our moralists who appear to be governed by some preconceived idea or might be suspected of systematic tendencies—La Rochefoucauld or Pascal, for example—it is always observation that prevails. They grasp the truth directly from life, and not via deduction or metaphysics.

In so doing they are only following an old French tradition. Imagine life as it was, from the Middle Ages on, in the small towns surrounded by their moats and ramparts: everyone has his place there and no one can escape it. Nothing ever changes; families live on in the same houses which they own. The small trader will never expand his business. There is no prospect of wealth or adventure. In the evening the people congregate, on the doorstep in summer and indoors in winter. They are sociable people, who swap yarns and drink wine; they are down-to-earth, restrained, and given to banter; and they watch their neighbours. Seeing how people live, weighing their character, catching them out on their weak spots, making fun of their oddities—that is an essential pastime with them, and their supreme enjoyment. I have been to countries where the people have to work and wear themselves out, every day, until the day of their death, without seeing how others live, or even themselves. You may find morality among them, but not moralists. I have known others where a great thought dwells in every heart and occupies every mind—national independence to be won, the country to be saved, for example: there may be more than morality there, but not moralists. A man is not a moralist in the United States, nor was he a moralist in Poland. One is in France, for there the penchant for applied, practical psychology, no doubt present a long time, has been brought

---

3 Of the many passages and essays in which Montaigne treats of this theme, the reader is referred in particular to Essay III, 2, "On Repenting", in Michael Screech's translation (Penguin Books, 1991) pp. 907-921.

out by sociability, leisure, communal freedom, moderateness in both climate and customs, the security of one's home, and the limited horizon. This penchant has subsequently been reinforced and sharpened. Anything can be done in France by the art of handling men. Genius alone does not open the doors of the *Académie Française*: what is needed also is psychology, and the feeling for human character. To be agreeable and amenable—amenable even more than agreeable—is the source of success, even in politics. Now being amenable means knowing how to deal with men, knowing their likes, their wants and their condition of life— what Pascal calls the 'principles of pleasures.' "They are different in all men," said Pascal, "and variable in each individual, with such diversity that there is no man who is not more different from another than he is from himself at different times. A man's pleasures are different from a woman's; a rich and a poor man's are different; a prince, a soldier, a bourgeois, a peasant, the old and the young, the ill and the weak, all differ. And the slightest incidents change them."

If the French, men and women alike, know how to be amenable, if amenability is more the thing with us than domination, it is because people have the gift of noticing and adapting to the differences, the constant and imperceptible variations and changes. For the fact is that the streets swarm with psychologists and moralists. The best psychologists in the world are assuredly the concierges of Paris.

This flair for psychology with us—practical, realistic, and matter-of-fact—comes out still better when we pass from fact to precept and from the recording of things to the response of the conscience. The Frenchman does not stop at observation: he has a deep-rooted moral sense in that he is prompt in judgement, and actively moral in that he is quick to try to impose his judgement. In other countries one finds a severer general morality, but this general morality saves one the effort required for individual moral judgement. In France, especially since the last century, all moral judgement tends to be individual and is not satisfied with general principles. And then, every Frenchman is fond of saying what he would have done if he had been the person judging: "Now, for my part . . ."

Our moralists, be they declared or covert, Montaigne and La Rochefoucauld as well as Montesquieu or Marivaux, even when they assume a purely objective attitude and wish to eschew a moral perspective, cannot avoid having opinions on morality. Moreover, they seldom take a detached attitude for long. Our best writers are never 'amoralists', as it is said. A Gabriel Naudé in the seventeenth century, albeit a lesser writer, is a rare exception; and any who nowadays claims to be an amoralist is obsessed with moral preoccupations.

What can we say is the nature of those judgements?

Firstly, they never invoke a written tradition, or a law laid down as a universal axiom, or a categorical imperative. They are prompted, first of all, by the inherent feeling for what is right and wrong, just and unjust, good and generous. You will hear: "That is all right; that is not done!" Secondly, there is respect for propriety, utility, practical good sense; a keenness to point out the stupidity and foolishness of people's mistakes and failings. The instinctive flair for bantering mockery, which finds its way into the stories and *facéties* of old France or even La Fontaine's fables, more often than not colours the disapproval expressed in a moral tone. Only serious offences and revolting crimes arouse indignation, without any consideration of what is useful or seemly—which explains why foreigners do not generally recognize the basic seriousness underlying joking and laughter. Thirdly and lastly, moral judgements in France are almost always underscored by an ideal which the great moralists alone have the ability to express, but which the people, or even the writers, experience unexceptionally, without even being aware of it.

The word 'ideal' will perhaps come as a surprise. How can 'realists,' skilled psychologists, conceive an ideal? The fact is that the term gives rise to misunderstanding; it would be better to say, to be quite correct, that each age creates a type of human perfection, both relative and attainable, which gives form to judgements of conscience.

There has always existed in France, beneath occasionally deceptive appearances, a taste for the poetic, a yearning for nobility, a feeling for human dignity, a respect for individual worth, in a word what Pascal called an instinct of greatness, which common sense has sought to check and control, but which it has never abolished or even diminished. At each period of our spiritual history, the French consciousness has created, not so much a notion (that would be abstract) as a living image which gives expression to its instinct of greatness. This living image is always made up of real elements, is always related to everyday life, to the circumstances of each period, to the potentials of each generation. So it is we have the gentleman in Montaigne's time, the cultured man in Pascal's and La Rochefoucauld's time, the civilized man in Voltaire's and Montesquieu's time, and the social man in Balzac's and Stendhal's time.[4]

---

4 The four terms used by Strowski are, respectively: *'le gentilhomme', 'l'honnête homme', 'le civilisé', 'l'homme social'*.

IV

To study the philosophy of man in French literature is, then, to study the art with which the great writers have depicted the human condition and the inner springs which motivate men. It is to describe, period by period, the ideal and real type of perfection which is created naturally in the imagination and the heart, in conversation and in books, in fashion and in philosophy. But that is not all.

A reader would be committing a serious offence against the truth if he were to study French literature and thought as isolated entities deriving their substance only from themselves, and irrelevant to the rest of the world. It would be doing an injustice to the other literatures, which have given us so much, and to ours which has given so much to them. One must cast one's eyes farther and higher, and have the courage to give thought to the human spirit—if only to determine the place and the mission of France in the spiritual development of mankind.

The human mind has two dangerous tendencies, which both work toward the same end, and they have their origins, respectively, in pride and in laziness. When the human mind has discovered or created what it believes to be a truth, it is so smug and proud about it that it wants to leave well alone. It is satisfied thereafter with the principle or image which it feels secure with; it shuns anything that might modify them; it is disturbed if they show signs of life—for does not being alive imply change? The mind refuses to subject them to new tests: that would be an admission of impotence! It is confirmed in that by its laziness. There is nothing more convenient than a general rule, because it encourages the mind to forget individual cases, relieves it of the burden of learning about things themselves, and frees it of the need to make a personal judgment in every circumstance. The rule does the judging for the mind and relieves it of the problem of examining, of deciding, of taking on a responsibility. It does this for it and so reassures it. The mind believes itself to be infallible, at so little cost and with so little bother!

Where the philosophy of man is concerned, how often has the human mind constructed eternal systems of thought, which gave refuge to pride and laziness alike! We learned incontrovertibly, once and for all, what man was, what the perfect human type was, and how they should and could be attained. Religion, science, metaphysics, tradition, poetry—each in its turn has decreed, irrevocably and for good, according to them, the rules necessary for the conduct of life. Generally these pretentious illusions originated outside France; but they soon found their way in and thought to prosper there.

It has often happened in the course of history that men of genius—philosophers or thinkers or even men of action with no literary ties—have conceived or created a noble human model. It has also often happened that groups of men and even whole nations have imposed certain rules of life on themselves which implied a new conception of man. Ordinarily in such cases our predecessors have been obliged to look back to earlier epochs for help from moral ideas and standards that were thought to have had their day.

Now when that occurs outside France, these human types and conceptions always tend to take on an abstract character and are transformed into definitions or general, universal laws. Pride thereupon invests them with an aura of infallibility: there is no further debate about them; and they then, thanks to laziness, become convenient means for judging and for coming to decisions in life without one's being compelled to go through the tedious business of looking and thinking for oneself.

So it is that, in modern times, we have had the humanist idea of man, the Jansenist idea, the 'naturist' idea, and still others. It is here that the French genius comes into its own.

In contrast to those rigid doctrines and the wooden or stone statues which the cultivated world accepts as the true human model, the French genius proposes the factual and analytic knowledge of real men involved in the real conditions of life. In contrast to the ideals and prescriptions of an artificial morality, it proposes practical ideals which it adapts to the real potentials of man and to our condition.

I do not mean to say that the French genius, because it points out their shortcomings, is inimical to those great European and universal ideas. On the contrary, it ingests them into its system and by cohabiting with them makes them, as it were, viable. It keeps what is new in them; it even preserves their beauty of form. For it destroys nothing. It is not radical. (I use this word, of course, in the intellectual sense, and not in the political sense, in which it has no sense whatever.) It is by this very sign that it can be recognized. And when there appears in France a truly radical doctrine, like that of Rousseau, a citizen of Geneva, we may be sure that it is not French in its essence.[5]

The French genius, with its experience and its sense of realities, moderates, transforms and improves on the philosophy of man which seems to thrust itself on each epoch. In its renewed and vital form it

---

5 What then of Calvin, who was French? Ed.

sends it out again to the world, which adopts it and makes it into a new idol. The *rôle* of our country, in brief, is to break down those petrified and ossified forms, and to preserve life in its suppleness, that is to say, its powers of continuity and vitality, the faculty which transforms lifeless statues into living beings.[6]

---

6 The last two pages of text have been omitted. They outline the author's method in the chapters that follow, which deal with individual writers. Ed.

6

French Art and Letters

by

Salvador de Madariaga

From: Salvador de Madariaga, *Englishmen, Frenchmen, Spaniards: An Essay in Comparative Psychology.* (Oxford University Press, London: Humphrey Milford, 4th Impression, 1937). Part II, ch. VI, "Art and Letters." Reprinted by permission of the Agencia Literaria Carmen Balcells, Barcelona.

*I*n the beginning of art there is passion. The first instant of art is a touch felt within—whether from beyond or merely from outside does not matter for our present purpose. This touch starts the soul vibrating. From the moment when it takes place in the passive soul of the artist till the production of the work of art and its further absorption by the artistic life of the community, there exists a long and complex gamut of phases in each of which new elements—intellectual, volitional, and, finally, extra-individual—come to complicate and enrich the initial stage.

In ordinary language, opinions on the art of this or that nation are based on the observation of the main facts connected with its artistic life; they include the quality of the inspiration of its artists, together with the average level of beauty of its household furniture and the aesthetic value of its folk-lore. Even if sufficient for everyday consumption, opinions thus formed would be more misleading than illuminating for our purpose.

II

If passion is the first instant in the creative process, the second or form-giving phase is controlled by the intellect; in its narrower and more concrete sense, the word 'art' means precisely the form-giving power of the intellect moved by aesthetic emotion. France is therefore the country which excels in Art. She is, we know, poorer in the raw materials of art than Spain. Her people cannot compare with the Spanish in those spontaneous manifestations of aesthetic life which we have observed in Spain. The stress in France comes a little later in the creative process; it is a moment in which conscious effort and constructive thought have a wider share. Compare French with Spanish dancing; French feminine elegance with Spanish feminine movement and grace. French excellence will be found to reside in a greater intellectual control over the aesthetic emotion, even if the emotion itself is found to be less vigorous at its root. Hence the typical French distinction in all manual arts which require a close intellectual co-operation. If we want to seek in France the equivalent of those popular manifestations of aesthetic life which are so abundant in Spain in a primitive and unconscious vigour, we must turn to the almost universal ability of French men and women to arrange materials for life's uses with refinement and taste. In such artistic productions, the person is less present than in their Spanish equivalents. He is no longer himself the raw material of his art, both

108

the channel and the flow of his emotion, but the artificer who, from the outside, works on the material and gives it shape.

Hence that sense of objectivity which we find as the key-note of all French art, in contrast with the subjective value of Spanish aesthetic manifestations. Even when the Spanish anonymous poet tells a ballad or drops a proverb in an impressive way, there seems to sound in his words a note of hidden lyricism. Objective as the truth may be as a truth, it is deeply subjective as an experience, and we feel it in the way it is said. Inversely, even in her most personal and lyrical moments, the French muse manages to keep a universal, an almost abstract outlook.

Lleva el que deja, y vive el que ha vivido,

(He takes with him who leaves behind; and he lives who has lived), says Machado in an immortal line, and this philosophical theory of general and abstract import is, nevertheless, inseparable from the poet who sings it, in a recognizable voice matured by experience. But when Baudelaire, in one of his most purely lyrical songs, draws the picture of the ideal land of love, he defines for all time the ideal features of the French mind in lines of cold and perfect beauty:

Là tout n'est qu'ordre et beauté,
Luxe, calme et volupté.

Nor is this the only way in which French art manifests the intellectual nature of French character. Thus, in contrast with Spanish art, we find in France a better balance between the critical and creative elements. This can be observed in all the arts. French artists are conscious, they know where they are going, they know what they want. Racine, writing to a friend: "I have finished my tragedy; nothing remains but to write it," is a signal example of the French attitude towards creative work. It is all planned beforehand. Method, foresight, all the qualities we know to be those of the intellectual, shine with special brilliancy in French art.

This importance of the critical element at work in the individual contributes to keep up the high standard of formal excellence in French artistic work. The critical mind it is which puts into shape the shapeless lava thrown up by the imagination, after having purified it of all the worthless material which usually comes up with it. France is the teacher of the world in matters of form and of composition.

Collectively, the vigour of the critical sense acts as a powerful stimulus to the continuous study of artistic methods and technique. In the community as in the individual the assiduous presence of the intellect leads to consciousness. France works always under her own attentive eye, and each epoch knows, while working, that it is fulfilling a specific mission in the history of French art. "We are the knights of the Middle Ages," sings a chorus of ironclad men in a somewhat naïve musical comedy. A French literary and artistic generation always feels happier when it is working under a banner and knows what it is doing.

Hence, those 'isms' which appear periodically in the fields of literary and artistic criticism in France: symbolism, parnassism, romanticism, classicism are the names of generations, banners, labels which the critical intellect affixes to this or that period of French literary and artistic life. They usually have but little meaning outside France, and if non-French critics were not, as they usually are, bamboozled by their brilliant French colleagues into believing that things must happen in the world as they happen in France, these 'isms' would have remained what they really are, mere accidents of French life, perfectly clear and plausible in a country which evolves according to plan but inapplicable elsewhere. The least exclusively French of them—Romanticism itself—when applied outside of France leads to such utter absurdities as classifying Victor Hugo and Lamartine with Wordsworth, Byron, Schiller, Espronceda, and Leopardi—a strange cauldron of eagles.

In point of fact these 'isms' of French artistic life must be considered in the same light as similar manifestations in other spheres of French history; for instance, the constitutions in French political life. They began like new political eras, with a manifesto and a fight. Victor Hugo's manifesto is a kind of declaration of the rights of man, and Theophile Gautier's famous red waistcoat is—if an Irish bull can be permitted in these matters—a kind of tri-colour.

This is of course another sign of the French tendency to plan out future work. Theory precedes practice; manifestos precede poems and plays. Schools, 'isms,' and literary generations bring intellectual order into the anarchical field of aesthetic creation. So much for artists. But what about their works? A similar effort towards intellectual order leads to their classification in genres. The garden of the Muses, as seen by a true French critic, resembles a botanical garden in which every work bears a label with its genus and species clearly set out. And it goes without saying that all these literary genres are rigorously defined by rules to which future artists must conform their creations if they do not want them to be branded as anti-natural monsters.

There is more than meets the eye in this invasion of literary lands by scientific preoccupations. A mind given to thought and thinking is predominantly interested in knowledge. France can no longer keep that wholly disinterested aesthetic attitude, spontaneous in the Spaniard. No sooner is he moved by an aesthetic emotion than the Frenchman instinctively and unconsciously deflects it towards intellectual aims, *i.e.* towards aims of knowledge. Hence the frequent use of a scientific vocabulary in literary spheres: *le document; un livre très documenté; qui révèle une observation pénétrante; recherches.* French literature would seem a branch of science, so keenly interested is it in truth rather than in beauty. Naturalism, 'verism' (the very word is a revelation) are the manifestations of this scientific invasion of art. Impressionism itself, the nineteenth-century revolution in painting, is little more than the application of scientific methods to the technique of the painter, and a French artist can put forward as his greatest claim to glory that he painted a haystack under all possible laboratory—I mean natural—conditions of light and shade.

By dint of intellectual pressure the French artist tends therefore to lay special stress on clearness, order, and composition. Hence a tendency to simplify, almost to schematize, to abstract irrational elements. French art in fine gives the same black-and-white impression which the French mind and language leave in us. Just as Spanish painting is based on colour, French painting is based on drawing. France, along with northern Italy, is the country in which black-and-white art reaches its highest excellence. But this observation, born in the sphere of the plastic arts, applies equally well to the other arts. French music, French literature are mostly line and composition.

More art than nature, more intellect than passion, more line than colour, French art is always on a high level of distinction and excellence, but shows no giants. Giants, in fact, are an insult to that sense of measure which we know to be a French psychological category. It is true that Victor Hugo, Rabelais, and Balzac may be mentioned as three living arguments against our case. But are they so very formidable as arguments? Balzac is impressive mostly as a man with an immense capacity for work and production. He is big rather than great. Moreover, in dealing with great French artists it must be borne in mind that they are *ex hypothesi* intellectuals with a greater proportion of passion in them than is usual in their country's type. This observation may suffice to explain many an apparent exception. Rabelais seems to have no sense of measure, but has it to such an extent that he can play with size without ever losing his proportions. And, moreover, when he sins against measure, he does it knowingly, and after having sized the leap. As for Victor Hugo, he is not wholly himself. Victor Hugo is not a self-contained artist; he is possessed of the idea that he is a genius, and that he must bellow genius-like and show big. In his way he also sins against measure wilfully and to show what he can do. But out of measure he is like a fish out of water—as a Frenchman is bound to be.

No, the strength of French arts and letters is not in its peaks, but in its general level. The truly specifically great French men are not geniuses but supreme talents: Voltaire, Racine, Anatole France. Like France herself, her art is even, cultivated, fine, and never overwhelmingly great. And this is one of the reasons why French culture is universal. It is the only culture which covers the whole world; for, being black-and-white, it does not lose so much in passing from country to country and from continent to continent, as other cultures more varied and coloured, richer in irrational and untranslatable elements. The same qualities and shortcomings which make French culture universal make it less apt to receive and understand other cultures. Of course, the small minority, the well-read and well-trained critic can understand anything. France possesses today perhaps the best exponents in the world of other than French cultures. But her cultivated mind is, as a whole, less open to other cultures than are the cultivated people of most other countries; for, again, it is a mind given to rationalize, simplify, and project everything on the two-dimensional plane of the intellect, so losing many of the vital elements in which the essence of non-French culture often resides.

7
The French Dialogue

by

André Gide & Charles Du Bos

From: I "*Le Dialogue Français*" by André Gide in *The Cornhill Magazine*, Winter 1946.

II Charles Du Bos: *Approximations*, 3ème série (Paris, Fayard, 1965), pp. 713-16, "*Introduction à Feuilles tombées de Boylesve*" (Décembre 1926). English translations © J. E. G. Dixon. The DuBos text is translated for this work by permission of Editions des Syrtes, Paris.

I

*I*t has often been remarked that what makes for the greatness, the merit, and the worth of our French culture is the fact that it is not, if I may put it thus, of local interest. The modes of thought, the truths it teaches us, are not especially of Lorraine or Provence, and consequently there is no risk of their rebounding against us when adopted by a neighbouring people. They are general and human, and apt to be of concern to the most diverse peoples; and since, in them, every human being can come to know himself, and can communicate and recognize himself, they make not for divisiveness and opposition, but for conciliation and understanding.

I hasten to add this, which appears to me of prime importance: French literature, looked at as a whole, does not enshrine a single view or opinion. (I am thinking of the exquisite saying of Mme de Sévigné, who wrote of herself: "*Je suis loin d'abonder dans mon sens*" ["I am far from abounding in my own sense", *i.e.* not in the least wedded to my own opinions][1]—meaning by this that she exercised a critical and uncomplacent judgement in respect of herself and the enticements of her sensibility.) French thought, throughout the course of its development and its history, presents us with a dialogue, a moving and continuous dialogue, one worthy above all others of occupying— for in listening to it one participates in it—both our hearts and our minds. I consider that the mind would be perverted if it listened to, or were allowed to hear, only one of the two voices of the dialogue—a dialogue not between a political right and left, but, much more vital and profound, between secular tradition, submission to recognized authorities, and free thought, the spirit of doubt and examination, which works towards the slow and progressive emancipation of the individual.

We can see it beginning to take shape in the conflict between Abelard and the Church which, needless to say always wins, albeit at the

---

1 After making recommendations for the moral upbringing and reading matter suitable to her daughter's young child, Mme de Sévigné adds: "Je ne sais si tout ce que je dis vaut la peine que vous le lisiez; je suis bien loin d'abonder dans mon sens." —"I do not whether what I say is worth the trouble of being read; I am far from attaching much weight to my own opinion." (Letter to Mme de Grignan of December 15, 1690. Pléiade edition No.1033, tome III, p.650.) For an account of this expression and its original meaning, which goes back to Rabelais and thence to St. Paul and Seneca, see M.A. Screech: *The Rabelaisian Marriage,* p.108-109. Ed.

expense of giving ground on each occasion and raising new positions well behind its original lines. The dialogue is resumed by Pascal's attack on Montaigne. There is no exchange of words between them, since Montaigne is dead when Pascal opens up; but it is he whom he has in mind all the same—and not only in the famous conversation with M. de Sacy: Pascal's *Pensées* is a book directed against the *Essais* of Montaigne, and on which it depends, so to speak. "*Le sot projet qu'il eut de se peindre*"—"The ridiculous idea of his of portraying himself"—he said of Montaigne, without foreseeing that the passages in the *Pensées* in which Pascal himself portrays and reveals himself, with his anguish and his doubts, affect us today much more than the exposition of his dogmatics. Similarly what we admire in Bossuet is not the antiquated theologian, but rather the perfect art of his exquisite language which makes him one of the most magnificent writers in our literature—the art but for which he would scarcely be read today. It is to form, which he considered profane, that he owes his survival.

A dialogue incessantly carried on down the centuries and in which its penchant for free thought is more or less concealed, out of prudence—that "wisdom of the serpents", as the Scriptures say, for the demon of temptation and emancipation of the mind speaks for preference in an undertone: it insinuates, whereas the believer proclaims aloud; and Descartes adopts as his motto: *Larvatu prodeo*—I advance masked; or better, it is beneath a mask that I advance.

At times one of the two voices carries the day. In the 18th century it is the voice of free thought, its mask now put aside. It prevailed to the point of bringing about, as an inevitable consequence, a regrettable exhaustion of the lyric vein. But the equilibrium of the dialogue is never disturbed for long in France. With Chateaubriand and Lamartine the religious sentiment, a source of lyricism, bursts forth again resplendently in the flood tide of romanticism. And if Michelet and Hugo rise up against the Church, it is nevertheless with a profound feeling for religion.

Rolling from one side to the other, the vessel of French culture advances and pursues its fearless path. *Fluctuat nec mergitur*[2]—"It sails on and will not be swamped." It would run the risk of being, and would indeed be swamped, the moment that one of the two interlocutors in the dialogue decisively got the better of the other and reduced him to silence, the moment the ship keeled over or heeled completely to one side.

In our day we are witnessing a prodigious flourishing of Catho-

2 The motto of the city of Paris. Ed.

lic writers: Huysmans and Léon Bloy are followed by Jammes, Péguy, Claudel, Mauriac, Gabriel Marcel, Bernanos, Maritain. But even without taking a Proust or a Suarès into account, the towering and steadfast figure of Paul Valéry would suffice to counterbalance them. Never had the critical mind been more masterfully brought to bear on the most diverse problems and more convincingly demonstrated its creative capacity. I recall the saying of Oscar Wilde's: "The imagination imitates: it is the mind that creates",[3] a saying which could have been Baudelaire's and which every artist would do well to meditate. (It is a question, it goes without saying, not of the criticism of others but of oneself.) For, among the many illusions that the imagination uncontrolledly presents to us, the critical mind must choose. All design implies a choice—and that is one school of design that I especially admire in France.

II

There exists a great dialogue which we must hope shall persist as long as our race, for it is the principle of the most comprehensive and solemn music which the French genius has drawn forth from the instrument which is proper to it—the Montaigne - Pascal dialogue. A Frenchman is profound in proportion as he is able to maintain this dialogue alive within him, according to his station. If a Boylesve owes to Montaigne the indispensable biological heritage, it is to him also that he owes the need "not only to define himself, but also to classify himself," in

---

3 It is unlikely that Oscar Wilde said anything of the sort. In his *The Decay of Lying*, in which he sums up his philosophy of art in the well-known paradox, "Life and Nature imitate Art," he says the opposite. For example: "Art begins with abstract decoration, with purely imaginative and pleasurable work dealing with what is unreal and non-existent."—"The whole history of these arts in Europe is the record of the struggle between Orientalism, with its frank rejection of imitation, its love of artistic convention, its dislike to the actual representation of any object in Nature, and our own imitative spirit. Wherever the former has been paramount...we have had beautiful and imaginative work in which the visible things of life are transmuted into artistic conventions, and the things that Life has not are invented and fashioned for her delight...Art finds her own perfection within, and not outside of, herself. She is not to be judged by any external standard of resemblance. She is a veil, rather than a mirror."—"The imagination is essentially creative, and always seeks for a new form."—"..when Art surrenders her imaginative medium she surrenders everything." It is possible that in attributing to Wilde the idea that *"L'imagination imite: c'est l'esprit qui crée,"* Gide is simply misremembering; probable it is, however, that he quotes—or misquotes—this in support of his thesis and own intellectual bias, as befits a critic who considered Stendhal the greatest French novelist. Perhaps also Gide derived a certain mischievous pleasure from quoting the persecuted Wilde back at his persecutors! Ed.

which Ramon Fernandez justly sees the specific value and significance of Montaigne,[4] and to which Fernandez himself would add today a concomitant need: the need "to be judged."

But the Montaigne of "the loving friendship", the man of: "Oh, the base and abject creature that Man is if he does not raise himself above humanity!" is neither the essential nor the definitive Montaigne. The one who speaks with "the implacable human voice" is the Montaigne of the last pages of the last chapter of the *Essais*—pages which are, and which shall ever remain, the charter of the most replete and at the same time of the strictest humanism. They are pages from which resounds this apostrophe of explicit declaration: "They want to get out of themselves and escape from the man. That is madness: instead of changing into angels, they change into beasts; instead of raising themselves, they lower themselves. These transcendental humours frighten me, like lofty and inaccessible places; and nothing is so hard for me to stomach in the life of Socrates as his ecstasies and possessions by his daemon, nothing is so human in Plato as the qualities for which they say he is called divine. And of our sciences, those seem to me most terrestrial and low which have risen the highest."[5] And then, unquestionably, immediately afterwards, with the sentence which, from its very deliberate choice of expression, derives so clear and utterly inexhaustible a significance— "It is an absolute perfection and virtually divine to know how to enjoy our being rightfully"—we re-enter the sun-drenched fields where we see spread out the harvest of a lifetime now grown to full maturity. But, in spite of its conclusive grace, how keenly we feel that the saying, "Stand aside from my sunlight,"[6] applies to all the rest. To which, "resounding in men's minds in its turn", engraving in its definitive form the charter of the supernatural and (in a thoroughly religious but in the widest acceptance of the word) that of the superhuman, Pascal makes his eternal riposte with man "full of needs", man "produced for infinity", and man "who infinitely surpasses man."

---

4 "The further we progress in our reading of the *Essais* and the farther we leave behind the somewhat rhetorical exercises of the beginning, the more concerned we find Montaigne becomes not only to define himself, but also to classify himself: his self does not fill the frame, there is space around him in the noble portrait which owes something to Epaminondas." (Ramon Fernandez, *Messages*, p. 155.) For Epaminondas, see especially *Essais*, II, 36. Ed.

5 The translation of this passage, and of the sentence following, is by Donald M. Frame. Ed.

6 The reply of Diogenes to Alexander in Athens when the latter asked him if there was anything he could do for him. Ed.

8

The Church of French Literature

by

Georges Duhamel

From: *Défense des lettres* (Paris, 1937) Part IV. English translation *In Defence of Letters* (London: Dent, 1938) by E. F. Bozman.

*J*n a page at once friendly and treacherous that he wrote for the *Liber amicorum Romain Rolland*, George Brandes said, just before he died: *'J'aime mieux les livres qui perdent beaucoup, s'ils sont traduits.'* ('I much prefer books that lose a lot in translation.') I quote this phrase of Brandes's word for word because it seems to be designed to prove that there is something untranslatable in every human idiom. Brandes was a great scholar. He understood and spoke several languages, and the opinion he expresses above is obviously coloured with egoism; it is the opinion of a dilettante of the mind. Every language has its esoteric rites and every literature its inner temple and only those who can give the password may enter the holy of holies.

The literary output of a nation or of a man comprises one part which is universally assailable. Given a good translation such work enters into the consciousness of other nations and may even take a place of honour there. The masterpieces of Swift and Daniel Defoe immediately took their proper rank in the French libraries, and moreover they came to our notice at a time when everybody in French wrote well and when anonymous translations were frequently models of style and good taste.

French literature is certainly rich in works which can easily be translated. It is not, however, through the medium of translations that it has made its way in the world and won its true glory. I once saw Molière's *Avare* played by an old Finnish actor in a theatre in Helsingfors. Disguised in the strange and beautiful dialect of Väinämöinen, Molière was still Molière; but one could feel that part of his unique genius stayed in the filter, as the chemists say, and that some of the qualities of this famous work are inseparable from the mother tongue.

It has been the remarkable destiny of French literature to win the attention of the civilized world, not only by offering it works of universal appeal but by converting it to the beauty of the original language. The educated world likes to read French literature in French. Great men of genius like Tolstoy and Dostoevsky have spoken for the whole world without teaching Russian to many of their readers; on the other hand I am sure that many foreigners have learned French conscientiously so as to be able to read our writers in the original text. French is not used much for commercial purposes and the man who wants to travel and handle big business had better learn English or German; both these languages, for material reasons, have extended their ideals, have benefited. With us it is quite different. Foreigners of all countries learn French so as to be able to share the spiritual treasures of French rather than for utilitarian reasons. Molière, Balzac, and Anatole France throw open doors through which our business men find excellent opportunities; for which service I must admit they show neither surprise nor gratitude.

This state of affairs is worth examination. It is not enough to say that French is extremely rich and varied; in addition it brings a message to the world, and we must consider the origin and the nature of this message.

Of all the remarkable phenomena which it is given to us of the twentieth century to witness, the most striking is undoubtedly the standardization of civilization. This phenomenon, which arises from improved facilities for intercourse between peoples and races, is now in rapid development. We cannot foresee all the consequences but we know very well that in a comparatively few years, with certain reserves owing to differing climatic conditions, there will be only one solitary system of civilization, monotonous and indistinctive, left on earth.

Until the time of the great colonial fever and the industrial revolution of the last century, in spite of travellers' tales and business enterprise, the world was ruled by diverse systems of civilization which would have no truck with one another and which guarded their treasures and their secrets jealously. There seemed to be no possibility of real fusion or compromise or alliance between the Asiatic civilizations and the so-called European or western civilization.

Western thinking men knew very well that the Asiatic civilizations were not to be despised, but they had many reasons for admiring the western civilization which was their own, and in which, through over six thousand years of history, several distinct primitive social ideas were incorporated. Egypt, the countries of the Levant, Greece, Italy, and North Africa had each evolved different and at first opposing civilizations which were finally united in one civilization that might be called Mediterranean and was thenceforward associated with Europe as a whole, a continent fertile in genius.

Although I have tried to do so all my life, it is difficult to distinguish between the spiritual and the material in this civilization. It can be said, however, that for sixty centuries a spiritual treasure has been accumulating in that part of the world whose shores are washed by the Mediterranean, the Atlantic Ocean, and North Sea, and that this treasure consists not only of works of art and literature, but, more important still, of intellectual methods and moral traditions, in fact, of metaphysical and religious doctrines.

Naturally this gradual and prodigious human experience has not been gained without setbacks and loss of continuity. But during the most troubled periods of history there have always been scholars to rescue the essence of our precious heritage, to recopy and annotate famous writings, to restore or corroborate intellectual traditions.

I know some distinguished thinkers who regard the French Renaissance as a disastrous event without which, according to them, we should have seen the development of a truly original culture in France. Brilliant though this paradox may be, it distracts us from our magnificent achievements only to surrender us to vain regrets for a hardly discernible shadow. The great French writers and poets before the Renaissance were all, or nearly all, saturated in Greek and Roman culture. Far from making us deplore the Renaissance in retrospect, they herald it and show it as a necessity that would not be denied.

Just as, at certain moments of their history, groups of human beings have shown their strong desire of forming a nation, so towards the middle of the sixteenth century the French writers and poets gave vigorous expression to their desire to form a literature, and to begin by codifying their language. They suddenly decided to revive the Mediterranean tradition, to reclaim their heritage from a rich and ancient civilization, the only one known to them, and to propagate that civilization throughout a whole nation.

Yes, the most remarkable event of the sixteenth century in France was this spiritual resolution to revive a tradition, not by the complete abandonment of all the original characteristics of a group of human beings but by the submission of those characteristics to an illustrious ancient discipline. In just such a way, in some families, one may see a son renounce his own original plans in order to devote himself to his father's business and maintain the good name and fortune of the house.

To tell the truth, everything tended to urge France to this succession. Among the peoples called Latin, for the reason that they were longer than others under the yoke of the Roman conquest, France occupies a unique geographic situation; she is closely hedged in by Anglo-Saxon and Germanic peoples, and, in spite of foreign invasions, she has always resisted Germanization. In giving evidence of her intention to remain Mediterranean by culture, and in affirming her inheritance of Greek and Latin civilization, she gave a fundamentally moral force to her resistance. Moreover she discovered political autonomy earlier than Spain or Italy. In the sixteenth century she was not, like Italy, bound up with the destiny of the Austrian empire, nor, like Spain, torn asunder by internal strife. Thus of all the so-called Latin nations she was the most capable of accepting a great heritage and developing it. Only a lover of shadows would regret what France might have given to literature and philosophy had she been resolute to follow the impulses of her racial genius alone. One can well imagine that this composite nation, so favourably placed in the rich territories of the Continent, would have produced some remarkable individuals and some interesting works; probably they would all have amounted to compared with that unique thing in the modern world, French literature.

In order to understand what this literature has meant during the last four centuries one must try to picture French literature as a single personality.

I realize that the genius of a language and of a people is always more or less comparable to a human personality, which is born, emerges from childhood, grows up, reaches maturity, the zenith, then wanes and dies. But this development often seems to be anarchic and casual. One notices, among those men who mark its stages, anomalies and asymmetries that are flagrant. There are often long periods of silence which are like eclipses of the genius of a nation. On the other hand, when one considers the life of the great thinker and writer whom I call 'French literature,' one is struck by the continuity of his effort, the good order of his experiments, the harmony of his history, and the logic of his development.

And so, round about the year 1548, France resolved to undertake a great work and to devote hundreds of years to the doing of it. All the Frenchmen who have been associated in this work have been conscious of the part they are playing in the whole and have accepted the strict discipline imposed on them by this majestic combination of effort.

What is this work of a whole nation? What is this monument with which French literature is associated? I should answer at once, a portrait of Man.

French literature has undertaken to depict man as he is, relentlessly; man individual, man social, the inner man and the outer man, man visible and man invisible, man subjective and man objective.

When we study works of art and their connecting links, we are struck by the regularity with which the labour has been accomplished, by shifts and by stages, through four centuries. Task succeeds task, and experience experience, as in a human life intelligently directed. French literature has behaved like a sensible person who travels prudently and always in the same direction.

Both thought and writing need a precise instrument; a language that is firm and sure. The first task of the great Frenchmen of the sixteenth century was to enrich and codify the language. I suspect that the word 'codify' may make some people uncomfortable. I know that a language is a living thing which, like the people it expresses, must absorb nourishment and undergo change, must live, in fact, but French has managed to live, and still lives, without abandoning the strict rules that are the guarantee and the very condition of all creation of the mind.

The poets of the Pleiad have been accused of having introduced into the language a host of words of Greek origin, foreign to our phonetic genius. The reproach is futile. Have we retained more than two hundred words or roots from the original Gallic? The philologist reminds us that we do not even know how 'yes' was said in Gallic. Spoken French has grown out of a number of different elements. Greek, from which either directly or via Latin we have received numerous roots, is one of the most important sources, and a source which is rich in bright tone colours.

Most notable is the constant care taken by writers and poets and philosophers to perfect their instrument, to fix the rules and usage of grammar, to extend and purify the vocabulary, to specify spelling and establish punctuation. It is really surprising to realize nowadays that Corneille had to fight for u and v to be represented by two different letters. This passion for law and order is not an abuse. I have had in my hands editions of Malleville and Benserade in which the poets' names were spelled out quite differently on different pages. It is interesting to watch the gradual codification of punctuation, too meagre with some authors, too plentiful with others (as, for example, with the abbé de Saint-Réal, who puts a comma after every other word); it is interesting, too, to note authors taking punctuation out of the hands of the compositors, and wielding themselves this important accessory of language and style.

Such pursuits are not, of course, the principal occupation of the creative minds which are the artisans of French genius; what is so striking is the unobtrusive way in which this team work is carried out, the mutual understanding, the dovetailing of the smaller perfections with the great works.

It may be desirable to try to discover a general trend in the mass of fact and fiction, but it would be a pity to diminish so glorious a page of human history by taking too systematic a view. The classical French writers and poets, while performing their important task of exploring the passions, endeavour to rediscover the guiding principles and laws of art, the laws established and tested by that antiquity which they admire and aim at perpetuating. Thus they restore what I should like to call the rule of economy and discipline.

If Shakespeare, incomparable poet, was barbarously treated by the French scholars of the seventeenth century, it was because their researches then led them very far from his adventurous genius. Our great writers were fascinated by the example of the Greeks and the Romans and yearned for literary bondage. They revived on the stage the three unities, they insisted on strict prosody in verse, and finally they set themselves to prove that their artistic principles of discipline and economy were borrowed from nature, which is not free, as it is mistakenly said to be, but is dominated by strict laws and stern necessities.

Can the austere classic art of Racine or Molière, which seems at first sight to be conventional and foreign to nature, possibly disclose the secret principles of animal and vegetable life? It is more than possible, it is certain. Almost all living beings instinctively practise economy and saving; instinctively all human beings know that, if they wish to live to accomplish their destiny and build lasting works, they must not spend all they possess but must put something to reserve. Man exists by robbing animals of their reserves of fat, vegetables of their reserves of sugar, all those humble provisions that life makes against famine. The peasant learns from the example of animals and plants and puts a similar economic law into practice. He learns to save. He builds granaries, silos, and reservoirs. He never spends all that he has. We may say he is a miser but he is preeminently wise and natural.

Strange that the fundamental laws of our classic art enable us to understand the French peasant, whom the entire world is now reproaching for his practical qualities!

The writer in the classical tradition does not spend all he has, does not say all he knows, does not undertake more than he can carry out, does not shout louder than his voice allows, keeps some reserves, controls himself, makes rules, and obeys them. The romantic tradition, on the other hand, not only spends everything it has to give, but runs into debt.

My opponents may suggest that my thesis is untenable because it would suggest that in France romanticism has destroyed or endangered the classics. Of course I do not suggest this, because in its romantic wanderings French genius has kept its respect for traditional values and proved possessions. We know well enough that in France, even after the worst follies, even after the most violent lurches, there has always been someone to take the helm and guide the ship back to the middle of the stream.

II

French literature is not a world of experiments in anarchy, but a society governed by strict rules, a Church, one and indivisible. The word 'church' implies assembly, and it is as an assembly that I regard French literature. It is not in my view a haphazard meeting or an accidental collection of men and personalities. Across space and time it is seen as a harmonious group of men and their works, ordered and controlled by a broad and unique design.

I know that great men are only men, that great minds seldom think alike, and that they may seem to contradict this superior order I am trying to visualize. Bossuet is cruel to Molière, Malherbe treats Ronsard with scant respect, Pascal is hard on Montaigne, Rousseau in *Émile* tears La Fontaine to pieces with ferocious joy, Balzac in his correspondence shows the most violent scorn for Victor Hugo. Like children who quarrel among themselves but are nevertheless united when the time comes to stand by the family, the great writers do not hesitate to give vent to their disputes; but they unite in respect and obedience: respect for the language they serve, and for the destiny of the literature of which they are part, obedience to the rules established by centuries of labour.

There is no Church, no true assembly without discipline and obligations. It is strange that our French people, long famous for their faith in the individual, should have produced this remarkable community founded on observance and discipline. Thanks to this discipline French is still a unique language, at once popular and scholarly, avoiding the dangers of corruption by dialect; and thanks to this discipline the writers of four centuries ago are today immediately intelligible to the average man of moderate education.

The Churches, even the strictest of them, could not, except at their peril, deny the laws of life, that is to say movement and development. French literature has never ceased to develop new and splendid growths but has always been afraid of heretics and has always resisted them. There has been no crusade hardly even a civil war; it seems rather that the people I am now calling heretics, apart from that especially favoured and beloved *enfant terrible*, lyric poetry, have constantly been smothered by indifference and oblivion.

To whom should this formidable epithet 'heretic' be applied? As far as French prose is concerned there can be no doubt. They are heretics who have left the beaten track, broad but well defined, of four hundred years of language and thought, all those who have tried to shine at the expense of others by frivolous experiments in schism and independent action which might deflect the true course of French thought and literature. It would be difficult to write a history of these heresies because, having been suppressed in embryo, they have no history. A few eccentrics of genius have succeeded in installing themselves on the frontiers of the literary empire, they have never succeeded in withdrawing from it entirely. Men of my generation came into the world of letters at a time when disruptive influences were at work. We know now that these experiments have proved to be without future. The style of Péladan, or even of Paul Adam and some others, has not obtained the assent of the council, and the work of these writers, despite undoubted merits, seem henceforward to be excommunicated.

I can well imagine how such a remark might wound the young men who bring to literature an ardent desire for regeneration. I appreciate and sympathize with this desire, because life is a dull and unprofitable thing without it; but I know from experience that the Church of French literature has always required of genius, even the most original genius, that it should observe her laws and respect her history and traditions. The mysterious thing is that through this subjection, voluntarily and finally accepted, our great writers have arrived at an effective principle of power.

If we wish to estimate the severity of the restriction we have only to consider the sort of reservation made by the literary Church—I am pursuing the metaphor—in respect of various regional tendencies in literature. I am not passing judgment on the phenomenon: it is not attributable, of course, to any deliberate plan, but to instinctive forces. Regional literature throughout France, before admittance to the Church, has had to accept her ritual; that is to say, to honour the one and indivisible French language, except for occasional eccentricities of vocabulary and syntax. This homage rendered, the works of enduring value have been carried away from their local habitation to be inscribed in the national treasure. Flaubert's and Maupassant's Normandy is first and foremost France; Mauriac's Gascony is already annexed. Authors who come to ask for a Paris imprimatur understand all this well enough.

French literature owns several provinces outside the borders of France which are not exempt from the common law. These provinces have some good writers and have made notable contributions to the common treasure. May they be obedient like us, and may they subscribe to no major heresy! For when they throw off the yoke of the Church they renounce her privileges too.

And the privileges are great, in return for this rigorous service. Every one who uses the French language experiences simultaneously the discipline and the joy of communion. The writer especially must be more aware than any one else of the humility and pride of his state, and if he has not the feeling when he takes up his pen of writing under the watchful and severe but friendly eye of an assembly of honoured predecessors and worthy peers, then, in my opinion, he is renouncing both the duties and the essential advantages of his calling.

III

The rigorous observance and discipline, the rule of the Church of French literature which so many great writers have followed faithfully, has always been waived in favour of lyric poetry.

In the most strictly brought up families there is usually one rebellious child who cannot adapt himself to the family law, a child tenderly loved but not properly understood; criticized, but tolerated with all his whims and tempers and extravagances.

Such has been the fate of lyric poetry in the French literary family. It has been, and still is, in France the spoiled child and darling, sometimes the prodigal child, sometimes the accursed child but always forgiven.

This odd state of affairs has not been properly understood by scholars, especially abroad. The oratorical splendour of a literature dedicated to the interpretation of man and the world and founded in order and discipline, seems to have dazzled many critics and induced them to take too simple a view. It has been said, and is still said in other countries, that France has no lyric poets as all, and that French, unlike English or German, is not a suitable medium for lyrical effusions. This is a very arbitrary judgment. The miracle is precisely that French, notwithstanding its splendidly luminous and analytical qualities, has always been responsive to the demands of the poets, and has proved to be an incomparably supple and musical instrument in their hands.

For centuries the best minds have been engaged in making French an unrivalled instrument of precision and analysis, but that has not prevented lyric poetry from flourishing on the side. I say 'on the side'; in the great century the middle of the stage was held by dramatic poetry, first cousin to lyric poetry, with which it shared duties and responsibilities; but lyricism has never lost its position. In a preface to an anthology of French lyric poetry I pointed out that the extreme difficulty of our lyric poetry is not due to some rare disease of the imagination, but is a veritable tradition, handed down from the fifteenth century to our times and renewed among the symbolists of today.

It is interesting to remark that the Frenchman, naturally a logician and a grammarian, has always admitted certain dispensations in favour of poetry, poetic licenses in fact. It is gratifying to see such licenses conceded to an art which in other respects is strictly and even absurdly regulated. Poetry is the prodigious prodigal son, the delicate monster. And so French lyricism has won wide acceptance by scholars, in folklore, and in our heritage of popular songs. Molière, right in the middle of the most disciplined period, honours folklore on the stage, and it is curious to hear the Misanthrope reciting verses which were then being sung, and had been sung for a long time, by the common folk.

This agreement to differ between the literary family and the poet, the spoiled darling and *enfant terrible*, seems to have been suspended by romanticism. During this extraordinary period we see poetry reinstated in the normal literary stream. Perhaps it would be more accurate to say that we see the normal stream overflowing its banks into the territories of lyricism. Immediately romanticism is exhausted the divorce becomes operative again. The whole symbolist movement grows in mysterious shadow, outside the main literary currents in which the tradition of thought and language is embodied.

Therefore let us have no heretics in the French literary Church; no heretics except poets. I find it right that it should be so, right that the poet should be free, a little outside the Church militant, that he should sometimes receive her protection and her consolation, that he should be sometimes chastised but finally acclaimed, that he should represent the divine and redeeming exception. I believe it is proper that the long triumph of order and reason should be secretly troubled by the noble faults of ecstasy; and I find it excellent that poetic madness, in constantly threatening the equilibrium of the ship, should effectively remind us of what equilibrium is, and of our need of it.

IV

For what is the equilibrium of an organism in movement except a perpetual struggle to restore the balance of conflicting forces and to create a harmony that is the fairer for being unstable and uncertain?

Once in my presence a man who knew both France and America well advised some French tourists who were about to cross the ocean, never on the other side to use such discredited expressions as 'measure, clarity, order, or Cartesian logic.' I know very well that these ideas, only too easily abstract, have suffered a certain amount of didactic abuse. To offer foreigners a tiresome and slightly ridiculous picture and to over-stress our greatest qualities, our clarity, for example, would be a great blunder, perhaps a disaster, and would be most damaging to this very quality.

What exactly is this celebrated French clarity which has been admired for so long and which cannot be laughed at with impunity?

I remember one day having delivered a lecture to a German audience, a lecture which I had carefully prepared and constructed according to our classical rules. As I was leaving the platform a university professor, an excellent scholar, said: 'You are a real Frenchman! We Germans, instead of beginning, as you did, by rapidly outlining the scope and the divisions of the subject, would have begun by casting a little shadow round it.' This remark is strangely reminiscent of one of Mallarmé's celebrated utterances. But Mallarmé was a poet, and the poet, even in France, has royal privileges. It is true to say that almost all French writers have used the French language as an instrument whose proper function is to classify ideas and states of mind and to render them intelligible.

That is a great and worthy undertaking. If it is admitted, in principle, that man is made for knowledge and that he can do better than to know, then we should praise those people who make a methodical and exacting and determined effort in the first place to understand exactly what they think and afterwards to comprehend what the objective world has to offer them. And if knowledge needs light, then let there be light, and may that light shine through our work!

Is it possible that excess of clarity may operate against the needs of perfect knowledge? It is possible. An excess of light can be dazzling. Therein lies a danger to the mind from which the real artists escape at the right moment by drawing a veil, or interposing a screen, or evoking a cloud. It is also possible that the full light of day may be not only blinding but corrosive and destructive, and that it may destroy both the colour and the texture of the materials exposed to its action. A skilful and resourceful artist can feel this instinctively. Needless to say the scholar and the artist do not make the same use of the light, and by analogy do not employ language in the same way.

In the most successful works of our national treasure, clarity may sometimes give a feeling, especially to foreigners, of avarice and parsimony, in respect of the object under illumination.

Beware of hasty judgments of this difficult question. The role of language is to 'resolve' at all costs, for our peace of mind and irrespective of our wishes. To resolve at all costs for the final salvation of mankind, even when, the operation done, we are going to think with a touch of disappointment, 'So it was nothing but that! And so that is all that is left us!'

Before asserting that any page of the great book of France is too clear, let us assure ourselves that we have fully savoured it, completely grasped its meaning. Lovers of the shade are often inclined to declare the world empty because they are incapable of seeing anything, because they cannot appreciate perfect nakedness. French psychologists and writers have gone as far in the knowledge of man and nature as they can go without compromise and ambiguity, and without counting on the good graces of luck and the powers of darkness.

Zealous propagandists spread the idea freely that France is, *par excellence*, the country of moderation. To hear them one would think that the hillsides of the Ile de France and Touraine were the only hillsides in the world, and that the view from these marvellous hillsides would suffice to imbue the soul of the inhabitants with a miraculous sense of moderation and just proportion and reasonable action. Do not let us trust this rather 'Tainian' sentimentality. The history of France proves again and again that the most charming geographical emotions are not sufficient to give rise to political and social wisdom. The country of moderation has had more revolutions that any other European country. It has not, so far as I know, always been a model of prudence and balance. Passions and crimes and sins work their havoc in France as elsewhere. And if France may be proud of the valleys of Normandy and landscapes of Poitiers, she also possesses wild mountains, desolate plains, rushing torrents, and barren heaths. No, let us guard against this vain and ridiculous eloquence. But let us remember that through her language and her literature, through the untiring energy of her civilized minds, France through the ages has at least made a praiseworthy effort to arrive at moderation. France is not yet, alas, the country of moderation; but she is the country where the master minds have made the most genuine efforts, through their works, to teach respect for moderation.

V

Is French literature, as it used to be said, a literature of moralists? Here is a problem that needs examination.

The word 'moralist' in days gone by used to connote observer and recorder of morals and manners. Without losing its original sense it has gradually taken on that of moralizer. Will French literature, the literature of moralists, become a literature of moralizers?

The majority of the great French writers have described the manners of their time and have proceeded thence to show the way of life of mankind in general, claiming by their descriptions to work for the betterment of the species. Ethical preoccupation is inevitably part of such literature, and the result is that the words 'moral' and 'moralist' take on a wider meaning. From La Fontaine to Molière and Voltaire this impulse to control manners and customs has characterized all the leading writers of our literature. Destouches is quite candid about it. He says: 'I can believe that dramatic art is worthy only when it aims at instruction through entertainment.' The impulse was often adventitious. Our masters followed their desire, which was to depict; and to justify this desire they made a pious pretense of having in view the perfection of mankind. We are at liberty to doubt the motive without in the least slighting the genius of these artists. However that may be, the avowed pretext was for a long time a moral, or rather an ethical one. Let us note this in order properly to understand the tendencies of the new century.

There is no writer worthy of the name who does not want to exercise influence. There is no writer who does not believe that his influence is salutary. Even the cynics themselves, when they publish their outbursts, affirm with touching candour their wish to work for the well-being of mankind. The madmen who dream of disorder and destruction are doubtless persuaded, in the bottom of their hearts, that annihilation is a desirable, and in fact a moral, solution for mankind. Most writers, because they work constructively whether for good or ill, necessarily proclaim an optimistic faith. We are forced to believe that they refuse allegiance to nothingness, and that they say with Sénancour, '*L'homme est périssable. Il se peut; mais périssons en résistant, et, si le néant nous est réservé, ne faisons pas que ce soit une justice.*'[1]

---

1 Miguel de Unamuno, who liked this phrase, told me one day that he would have preferred it to read as follows: '*Faisons que ce ne soit pas une justice.*' Unamuno was a great believer in the power of the will. I approve his version, while modifying it slightly to the form: '*faisons que ce ne soit pas justice.*' ("Man is perishable. That may be so; but

131

Of course I do not disapprove of the wish expressed by so many writers whether sincerely or not to improve behaviour and to better mankind. It seems to me, however, that the writers of the twentieth century express this wish less frequently than their predecessors, and I do not blame them. One important reason for this development is to be found in the change in public morality. I do not think that morals are lower today than yesterday or that licentiousness is more tolerated. I believe, like everyone else, that a greater liberty of writing is admissible, at any rate in France. The recorder of manners and morals has no longer any need to search for a pretext or an excuse. Choderlos de Laclos wrote in the preface to *Les Liaisons dangereuses*: 'It seems to me, putting it at its lowest, that it is a service to morals to expose the methods used by the wicked to corrupt the good.' Self-deception! Laclos does not care a rap for rendering 'a service to morals.' He is concerned only with observing them and portraying them, and I notice that he is more interested and curious, happier perhaps, the more the spectacle is improper and cruel. But still he thinks it prudent to invoke the classic excuse. He does so very superficially, and it is obviously only as a matter of form.

Nowadays we can afford to dispense with this hypocrisy and illusion. For the idea of moral improvement there is gradually being substituted the stricter and sadder and purer idea of knowledge. The writer of the twentieth century portrays conduct in order to make a show of learning, to bear witness at the tribunal of humanity. If his evidence happens to be of some effect in reforming some people, well, the writer does not object to such a beneficial result.

We may, and we should, hope that the stories of the novelists and the dissertations of the essayists, the chants or the songs of the poets, will have a favourable effect on moral life. It remains to consider along what lines such an effect may operate.

I do not suppose that it can be possible to effect any profound change in the physiological and moral habits of man, the finished article. We can interest a man when he is in the prime of life, make him reconsider his reasons, shake his beliefs, disturb his leisure, perhaps even help him in his orientation if the wind is blowing in the right direction. We can amuse him or attract him, or, conversely, annoy him, and disappoint him. Perhaps it is just possible to move him a little in the direction of his powerful, instinctive, and sentimental forces, but I doubt whether it is possible appreciably to change a fully matured man, either by force of

---

let us perish while resisting, and, if we are destined for oblivion let us see to it that it is not with justice.")

argument or by description, or by eloquence, or by the music of words, or by all these elements combined.

It is not at all the same with young malleable minds, which are capable of receiving and retaining new impressions. In the moral sphere one can exert a great and a lasting influence on children. The essential influence of a writer is not that which he exerts immediately on the public by the first distribution of his works, it is what he exercises, even unknown to himself, through the intermediary of teachers and scholars on the children of the generations to come. I realize fully that one must first be accepted by the teachers, and that their intelligent understanding must be enlisted in order to obtain their mediatory action and collaboration. Because of this function teachers are always in the front row of the audience; they preserve, even in maturity, the freshness and vivacity of the youth whom it is their duty to instruct.

Thanks to the assistance of teachers, writers find eventually their best response among their remotest public, which is the final justification for a work of art.

This presupposes a friendly and continuously active collaboration between practical and scholarly literature, between the literary world and the university. Such collaboration we should not have dared to hope for thirty years ago. Alarmed by the excesses of realism and the alchemy of the symbolists, the university showed extreme distrust, or at least a frowning reserve, towards living literature—by which I mean the literature of living writers. It was a time when the literary manuals in use in the schools made only a derisive mention of Baudelaire, who is now honoured among us as a god of the written word. It was a time when the life of French literature appeared to the student to stop dead at the beginning of the nineteenth century.

Such a state of affairs could not have lasted without serious danger to all concerned. Enthusiasm and anger were aroused simultaneously among the keen intelligentsia by the paradox that authors whom the French universities insisted on misunderstanding or belittling figured in the courses of schools of Romance languages abroad and furnished subjects for theses to university students in Scandinavia and America.

Things have changed very much for the better in literature. The university of our day, under the control of broadminded men, has shown that criticism affirms its power and assumes its highest responsibilities in applying itself courageously to contemporary work. In all departments of the university numbers of qualified teachers have begun to illuminate their teaching by comparison of ancient and modern, and to accept the assistance of present-day minds in explaining the world around us.

Whether the writer admits or pretends to despise the function of instructor and teacher, there is another role of which, however sceptical he is, he cannot think without tenderness. Many writers who have no intention of being guides and philosophers are really, and they know it themselves, comforters and friends. I am not misusing words. There is no consolation for our deepest sorrows. Nevertheless, let us try to imagine what existence would be like without reading, let us estimate the grip that trouble, sorrow, sickness or any other adversity would have over us. Even in its most despairing melodies art is a living work. Even when it portrays fatality, suffering, death, art is light and life. Because it interests us in life, art is very near making us live life. If only because it helps us to endure life, art deserves our gratitude.

It is quite obvious that French literature, in its contemporary adventures, is not far removed from its illustrious traditions. The great discourse on man, as it develops, naturally becomes also a discourse for man. The work of the humanists from century to century is fulfilled in human work. That this precious treasure may be enriched and increased is the fervent wish of all good men. Do not let us forget that the treasure is in our hands and that we are responsible. Let us love it and honour it as our surest wealth, our inalienable possession, our bread for the days to come.

9
The French Literary Mind

by

Wallace Fowlie

From: Wallace Fowlie, *A Guide to Contemporary French Literature* (Cleveland: Meridian Books, 1962). All attempts to trace the copyright holder at Duke University and the original publisher failed.

*I*n the literary tradition of France, eloquence, both oral and written, is a ceremony. It is true that in every literary tradition, eloquence, by its very nature, must become to some degree the stylization of language, but in France the instinct to make of language a highly formalized expression is deeper and more permanent than in other traditions. Each of the great masterpieces in French literature seems extraordinarily aware of the public to which it is addressing itself, of the presence of a public, of a public mind which must be subjugated and enchanted according to well-established rules of subjugation and enchantment.

And that is why the first trait of the French literary mind always seems to be its sociability or even what we might call its worldliness. The French writer is always addressing some one, even when he is speaking on that subject which has become a favorite since the days of the Renaissance when Montaigne wrote his *Essays*: the subject of solitude. Because of this attitude of the French writer, which is more an instinct than an attitude, born of a need to communicate and to establish a relationship between his thought and the minds of other men, his works are characterized by a tone of bareness, of separateness. They often give the effect of arias sung in the midst of great silence, sung at some distance from the world, even if they are directed toward the world. This is sometimes described as the classical spirit in French art, and works composed in this spirit have the inflections of a pleader and a lawyer whose skill is used to combat and convince and seduce.

Such works, and they have occurred in all periods of French history, illustrate the solitude of literary speech. But such speech solitude, because of its ceremonial aspect, is floodlighted. Its contrived effect, so carefully planned to provoke, hold, subjugate and enchant, may often appear a pure theatricality. The writer in the French tradition resembles a performing artist. In French schools the primary literary exercise is that of textual explication, by which a single page of a writer is made to serve as a revelation of his particular art and thought, and even the art and thought of his period. Only a very highly self-conscious and even histrionic art permits such examination and such treatment, whereby a novelist is studied not in his novel, but in a single paragraph from his novel, and a poet is studied in a single sonnet. This habit of study has helped to convert French literature into a series of celebrated set-pieces. Renan is known for his prayer on the Acropolis and Proust for the passage on the madeleine cake dipped in a cup of linden tea.

A single page can be separated from its book and exist autonomously in its own brilliance, in much the same way as a speech in a French conversation may be taken out of its context and seen to be a distinct and singular creation. At French dinner parties the general effect may be that of conversation, or at times of hubbub, but when listened to more attentively, the conversation of each dinner guest will be seen to be a monologue, recited both simultaneously and independently. French eloquence, whether written or spoken under the stimulus of a physically present public, is expression ritualistically conceived.

The reason for this solitariness of the French literary voice, what we might name the primary secret of the French literary mind, is the fervent identification it establishes with the past. If the finished product of French writing often gives us the impression of an aria sung in the center of a vast space, of a form stripped of nonessentials and bare in an almost heroic vulnerability, we know that its strength comes from its alliance with an allegiance to the tradition of its past. The dependence of a French writer on other writers who preceded him is acknowledged and emphasized. French art is knowingly the renewal of tradition and not the discovery of the new. The writer in France learns his particular role and vocation in terms of those past writers with whom he is in sympathy as well as those with whom he is in disagreement. Many French masterpieces have been born from a quarrel. The loneliness of the French writer, which now might be termed his uniqueness, comes from this will to determine himself by his affiliations and disagreements. The French writer knows that originality is an unimportant and even an illusory goal in art. The seeming new really draws upon the old....I have taken courses in French literature both in America and Paris where the professor actually never got to the author announced as the subject of the course, where all the time was spent in discussing the forerunners of the author. We learned all about the writers whom the author had read during his lifetime and to what degree he had been influenced by them, but by then we had reached the final lecture, and although we had learned much of what lay behind the literary work in question, we had no time to consider the work itself.

Such an approach, which treats literature as a renovation of the past, as a prolongation, rather than as an original creation, explains to some degree the attitude of the French people toward their writers. The pride which the French feel in their writers and their awareness of them even if they do not always read them, are singularly French traits. The recent death in Paris of Paul Valéry, in July 1945, became an event of national significance. I refer to the example of Valéry in this connection because he is as far removed as it is possible to be from the type of popular writer. As a poet, he is one of the most difficult France has ever produced, and one who will rank among the greatest; and as a prose writer, he is even more difficult. The stylistic and philosophical difficulty of Valéry's art would seem to relegate him to a very small circle of initiates, but it is a fact that, even long before his death, he was a universal figure in Paris, a symbol and justification of French pride in literary tradition.

In the homage which France paid to Paul Valéry, the dignity of the literary mind was extolled once again. The case of Valéry signifies that once more in France acknowledgement was made to the belief that the literary artist, no matter how esoteric or difficult, represents a significant fusion between the present and the past. Valéry had not always been kind or approving in his treatment of the past. He has derided, for example, and in a tone of considerable malice, some of the most hallowed sentences of Pascal, sentences which have been explicated for generations in the lycées and universities, and precisely those belonging to passages which we have been calling arias. But the French, as well as possessing a sense of tradition, have an iconoclastic sense which rather enjoys a scene of destruction when it is carried out with deftness and critical sharpness. Valéry's very attack on the sentences of Pascal has thrown them into greater relief than ever, and one day there will be books written for and against Valéry's attack on Pascal....

If Valéry is anti-Pascal and anti-philosopher in general, he is on the other hand a disciple of Mallarmé, who directed him closely in his vocation as poet. The discipleship has helped to define Valéry's particular position in French poetry and to redefine the art of his master. Valéry's debt to Mallarmé is so significant that professors in future courses on Valéry will perhaps not feel compelled to go beyond a discussion of Mallarmé's poetry.

The French, more insistently than other national groups, use the names of their writers as symbols which stand for much more than their actual literary work. They represent attitudes of mind and varyingly successful efforts to study the mystery of man. The French use the names of Racine, Descartes, Villon, as others say Orpheus, Socrates, Venus. And French writers also use these names almost as talismans or as epithets of saints and sinners invoked during self-examinations. The literary past in France is constantly testifying and representing. Thus Valéry orientates his own thought by declaring himself a critic of Pascal and a disciple of Mallarmé.

The art of speech in France is almost identical with the art of persuasion. One of the surest means to persuade is to speak intimately and personally, to take the reader into confidence, to speak confidences. When the French writer employs this device, he speaks, not about his mother or wife or child, as the writer of another tradition might do, but about the author whom he reads passionately and with whom he has formed a spiritual liaison. Baudelaire is most personal when he writes of Edgar Allan Poe; Claudel when he tells the effect of Rimbaud on his life; Valéry when he describes his conversations with Mallarmé.

At moments of national crisis, the French turn to their writers, because the writer is by definition in France the man who writes about the world of his heart but who also looks at the world itself and seeks to integrate in his writing some considerations concerning the affairs of the world. On the one hand, Valéry can compose such a pure poem as *Narcisse*, which contains the description of a forest scene and the exploration of a psychological dilemma. And on the other hand, he can write such an article as *La Crise de l'Esprit* which, although it was written soon after the end of the first World War, stands today as one of the most penetrating statements on the political and sociological dilemmas of modern man. The first sentence of the essay has become a celebrated exordium in France: "*Nous autres, civilisations, nous savons maintenant que nous sommes mortelles.*" It is this kind of sentence we have been trying to describe as the beginning of an aria. It is both resonant and arresting: "We civilizations know now that we are mortal." It has the solitariness of a single voice speaking to a vast public which in this case is both France and the modern world. It is the voice of a pleader who is going to speak, through deep sensitivity to the past, to his world on the subject of the abyss of history.

So the literary mind of France, nourished as it is on the past, may analyze whatever subject persists in tormenting man: politics, morals, theology, philosophy. Literature, the most complex of the arts, involves all these subjects and many others, and in France, more than in other countries, the people turn to the particular form given to these problems by the literary artist. The ideas of the sixteenth century are perhaps best expounded in the *Essays* of Montaigne; the moral and religious problems of the seventeenth century may be studied in the sermons of Bossuet; modern man's psychological barriers are for the French more significantly analyzed by a Baudelaire or by a Proust than by a Freud. When we read such a passage as that of Valéry which begins with the words, "*Nous autres, civilisations, nous savons maintenant que nous sommes mortelles,*" we realize that the writer in France has replaced the prophet. The writer has learned, through the exercise of his form, which is the practice of lucidity, of stripping and condensing, how to see everything in its absolute meaning. Valéry in his passage on the mortality of civilization, and Péguy, another writer-prophet of France, when he speaks of the modern tendency of changing a mystical state into a political state, both attain in their writing to the absolute meaning of an event.

But this role of tradition in the make-up of the French literary mind is only one aspect. It gives to the writer a feeling of solidarity with the past and an urgency to continue a movement rather than to found a new one. This dependence of the French writer on earlier writers, which grows in many cases to something akin to religious fervor, is not however an enslavement of mind, but, paradoxically, a liberation. Montaigne is better able to formulate his thoughts when he reads Seneca and Sextus Empiricus. Pascal, in denouncing Montaigne, found his own voice in the seventeenth century; and Gide, in our day, in his approval of Montaigne, received confirmation in many of his own attitudes as writer.

The French genius, however, cannot be defined solely by this habit of integration with the past. French genius is not just one thing. It is characterized by infinite variety and richness, by the most opposing traits. After establishing a relationship with the past, it then establishes another kind of relationship with the present. The second secret of the French literary mind is the dialogue it creates with another mind of its time. No major view on man, and no particular kind of sensitivity is allowed to exist alone in France for very long. The French genius asserts itself by creating some miracles of equilibrium. It discovers in its own age an opposing voice, usually of power equal to its own, and therefore is able to grow more vibrantly according to it on distinctive qualities. French art seems to develop in the form of a dialogue. But this dialogue is conciliation, or rather balance and counterpoint. Each of the two voices remains independent and clear, but much of its clarity and independence is derived from the existence of the other voice.

The provinces of France, each one so different from all the others, prefigure and control to some degree the multiple varieties or variations of French art. Long before the classical opposition of Corneille and Racine, so minutely studied in the lycées, there existed at the very beginning of France in the twelfth century, one of the most dramatic dialogues between French minds. Throughout the history of France, Brittany has produced literary minds which seem to be characterized by agility and suppleness on the one hand, and by a tendency toward mysticism and poetry on the other. Pierre Abélard, the twelfth-century philosopher, who was also poet and lover at one time in his life, had this kind of mind: both critical and mystical, both lyric and independent. He is usually considered one of the forerunners of the French analytical and rationalist spirit, adept in argumentation and subtlety. But Abélard's philosophy and theology were attacked by a contemporary, a man equally powerful but in a different way. Saint Bernard was Abélard's adversary. He was a Burgundian, of a race vastly unlike the Breton. The genius of the Burgundians is that of organizing, constructing, synthesizing. The Roman legionnaires had settled in Burgundy and had perhaps bequeathed some of their respect for authority and their sense of order and even their physical prowess. It is still believed that the best soldiers in France come from Burgundy.

A clash was inevitable between these two men. Abélard's spirit was critical, analytical and even destructive; whereas Bernard's spirit was bent upon protecting authority and tradition, eager to preserve and synthesize, and determined to use his full power in accomplishing those ends. So Bernard, the man of action, opposed Abélard, the reflective thinker. The passion of order and synthesis opposed the passion of thought and analysis. The same warning, which, Saint Bernard gave to Abélard in the twelfth century has been spoken in our day by Valéry in the essay already quoted, *La Crise de l'Esprit*. Man's investigation and knowledge may grow to such an extent that they become dangerous for himself and for the world. That was why Saint Bernard intervened in the career of Abélard, and that is the reason today for Valéry's question about knowledge. We can easily realize the threat which such knowledge represents for civilization. It is not an exaggeration to say that today a civilization appears as fragile as a human life.

The twelfth-century dialogue of Abélard and Bernard, which was a pattern of counterpoint established between a spirit of analysis and a spirit of synthesis, continues in varying ways in each great period of French history. In the Renaissance, the humanism of a Rabelais who believed in the natural goodness of man, was offset by the humanism of a Calvin who preached the corruption of human nature. In the seventeenth century, one of the most significant dialogues for the subsequent development of French writing was that between Descartes and Pascal. Descartes furthered his so-called method of doubt so that human reason might attain to truth. It would not be fantastic to consider Descartes' philosophical treatise, *Discours sur la méthode*, as the first of the psychological novels in French literature wherein reason in its purest state is the protagonist. But Pascal, in the same years, and in no uncertain terms, was asking mankind to humble itself: "*Raison, humiliez-vous;*" and telling mankind that, "The heart has its reasons which reason does not understand." Thus the intellectual enterprise or adventure of Descartes cannot be separated from the more deeply tormented and spiritual adventure of Pascal. One was necessary for the other in this persistent pattern of French thought where each age seeks to conciliate opposite tendencies, where analysis is opposed to synthesis, realism to idealism, action to contemplation, thought to sentiment.

More than other countries, France favors and supports and values the existence of opposing minds at any given moment of its history. In that country which has developed to such a high degree the art of argument and discussion and conversation, no single voice is ever allowed to be heard for any length of time. I suppose that no teacher ever had such abundant and hysterical success as Abélard, and yet his revolutionary spirit, brilliant as it was, negative and demolishing according to that form which holds and stimulates young students, was not unchallenged and was finally subjugated by sterner, more dogmatic, although far less subtle and scintillating, spirit of Saint Bernard.

There exists throughout the history of French literature, from the earliest writings in the French language, the courtly romances, for example, of Chrétien de Troyes in the twelfth century, up to the plays and novels of the Existentialists in Paris today, a profound and persistent unity of inspiration. What unites all the major works of French literature is the psychological inquest of man, an inquest to which each one seems dedicated.

The effort to study man, to explore the secrets of his mind and his desires, to define his position with respect to life and death, to the cosmos and to truth, is the motivation and the activity of the French literary mind. Many answers have been given to these questions in the various periods of French history, but all the individual questions might be summarized by the one large question: What is Man? And this question provides the stimulation and subject matter of French writing, whether it be the ballades of the gangster-poet Villon in the fifteenth century or the involved psychological novel of Proust in the twentieth. The French writer turns instinctively not to the collective problems of mankind, but to the personal, more secretive and individual problems of a man. He believes that only through the laborious exploration of self can he attain to any aspect of universal truth.

In the so-called central period of French culture, in the classical age of the seventeenth century, there occurred an exceptional harmoni-

zation between this permanent interest of the French writer in psychological study and the philosophically Christian view of man which lies at
the basis of everything we call French. The study of man became at that
time, more uniquely than it had previously, the study of man's corruption. Classicism and Christianity were united by the doctrine that man
is not born good. The mystery which man brings to the world is not his
innocence, but his knowledge of evil, his corruptibility. The experience
of evil is the subject matter of the tragedies of Racine, the maxims of
La Rochefoucauld, the fables of La Fontaine and of every other literary
work of the classical age.

Descartes' very method itself, which was expounded in France as
well as in Holland and elsewhere in Europe just prior to the reign of
Louis XIV, consists in a descent onto one's own mind and a removal
from one's mind of all those notions falsely acquired which cannot be
arrived at by rational intuition. We have already mentioned Descartes'
Discours sur la méthode as a kind of introduction to the impressive list
of psychological novels, the type of writing which, since the tragedies of
Racine, has dominated French literature. Descartes' celebrated "*Cogito,
ergo sum*" is the axiom on which he built his metaphysical system. It
is the point of departure in a revolution not so much of ideas as of a
method which has had a long history and which is not yet terminated.

Pascal, contemporary with Descartes, initiated a further revolution, which has had an equally fertile history. Descartes' analysis of the
basic simple truths which man discovers in himself by means of his rational intuition is paralleled in time by Pascal's revolution of the human
heart and of sentiment. The logic of Descartes, which is always however
that of a single hero, is offset by the turbulent dark poetry of Pascal's
torment. The "abyss" which he bears within himself is Pascal's symbol
of the barrier which separates him from truth and helps to objectify the
personal anguish generated by his self-inquisition.

The psychological inquiry which has been carried on uninterrupt-
edly by the French literary mind since Descartes and Pascal, continues
in varying proportions the influence or the example of these men. On
the one hand, the spirit of a method may be primary. This becomes
equivalent almost to a cult of evidence, analysis and synthesis where
structure and compositional form are uppermost in the mind of the creative artist. Flaubert is a leading example of this type of writer. And, on
the other hand, a spirit of disquietude and even of anguish, manifest-
ing itself in the lineage of Pascal, where the study of man is carried on
in an austere trembling and fearfulness, where the complexities of the

heart overbalance the logical reasonableness of the mind. Some of the great artists belong to this: Racine, Baudelaire, Rimbaud, Mauriac, Malraux. To them I would attach the contemporary group of French writers known as the Existentialists.

Existentialism illustrates all the permanent traits of the French literary mind, but especially the close, fervent exploration of psychological man. In Sartre's play, *Huis Clos*, he forces each of the three characters to turn inwardly upon himself and to reveal to the other two his most personal secrets and motives. The first part of the play is a reduction to zero of the pretence and deceit and even imagination of the three characters. It is an effort to begin all over again from the most basic and simple truths concerning three case histories. This is in a way an application of what is usually called the Cartesian method, which is the most lucidly rational approach to any given problem. But this is only the beginning of the play. The three characters find themselves in hell, which appears to them in the form of a Second Empire living room, and here we come upon the Pascalian aspect of the play. The room is hell for the three characters because they are not free to escape from it. It is what Pascal calls the "abyss" or the obstacle in one's nature which prevents happiness.

This play by Sartre contains therefore two subjects which we associate especially with French literature. First, the logic of an analysis or an inquisition which may be called the Cartesian influence; and secondly, the problem of man's happiness or salvation, which may be called the Pascalian influence. Cartesian and Pascalian are two adjectives which designate method and problem, and their commingling in the writings of Descartes and Pascal themselves, as well as in subsequent writers like Baudelaire, Rimbaud and Sartre, is the specifically French quality and paradox in literary art.

We use the word "paradox," or we might have used "irony," because of the extreme logicality and sense of order with which the French artist approaches the problems of the most dizzying illogicality. The towering disproportion between man's desire (idealism or thirst or aspiration) and man's capacity (realism or limitation or existence) is the subject matter of literature, and the French consider it with a disarming clarity of vision and a mathematical preciseness, whether the work be the seventeenth-century *Méditations* of Descartes or the twentieth-century treatise on *L'Etre et le Néant* of Sartre.

Existentialism, as the newest expression of the French paradox, takes its point of departure from a fundamental axiom, "Existence precedes essence," as fundamental as Descartes' *Cogito, ergo sum*. Sartre has often repeated that man exists first and then defines himself later. Man is only what he makes himself into. He projects himself into his future. With such statements, Sartre immediately defines doctrines on human liberty and responsibility which are strongly reminiscent of Pascal's. If the key words used by the Existentialists in describing man's state: despair, abandonment, anguish, nausea, have their counterpart in Pascal's vocabulary, Descartes' sentence about man conquering himself rather than the world (*"se vaincre plutôt soi-même que le monde"*) is likewise applicable to Sartre's belief that man is the ensemble of his actions and that every human project has a universal value.

Existentialism has its roots in the past. Its writers have established a debate or a dialogue with other contemporary writers. And it has revised all the basic metaphysical and psychological problems of man: action, liberty, responsibility.

The outstanding trait of the French genius, that on which all other traits depends, is its spirituality. I believe that the equilibrium which the French writer establishes between himself and the historical past, between himself and his contemporary world, and between himself and the problem of man, is due to an exceptional power of spiritual discernment. It is a willingness to avow and unmask the spiritual turmoil and aspiration of man. More than a willingness, it is a habit, centuries old, of considering virtue common sense, of considering intuition that faculty by which one attains truth. Literature in France has had an incomparable tradition in its awareness of a spiritual mission. No matter what the subject matter may be, and no matter what philosophical stand the individual writer takes, the most apparent word in his vocabulary and, I dare say, the most frequently used word in French literature, is *esprit* and its derivatives, *spirituel* and *spiritualité*. No matter what kind of writer is speaking on human destiny, a Villon or a Pascal or an Existentialist, the mystery of the subject is best articulated by the word "spirituality."

Everything that can be designated as essentially French seems to come from their understanding of the individual, of their prized concept, *la personne*. For the French, to comprehend the destiny of their country is to comprehend the destiny of man. France is the vocation and the study of the individual.

Throughout their history, the French have never ceased believing in what we might call the "absolute of man." I mean the absolute which exists in each man and which can be attained only through perpetual analysis of himself and struggle with himself. This belief in the absolute of man is what might be designated as French pride, vastly different from the humanistic pride of the Renaissance, when man was sensuously glorified by painters and poets, and vastly different from the racial pride of a culture myth. French pride has its roots in a profoundly pessimistic view of man: he has lost through greed and perversity a great heritage of peace which has to be won back by relentless struggle and purification.

This is the key to French writing in every century: in the poetry of Villon, in the story of Rabelais's giants, in the thoughts of Pascal, in the novels of André Malraux, French pride comes from this extra-ordinary awareness of man's imperfection and a courageous measuring of his dilemma. André Gide has summarized this in one of his sentences: "*Je n'aime pas l'homme, j'aime ce qui le dévore.*" ("I don't so much like man as what consumes him.") But to this very special form of pessimism is added a particular kind of optimism: a belief in the dignity of this struggle, in the ultimate capacity for reform in man and society. Behind every limpid portrait of man which French civilization has produced, behind every Gothic representation of Judas, behind every character of Balzac, behind every clown of Rouault, rises the archetype of human greatness. France has given to the meaning of freedom the will to bind oneself to the ideal through a fierce embracing of what is actual and real and even debased in man.

I suppose that no nation in the world is so diverse as France, so divided, so made up of contradictory individuals. France to the outside world often resembles a multiplicity of political parties, of social classes, of beliefs and ideas. But especially, at those very moments in its history when France appears to us the most divided, it appears to each Frenchman as one and unified. At the moments of greatest fever when France seems split asunder, it is then that she is magically composing past and future, fusing them, unifying, uniting and resolving. Its literary mind never allows France to lose its conscience.

Literature is the deepest memory of the world. In France, in particular, literature is the most powerful reassembling force of conscience. It is true that dogmas, philosophies and ideals will appear contradictory in France, and in any other country for that matter. But if these contradictions, which are the product of the mind, become also the product of the literary mind and are cast into a formalized product, the artistic work, they have the chance of becoming a stabilizing factor in periods of turmoil and crisis. Literature is a vast register of everything: myths, psychology, philosophy, theology; but it is a reality, because of its form, which helps us to bear and understand that nightmare, infinitely more chaotic and contradictory, which is life.

France recently passed through a military crisis and is now engaged in an economic crisis. But there is a third kind, which implacably follows the other two, and which is the most subtle and significant of all: the intellectual or spiritual crisis. Here, on the third crisis, the focus and strength of literature are felt. I have already referred to the example of Paul Valéry and his lecture, *La Crise de l'Esprit*, written at the close of the first World War. At that moment of depletion France was able to turn to one of her literary minds in order to see more clearly into the problems facing her. Valéry belongs to no recognizable group of writers, such as Communists or Catholics or Existentialists. He is, therefore, as Gide is, a more purely literary figure, disinterested and supremely independent.

His death coincided with the end of the war, and again, as in 1919, France turned toward him as a clarifier of contradictions. The long creative effort of Valéry's life was directed toward a study of the activity of man's spirit or of man's mind. The word *esprit* in French means both spirit and mind, and it is one of the most frequently used words in Valéry's texts. In one of his earliest writings, published before the end of the nineteenth century, Valéry asked the question, "What can a man do?" (*Que peut un homme?*) and he was still asking the same question in the pages he was writing at the time of his death in 1945.

He never deviated from the most central problem of man, from a consideration of the deepest part of man's being, of what he called *le moi pur* ("the pure self"). Valéry's enterprise of fifty years, twenty of which were spent in total literary silence—an admirable lesson of rigor and severity toward oneself—was an enterprise of denuding the intellect, of stripping off false notions and precepts and prejudices from the mind. The activity of the mind consists for Valéry of two parts: transformation and conservation. By these two activities the present and the past are harmonized.

This enterprise of the literary mind, which is spiritual in its deepest sense, stimulates the demon of knowledge who always represents a grave danger for spiritual man, but Valéry pursued his adventure with an admirable French balance of wit and seriousness, of science and maliciousness, of incredulity and *naïveté*. There was always in him the trace of the young student's mind: brilliant and supple, affectionate and destructive. He likes to demolish traditions and then walk about joyfully in the debris. He used to call the devil "a very attractive literary character." But levity was always offset by seriousness. Valéry composed out of the problem of knowledge a work in prose and a work in poetry where light is juxtaposed with nocturnal shadows. The experience of being human for Valéry is, in its spiritual sense, equivalent to feeling that "there is something of all men in each of us and something of each one of us in all men." (*Il y a de tous dans chacun et de chacun dans tous.*)

The most constant theme in the writings of Valéry he learned from the example and methods of Leonardo. It is a theme which, more than other literary themes, defines and limits the work of the artist and emphasizes the primacy of the spirit in the activity of the artist. An artistic work, according to this doctrine, is never terminated. It is abandoned. A poem or a painting, therefore, represents a fragment of some greater exercise or adventure carried on, not within the realm of matter, but within the realm of the spirit.

10
The Classic Objection

by

Jacques Barzun

From: Jacques Barzun, *Classic, Romantic and Modern* (New York: Doubleday & Co., Anchor Books, 1961) Reprinted with the permission of the author.

*T*wo conclusions have so far emerged from our concern with romanticism. One is that it is a complex movement, whose direct connection with any doctrine in our own day cannot be asserted offhand or light-heartedly. The other is that romanticism has to do with creating a new society different from its immediate forerunner. Since we ourselves are living in an epoch of travail, perhaps of creation, and since there is fear of what some are pleased to call a new romanticism, we must, before going further, attend to the pre- or anti-romantic outlook; the old order which romanticism left behind when it repudiated—as the phrase goes—classicism and rationalism.

Given the native absolutism of the human mind, we may take it for granted that every epoch looks for unity—unity within the human breast and unity in the institutions sheltering man. Now the straightest path to unity is to choose from all possible ways of living those that seem to the ruling powers most profitable, most sensible, most general; and to enforce these as a code for public and private behavior. The laws soon give rise to attitudes by which any man may shape his feelings, and this in turn brings about a ready understanding among men. For no matter how arbitrary, conventions are useful and can be relied upon in proportion as they are held inviolable.

Such a system produced stability in the state and with it all the attributes of the static: fixed grandeur, dignity, authority, and high polish; while in the individual it produces morality and peace by showing him that values are rooted in the universe, rather than dependent upon his fallible and changing judgment. This, I take it, is the view of life properly called "classical," irrespective of whether it is enforced upon Europe under Louis XIV, or advocated anywhere today by the proponents of a new or old order. It is an attractive view and it draws out the best in those who make themselves its masterbuilders. It calls for intelligence, discipline, unselfish renunciation of private desires, a sense of social solidarity, and punctilious behavior towards other members of one's own caste.

From these premises, it follows that everything the romanticist thinks and does is wrong: far from taking the short cut to unity and peace, he insists on the reality of double-mindedness and self-contradiction. He denies the beauty and fitness of the conventions that bind men together and prefers the loose human diversity. Sharply aware of his own desires, he argues that the social rule is oppressive and unjust, so that he becomes, potentially at least, an anarchist. Being an anarchist in an anarchical world, he places a high value on effort, strife, energy. He is therefore in the position of constantly bewailing a condition for which he is solely to blame: Having refused all help from social conventions, his art, philosophy, and religion are bound to remain diversified, many-shaped, chaotic—hence unsatisfying.

This, I believe, is a fair copy of the classic objection—classic because it has been so often uttered and because it has been uttered in the name of classicism. In common speech, certainly, the sentiments aroused by the word 'classical' are those of repose and serenity, while the connotations of 'romantic' suggest restlessness and disorder. It is perhaps inevitable that something of these associations should always cling to these two words; but it is desirable for the moment to make a conscious effort at forgetting them, in order to look upon both classicism and romanticism historically. Instead of two neatly paired abstractions, of two contrasted ideals falling into familiar formulas, consider classicism and romanticism as recurring facts. Let us try moreover to imagine some concrete case for every generality and to generalize from the examples we are about to take up.

For the contrast I began by describing is obviously and falsely heightened. It takes the abstract perfection of classicism and matches it with the concrete imperfection of romanticism. If the comparison were historically fair, we should properly expect the men of a classical age to be as completely happy as it is possible for humans to be, and we should expect the men of a romantic age to kill themselves en masse, like lemmings. But this has not happened. The wails of the classical gentlemen about existence differ in tone, but not in subject matter, from those of the romanticists, and beneath the difference in tone we shall find certain facts which afford a better test of cultural meanings than the routine antitheses about the classicist and the romanticist.

To begin with, the opponents of romanticism are strong on generalities but rather weak on particular cases. This is indeed consistent with the other tastes that make them prefer classicism. It is because they are bewildered by romanticist concreteness and diversity that they seek refuge in the simplicity which classicism achieves by generalizing and abstracting. And here comes the pragmatic test: how far can abstracting and generalizing be carried as a device for organizing society? Clearly some unity of opinion, some common ground, is indispensable to every social order. Romanticism does not deny it, either in theory or in practice. The romanticists may have defied certain conventions, but they did not go about naked. They praised originality but they did not talk each in his own private language. Still, let us suppose for the sake of argument that on the basis of some degree of uniformity one desires to abstract and generalize, so as to build a stable classical order. One decrees that Man is a clothed creature, whose proper, because logical, language is French, and whose destiny is to live according to the Christian religion under an hereditary monarchy. How far can one go without meeting some actual instance that defies the universal rule? The world being what it is, not very far. There are then two courses to follow: one is to remove the exception by pretending that it does not count; the other is to remove it by enforcing conformity.

The reasoning here proposed is not so fantastic as it seems. It is neither a straw man nor an imaginary instance, but simply one feature of the historic ideal embodied in seventeenth-century French classicism. The absolutist temper of that century removed the "exception" of the unclothed man by calling him a savage "who does not count," while the unorthodox habit of speaking a foreign tongue was removed by declaring French the universal language and successfully imposing it on all Europe.

This suggests that if a just comparison is to be made with the historic romanticists, we must look not at a theoretical classicism found in books or fancied in ancient Greece, but at an actual classicism found at work in modern history. This is another way of saying that we must look behind the Versailles façade of the Age of Louis XIV, with its alliance between an absolute monarchy and an absolute church, and assess the work of the half-century 1661 - 1715, which established a new order and succeeded in enforcing it upon manners, behavior, language, art, and thought. This classical age followed appropriately upon a period of political disorders, national disunity, and dynastic troubles. Once established, it entered upon a career of territorial aggrandizement and it spread its culture by snobbery and force of arms to the rest of Europe. The pattern of conformity came to England with the restored Stuarts who had lived in exile at the French court; and everywhere in the following century it evolved into a cosmopolitan classicism, during which its ideals became less and less compelling or productive, until the ground was cleared for the romantic revival.

To sketch in this way the career of a modern classicism is to treat it as it were from outside. Within, the first important fact confronting us is that classicism must begin by making, by manufacturing, its unity. Then, when this artificial unity has been enforced long enough to have become habitual, classicism is sure that it has been found ready-made in nature. This explains why the classical period used the two words Reason and Nature interchangeably, and why the romanticists, in repudiating classical Reason, had to give Nature an entirely different meaning.

What leant support to the seventeenth-century view that reason and nature are one is that the classical scheme of society coincided with a great scientific epoch; an epoch, moreover, specializing upon the one branch of science most congenial to the classical temper. I mean mathematics. For mathematics also abstracts and generalizes and yields simplicity and certainty while appearing to find these ready-made in nature. Seeing the beautiful demonstrations of Descartes and Newton as they explained the heavens with their coordinates, the great classical minds sought to rival this perfection and simplicity on earth. Philosophers used the geometrical method to arrive at moral and religious truth; social scientists reduced government to mechanics; the tragic muse imitated the tight deductive gait of Euclid; and I am not merely playing upon words when I say that poetry itself adopted one common meter as if scientific accuracy depended upon it. In all the imponderables of life, conduct, and art, the test was no longer the flexible, "Is it good, true, or beautiful for such and such a purpose?" but "Is it correct?"

As the classicists are wont to boast, the tremendous pressure of all these restrictions and rigidities produced some magnificent expressions of human genius. Racine and Boileau, Dryden, Swift and Pope, Lully, Rameau and Handel, the English portraitists and the French landscape school, created an abundance of great works to which we return with ever-renewed pleasure and admiration.

Yet there is to this brilliant period a darker and a neglected side. It is surely no accident that Pascal's *Thoughts*, written at the height of classicism, but undermining it, should begin with a distinction between the geometrical mind and the intuitive. Pascal's actual phrase to express the latter is *esprit de finesse*, which means the ability to distinguish and deal with concrete things, with living beings, as against the geometrician's ability to manipulate the abstractions and definitions of the nonexistent. The geometrician's universe is articulate, colorless, and clear-cut; the *esprit de finesse* on the contrary sees the color, continuity, and indefiniteness of things. The *esprit de finesse*, in short, is the instrument of romanticist perception, though romanticism does not necessarily begin and end in the realm of concrete detail.

The two types of mind contrasted by Pascal are alike capable of subtlety and greatness, but the geometrician works in a closed universe, limited by his own axioms and definitions; the romanticist works in an open universe, limited by concrete imperfections—imperfections which have not all been charted, which may change, and which need not be the same for all men. Classicism is geometrical in its assumption that human shortcomings must be disregarded in order to be corrected, correctness being stated in the form of an exact rule. Romanticism is *finesse* in the belief that exactitude is only a guide to thought, less important than fact, and never worthy of receiving human sacrifices. Classicism is therefore stability within known limits; romanticism is expansion within limits known and unknown.

An enforced choice at this point would, it is true, probably still incline us toward the classical as meeting more nearly the requirements of such a wayward creature as man. Since man wants certainty and stability, it seems better to have known limits and known ways of moving towards them. As a seventeenth-century English poet, Robert Herrick, phrased it under the title Rules for Our Reach:

> Men must have bounds how farre to walk; for we
> Are made farre worse by lawless liberty.

But there is a great doubt concealed within the safer choice: does a geometrical order yield stability when imposed on life? The question can perhaps be answered by comparing this same seventeenth century with the agreeable fictions that are current about it. Modern critics who are avowed enemies of our century and the last, yearn for the classical order as having given to the best men full scope, high honors, and true peace. Under classical rules, they say, the artist is not a rebel at war with society and his public; he satisfies a settled taste and is a willing supporter of the established régime. Under classical morality, the good man is reasonably happy; he is not, as with us, driven by the chaos of manners and codes into morbid guilt and fanatical efforts at reform. Lastly, under classical religion, the human mind finds an unshakable embodiment of its own permanent values, making impossible that modern freakishness or irresponsibility of belief which turns every man into a puzzle or threat to every other man and robs the state of all cohesiveness. In a word, the classical order acts as an infallible balance wheel to steady the human emotions.

Yet on looking at the classical centuries in biographical detail, one is struck by the amount and kind of ill-repressed human feeling beneath the crust of serenity and politeness. The number of converts to the forbidden religion of tears, self-mortification, and enthusiasm which goes by the name of Pietism was considerable. They include Pascal, Racine, and Fénelon. The names of Mme Guyon and of the convent of Port-

Royal will suggest many more; and a famous chapter in Voltaire's *Age of Louis XIV* tells us in a satirical vein about the unhappy quarrels and tribulations of those the historians mock as fools and bigots. Far from keeping a religious balance, Louis XIV and Mme de Maintenon themselves ended their reign as extremists in superstition and devoutness, an excess which swung the early eighteenth century into libertinism and atheism.

As for the standard comparison between the classical geniuses, thoroughly in harmony with their age, and the romantic rebels divorced from their society, it is simply not true. To take France alone, the first case we meet is Corneille's compulsory retirement after his quarrel with the Academy. Some may feel that Corneille was a belated romanticist harking back to the Renaissance. We must then recall Racine's struggles with his critics and the cabals which cut off his career at thirty-eight. Another genius, La Fontaine, was forgiven his nonconformity only because he seemed a child, a "natural," who loved the woods, and would not be acclimated to the only classical life—city life. Molière himself, supposedly the great interpreter of classical moderation and social sense, harbored a dissenter within. It was the dissenter who created the Alceste of the *Misanthrope* in his own image, who maintained the tradition of popular speech against refined diction, and whose death robbed the world of a projected satire on the highest classical product, the courtier.

The poets were not alone in feeling out of joint with the times. What we find among the philosophers, from Descartes to Voltaire, is one long story of persecution and flight from authority, only a little less violent than the harrying out of the Huguenots after the Revocation of the Edict of Nantes.

Because of the force of authority in all departments of classic life, it has become a commonplace that the romantic cry for freedom reveals an egotist. We take it for granted that the classic ego is silent if not subdued. But this is mere forgetfulness on our part. Compare the prefaces of Boileau, a classicist, with those of Victor Hugo, a romanticist. Contrary to your expectations, you will find that whereas Hugo is chiefly concerned with the principles of the artistic battle he is waging, Boileau seems to be interested only in reporting the praise that has been lavished on him and in disputing the statements of fault-finding critics. Hugo is "objective", historical-minded, occasionally grandiloquent; Boileau is "subjective", autobiographical, downright pettish. Or again, turn to Racine's prefaces—there are usually two to each play, the first rather grumpy and quarrelsome about the play's reception, which was seldom satisfactory; the second more complacent, because, after all, Racine knows what he is worth.

I am not saying, of course, that Racine and Boileau were egomaniacs. I believe rather that the reason their egotism seems so personal and small is to be found in the very nature of the classical scheme of things. It is the worst of the classicist beliefs that all true judgements are absolute and universal. As the King rules, so is the law. By extension, what is decreed by the vague abstraction, polite society, must be correct; for standards are common and public and there is no such thing as individual taste. In reality the polite world is a single cabal or critic. Hence any attack on an artist is fraught for him with grave consequences. Unless repelled it may mean ostracism, because society pretends to be unanimous. In any case it means battle, which explains the fate of Corneille and Racine, and the narrow escapes of Molière and La Fontaine. Indeed, the story of Poussin's or Bernini's misadventures with officialdom, and the function of the Royal Academy under the dictatorship of the First Painter to the King, Charles Lebrun, form a tale of coercion, jealousy, subservience, and war against all but mediocre talents, such as must give pause to the most sanguine neo-classicists. Pascal himself was not secure in his private retreat from a classical church and state jealous of all individualism.

In other words, the classical hierarchy maintains an unruffled front behind which all the fighting passions of men go on just as usual. But these passions take an especially heavy toll because there is no legitimate shelter in some other group—a second, or third, or fourth party—based on diverse interests and tastes. For the artist, the classic society is like a disunited family that is compelled to live together in a single room. There is hatred but no fair field for it. At the same time the issues lack magnitude; they are personalities. To read the memoirs of Saint-Simon gives one a painful impression of frivolity, even of immaturity at the root of the system. His admirably drawn figures are like schoolboys, kicking and cuffing one another under the table while the royal master is not looking.

These conflicts of authority and individual wills are not peculiar to classicism; only their form, and the pretense that no conflict is there. All of which naturally brings up the classical antithesis between Reason and Emotion. With its bent towards social unanimity how does classicism cope with man's emotions? Classicism does not of course deny their existence. It merely says that for the sake of decency certain feelings only can be exhibited—pleasure, amusement, ridicule, surprise, a few others—and these in their mildest form. For the same reason, gestures, fervor, eccentricity, must be suppressed, so that the social stage—the salon or the court—shall be peopled by human beings whose contacts will resemble those of perfectly smooth and well-lubricated ball bearings. With this ideal, incidentally, go some admirable rules of conversation which it would be well for modern man to meditate. But the trouble with the social device of repression throughout is, again, that there is no outlet, no elsewhere, for the force generated by pressure to expend itself, either harmlessly or productively.

This force, it may be said, has no right to intrude itself on society's attention. It is for the individual to dispose of it, since it is, by definition, irrational. More than that, it is the Irrational. Granted. But it is precisely called the Irrational because it cannot be argued out of existence, 'it' being the blind and the resistless force that we call life. Abstract reason is here simply irrelevant. Rather we must look for the socially accepted channels that may help drain off these energies. Whether admitted or concealed, these channels exist.

What investment, so to speak, could the classic century make of its fund of unreasoning passion? Taking for granted the ancient tradition of love-making, we discover several other institutions for expressing emotion. One excellent object of enthusiasm was the person of the King. Whoever thinks the romanticist worshipped heroes foolishly had better see for himself how much time and effort went into deifying the *Roi Soleil*. Certainly there is no extravagance in the nineteenth century comparable to the folly uttered and acted out when Louis XIV crossed the Rhine in 1672. One would suppose he had actually fought a battle and built a bridge like Caesar. His virtue, his grandeur, his words, his appetite, his form—nothing seemed too slight to deserve exaggeration. Perhaps the nation was worshipping itself through the King: it was a time of aggressive imperialism; the fact remains that it was hero-worship, and concentrated upon a non-hero.

At all times, in spite of his title of Most Christian Majesty, the monarch was reverenced—and painted and sculptured—as a pagan emperor-god, and the state followed imperial precedent by exacting (or purchasing) from its most brilliant talents the most profuse expressions of praise. The King could see his figure reflected from every wall and outlined in every square. In an Academy presumably devoted to letters, it was customary rather than strange to hear a new appointee—often an ecclesiastic who had never published a line—signalize the cultural greatness of the régime by saying:

What have I been doing thus far? Why have I spent so much time admiring in Antiquity examples of virtue which I deemed without equal? Our age has gathered them all up, greater and more pure, in the person of the monarch to whom Heaven has subjected us for our greater happiness . . . (and to whom we owe) a great state better organized in all its parts, order more solidly established . . . our frontiers more gloriously extended, our enemies more promptly conquered, our neighbors put in greater fear or respect towards us, . . . everywhere a more perfect union between the Head and the Members . . .

All these great and wonderful qualities . . . united in him whom we have the honor to obey . . . will henceforth furnish me with a nobler object for my admiration and my studies, and a fitter subject for any praise than any of those I have found in ancient history.[1]

Though the pension system will account for much of this adulation, we must remember that even without bribes flattery is a binding medium between the layers of classical society. For in its effect upon the emotions the theory of rank serves a double purpose. According to it, each man is absolutely better and nobler than the man below him, hence energy can go into emulation, *noblesse oblige*—and social climbing. But at the same time, the single code common to all men of honor restores a kind of equality and releases a certain amount of passion, by giving egotism an outlet through the point of honor.

King-worship, love-making, intrigue, etiquette, dueling, will certainly take up a good deal of slack in the sphere of the irrational, but there were still other socially approved channels for feeling in the seventeenth century. The playhouse—not quite so orderly then as now— was one. Watching public executions was another, a pastime which in eighteenth-century England degenerated into the worship of the highwayman. The life of leisure and the constraints of politeness encourage pleasures that were violent and exhausting. Sport embraced gaming, hunting, and the playing of murderous practical jokes; not to mention lavish entertainment, which was often so extravagant that the expense ruined the host if the King did not rescue him in return. In all these it is

---

1 L'abbé Huet: *Discours de réception à l'Académie*, quoted in J.F. Thénard, *Les Maximes de La Rochefoucauld*, Introd. p. 26.

not the thing itself, but the lengths to which it is carried that is a significant comment on reason.

Such were the energetic manifestations of feeling tolerated under classicism. There were also more passive ones. The literature of the seventeenth century, we must not forget, was not limited to the high tragedies and comedies that we still read. The age consumed a great quantity of long-winded romances about Grecian heroes, shepherds and shepherdesses, swooning lovers, and marvellous adventures. Books like *The Great Cyrus* and the *Astrea* were not read by the lower classes but by the aristocracy; they were not confined to France but were translated or imitated abroad. Parlor games grew out of such reading, and nature imitated art to the pitch that Molière records in *Les Précieuses Ridicules*.

Lastly, classicism had to recognize, though perhaps it did not relish, two flaws of temperament that we are likely to forget in speaking of classical balance. One was melancholy, a familiar yet half-hidden manifestation of the strength of the feelings. The other was vindictiveness. We should like to know more about the settled sadness of the moralist La Rochefoucauld, whose melancholy, as he tells us, came not only from his constitution, "but from elsewhere." We ought also to ponder the strange irresoluteness of Dryden's faith, the true source of Swift's "savage indignation," and the mental depression which the young Alexander Pope suffered during his four years at Binfield. Perhaps Pope recovered by main strength of Newtonian reason. Certain it is that in *The Dunciad* he discharged passion enough for a lifetime. Yet characteristically this passion was the undiluted one of hatred, turned upon men whose crime was either to have offended him or to have remained lowly and poor. Finally, in the supposed paragon of sound eighteenth-century common sense, Dr. Johnson, emotional troubles and the fear of death were so deeply implanted that a sympathetic critic can only describe him as "melancholy almost to madness, radically wretched, diseased, indolent," and unpredictable in his actions.

Historic classicism is therefore not the blessed epoch that some modern critics like to imagine. Without taking Pope or Racine or Dr. Johnson as typical—for they are the finest products of the age and its best recommendation—we can nevertheless infer something from so much covert rebellion, hate, and misery. The least we can infer is that classicism does not necessarily bring peace to the individual and stability to the state. Making "admirable rules" is one thing; enforcing them, another; and still another, having the enforced upon oneself by the eternal knaves and fools whom Racine suffered or Pope pickled in vinegar.

If it is objected that the facts I have presented are only the by-products of a fine distillation, I fully agree. No one should argue that classicist art, philosophy, or science are diminished by stating the conditions under which they were created. Nor is personal taste involved. I for one enthusiastically admire many of the seventeenth-century masters, and am not so foolish as to think less of Johnson as a critic because he showed psychiatric symptoms. The argument is not about the undisputable merits of classical genius; the argument is about the feelings and behavior of representative classicists, and the political, social, moral, and esthetic forms within which they worked. The point is quite simple: the usual comparison between classic and romantic depicts a wonderfully ordered greenhouse as the nursery of the former and a desperate battleground as the ungrateful soil of the latter. That comparison is false.

More than that, the catchword "tradition," which is monopolized by the proponents of classical order, helps to conceal the important fact that seventeenth-century classicism was nearly everywhere a break with European national traditions and a return to an imaginary Graeco-Roman past. It was just such another "break" as that of the Renaissance before, and Romanticism after. Classicism naturally borrowed from the Renaissance, but looked upon itself as civilized order replacing barbaric chaos. Quite specifically, the French classicists were asserting their independence from the Italians who had been their masters during the previous century and a half. But whether in politics or art, nothing could be further from the ancient classic spirits than the products of seventeenth- and eighteenth-century Europe.

To be sure, poets, painters, and academic critics ceaselessly invoked the ancients and pretended to follow them humbly, but the rules they tried to respect and enforce upon one another were as arbitrary and as "original" as those of any "revolting" romantic. It is precisely because modern classicism was an original creation, and not a copy, that it deserves to be called great. It differed from romanticism in seeking greatness through the adoption of common forms which it tried to make exclusive. In this sense it is "traditional" and resembles other periods of thoroughgoing orthodoxy—including the earlier phases of ancient civilizations—where individualism in art, action or belief is sternly repressed.

Pro-classical critics are wont to say of some romanticist they half admire, "If only he had had discipline!" It would be easy to retort of a classicist, "If only he had been let alone by rule-ridden mediocrities!" Both statements are anti-historical. The choice does not exist, for artists find themselves inspired or crushed by institutions which they are not alone in making. That is why it is important to know what is achieved when the general will produces a classical order, and at what cost. To suppose that one can have classicism without authoritarianism is like supposing that one can have braking power without friction. Conversely, romanticism is not simply love of ease or impatient rebellion. It is a different way of fulfilling human wants after the breakdown of an attempt at eternal order.

The question of human wants brings us back from historic to *intrinsic* classicism, for a second look at the classical meaning of Reason, Nature, and Feeling. The classic objection to romantic psychology is that it accepts an inner dualism—the "two souls in one breast" which publicists in wartime like to think especially German, if only because it is exemplified in Goethe's Faust. In romanticism, the two souls can be variously interpreted. I have chosen as most basic man's double consciousness of power and weakness. Another expression of the feeling is the Christian awareness of grace and sin. A third is the conflict between man's sense of values and his knowledge that nature is indifferent, this last being another form of Pascal's loneliness in the eternal silent spaces.

The classicist view of a man's mind also recognizes the split but makes it fall in a different place. Following one of Plato's myths, it sees the soul as a charioteer driving a team of wild horses. The charioteer is Reason, the wild horses are the emotions. Some emotions are good, some evil; the driver is of the same sort as the good. Classic man is a kind of Centaur—man above and horse beneath. Now, one of the features of classical Reason is that it can be put into words and become common property. Hence a society can be built which embodies Reason and helps each individual to drive his equipage on the straight road of duty and decency.

So natural is this psychological metaphor that we still speak of reason and emotion as opposites, we use the Head and the Heart as images of rival powers. Even when we repeat Pascal's phrase "The heart has its reasons which the reason knows nothing of" we tend to mistake its meaning and to use it as an equivalent of: "It is sometimes good to do something of which our judgement disapproves." We go so far in our slipshod use of words on this subject that we commonly characterize certain people as "emotional," as if they were cursed with pure emotion, or with more emotion than others. Freudian psychology is doing something to correct this error by pointing out how deceptive is the calm of so-called repressed personalities. The task is difficult because common speech imputes the wish to go berserk to anyone who challenges the classic figure of the charioteer.

Fortunately, in this same classical seventeenth-century there lived a philosopher of blameless and even stoical life, who can act as a character witness for the anti-classical view of emotion. I refer to Spinoza, and to his demonstration that the only way the human mind can conquer an emotion is by attaching its thought to another and stronger emotion. According to Spinoza, Reason is not a charioteer; it does not play the role of a guardian angel pushing back the demons into the pit; reason is but a guide, always moved by some emotion and pointing to an object. By effort and training, ideas can be detached from one deep-lying motive and reattached to another. As William James showed, will power consists in the ability to sustain an idea against its competitors from within the stream of thought. It is imagination plus attention. Hence there is never an emotion without an idea, nor an idea without an emotion. In the so-called reasonable man there is an awareness of motives and consequences which gives the impression that reason is wholly aloof from passion; but this is an illusion—the illusion upon which classicism builds its society.

This corrected view of the human passions explains why it is not sufficient to know the good in order to achieve it. It explains why copybook maxims always seem empty words until "something hits us." If this is true, we should cease to qualify a man or a mob as "emotional" when what we mean is that the ideas of the one or the other are crude, oversimple, and destructive. If we ever come to feel this difference clearly enough to change our clichés, we shall know that it takes as much emotion to solve a differential equation as it does to write a sonnet, and we shall stop speaking of "cold reason" and its counterpart, the "hot fit of inspiration," as if the categories of the plumber would suit the psychologist.

Spinoza is a doubly telling witness, for it so happens that, like Pascal, he was neglected by his classical age and rediscovered by the romantics. On the point we have been discussing, they all saw alike, and what they saw was not a need to glorify emotion or to give up thinking; it was something much more subtle and important, namely, the need to find organic unity within the human animal—the mind harmoniously expressing the demands of the feelings. Pascal who said "The whole duty of man is to think well"; Spinoza who said that the freedom of man lay in concentrating his passions on a proper object; the romanticists who said that the highest development of the self was true morality—all agreed that the task was one of reconciling the two souls as a prelude to social harmony. Blake put it with his usual forthrightness when he denied "that energy, called evil, is alone from the body; and that reason, called good, is alone from the soul." Contrary to the charioteer theory, he asserted that "energy is the only life and is from the body; and reason is the bound or outward circumference of energy."

It is urged against this view of reason and emotion that it sets men no common goal, and that the romanticists in particular did not seem to agree on the good life. Shall a man be a saint or a civil engineer, a gentleman of leisure or a social reformer? The disagreement exists, but may point to an eternal feature in the world of men—its pluralism. In any case, Romanticism declined to be deceived by the sleight-of-hand with which classicism pretends that the truth has been found and can be handed to each shareholder in its limited-liability company. Classicism forgets that its truth has not been found but made; that its social order does not represent concurring wills but is imposed by a caste; and that its boasted reason is mere maxims of prudence, useful in their place, but incapable of stilling forever the diverse claims that men do in fact make upon life, and make good. There is, in short, as much weakness in mankind as classicism sees and tries to conceal, but there is also much more power than it allows room for.

In calling classicist reason "maxims of prudence," I mean that they are negative commandments, whose application to life can only be mechanical, since they fail to recognize temperamental differences among individuals and the organic bond between feeling and thought. Too much ignored in the seventeenth-century, this bond was rediscovered in the eighteenth. The men of the Enlightenment did not underrate the irrational, but they still dealt with it abstractly. Voltaire's *Candide* is a complete demonstration that the world is largely the product of impulse. But of what use is the maxim "Cultivate your garden" except to a wise old man like the author, who has indulged his passions for many a year before prescribing this capsule of wisdom? Surely it is rank unreason to expect of the young Candide, at the beginning of the book, that he should cultivate his garden instead of the lovely Cunégonde's acquaintance.

The difference, then, between classical man and romanticist on the point of irrationalism lies wholly in a difference of judgement and intellectual bias. It is not a factual difference. Nothing can be more false than to represent the rationalist as natively able to get on without trouble from his feelings, or even as wishing to forget them. Those who have tried to palm off this picture of a rationalist superman might be surprised if one asked, "Who was the first great French writer to say that the passions were all good?" They would certainly shout "Rousseau" with one voice, but the correct answer is Descartes, who concludes his *Treatise on the Passions* with that blanket approval. His rationalism lay in recommending a "simple method" for controlling these all-good energies. Hume, too, saw very clearly that "without passion, no idea has any force": and the psychologist Hartley was far from ignorant of the importance of the sexual passion in shaping human character. But they all believed in a simple common rule of reason, almost a recipe, for maintaining equilibrium and keeping not only the individual but society static.

When reason itself suggested that society might stand in need of improvement, what did classicism offer on the perplexing subject of social change? Nothing, unless we adapt the words that Pope applied to fashions:

Be not the first by whom the new are tried,
Nor yet the last to lay the old aside.

In other words, let a romanticist begin. Let Columbus discover America: the classicist will come when de luxe passage has been provided. In truth, under classicism, innovation and discovery cannot be underwritten by society, because they are destructive, venturesome, uncertain; and because all the necessary forms and truths are known. Classicism assumes its own highest perfection and the individual who departs from it does so at his own risk. Rousseau is accordingly compelled to define genius as that which has the power to create from nothing, and to add that only fiery souls ever accomplish anything.

But why should there be creation and social change? Because although the great classical word is "restraint," classicism is impotent to restrain the forces that keep society alive. In the eighteenth century, the most perfect of neo-classical ages, the stirrings of unchanneled emotion were the most tangible force disrupting the old order. No sooner had "civilization" reached its high point, as all agreed, than restlessness set in and the South Sea islands began to seem a better world. Throughout Europe new interests developed—in popular ballads, in Gothic architecture, in natural scenery, in sentimental stories, in informal gardens, in tales of horror and mystery, in the Celtic and Germanic literatures as against the Graeco-Roman—all having the common feature of a pleasing irregularity.

All these new tastes were at first affectations, for things which have been formerly neglected can only be taken up by a conscious steeling of the person against public censure. The innovator has to pretend that faddishness is a merit, and the new does not sit as lightly upon him as upon his successors. The modern connoisseur of cathedrals is a man like any other, but the first gentleman to like Gothic architecture made himself ridiculous by building false ruins.

The significant fact is that the new taste was for pleasing irregularity. Each innovation was just another fad, but all together amounted to a shift in outlook. The results were to mark an epoch not only in art and society, but in political forms and natural science. What happened in these four realms may be summed up in the words which apply particularly to science; it was a Biological Revolution. The term says plainly enough that the absolute reign of physics and mathematics was over, and with it the dominance of the Reason patterned upon these two sciences. By the end of the eighteenth century new branches of knowledge—the sciences of man—had come of age: anthropology, ethnology, and zoology were offering new facts, new analogies, new modes of thought. Cartesian and Newtonian mechanics were taken for granted; the new principle was vitalism and the new theory, evolution. The mechanical materialism which had threatened to overcome all rival philosophies was in full retreat.

The clearest manifestations of this unexpected reversal are to be found in the careers of three famous rationalists—David Hume in England; Diderot in France; Lessing in Germany. All three had won fame by battling for the Enlightenment, for Deism, for the classical view of art and life. But by dint of sticking to their method and leaving nothing untouched by it, they dethroned Reason herself—Reason, that is, with a capital R, the Reason of the eighteenth century. A curious parallel unites the last thoughts of these men—they are consigned in dialogues, all three posthumously published. Hume's *Dialogues concerning Natural Religion* undermined Deism, and did so by means of biological comparisons and suggestions, including the notion of survival of the fittest. In France, Diderot adopted the evolutionism of Buffon and Bordeu and became a virtual pantheist. At the same time, in his extraordinary dialogue, *Rameau's Nephew*, he plumbed the irrational depths of a human specimen chosen as if on purpose to disprove that man is a machine and to forecast the dilemmas of the romanticist.

It was Goethe who first drew Diderot's masterpiece to the world's attention. Meantime, Lessing in Germany had been having conversations with a young publicist named Jacobi, of which the burden was Lessing's enthusiastic adherence to Spinoza's psychology and Spinoza's religion. When Jacobi published an account of these conversations it caused a scandal throughout Germany: the philosophy of the Enlightenment had been dealt a mortal blow.

Why should this be so? What does biology imply that mechanics does not? It implies that life is an element and not merely a combination of dead parts. It implies organic structure and organic function. It implies that the primary reality is the individual and not either the parts of which he is made or the artificial groupings which he may enter into. This is, in a word, individualism. Within the individual, the motive power is, as its name reveals, emotion. Consciousness and intelligence remain at the top of the hierarchy of values but they are not disembodied or centered upon themselves. They serve larger interests, which are those of life itself—the survival of the individual and the species.

Survival in turn suggests that the first law of the universe is not thought but action. As Goethe has Faust say, "In the beginning was"— not the Word, or Thought, but "the Deed." Action means effort, energy, possibly strife and certainly risk. The world is a world of novelty, in which changing situations cannot always be met by rules previously learned, though imagination can foresee and forearm the creature, who thereby becomes also an agent of creation. But imagination and creation carry with them no guarantee of success. The sustaining principle in man and his new world is therefore not reason—which is merely the already acquired and codified experience—but faith, which is hope plus the power of hope to realize itself. Why this power should work as it does is a mystery. It is the mystery at the heart of nature, which reason can guess at but not pluck out. When successful, man's reason—man's sense of power—is justified, and equally justified when he fails is his sense of weakness: in denying neither he has become a romanticist.

As a romanticist, his task is to reconcile the contraries within him by finding some entity outside himself vast enough to hold all his facts. He has become once again a religious thinker. For religion is more than a description of the Unseen. It is a theory of energy—the energy that animates nature and that animates him. To the romanticist, religion is no longer a superstition or a bald statement that the universe must have a First Cause; religion is an intellectual and emotional necessity. As Pascal said, man must wager on the existence of God, "because he is embarked."

In the romantic period, man wagered on the existence of the Catholic or Protestant God, on pantheism, on art, on science, on the national state, on the future of mankind: but in all the pattern is the same. The solutions differ in concrete particulars only because salvation is ultimately individual.

With these premises, classicism—at least in its old form—cannot subsist. It had built a shelter for man on too narrow an enclosure. It had supposed society to be static, emotions compressible, and novelty needless. It had selected what seemed to it best and truest and most eternal—monarchy, orthodoxy, courtly etiquette, mathematics, and rules of art and morality so simple that their universality could be deemed self-evident. But what had it selected these elements from? Clearly from a previous romanticism, that of the sixteenth-century Renaissance, an age of exploration and creation.

That is why, when classicism had twinges, they were like pre-natal recollections of romanticism. When Corneille drew his heroes, they were medieval knights and religious martyrs in seventeenth-century dilemmas. When Molière drew Alceste, the prospect of retiring to the country did not frighten the so-called misanthrope, but only the co-quette and the flatterers he left behind. When Racine was melancholy, he wrote a simple song in which he says he feels two souls within his breast, two men struggling with each other; and hearing the song Louis XIV is reported to have leaned over to Mme. de Maintenon and said, "How well I know these two men!"

In short, the protection and certainty that classicism gave were only temporary. It is no discredit to the genius or the strength of the classicists that it should have been so. It is merely a reflection on their self-knowledge, and a damaging flaw in the anti-romantics' classic objection, that they should mistake the man-made and temporary for what is given and permanent.

11
The Morality of French Literature

by

Gustave Rudler

This essay constitutes an address given in French to the Alliance Française of Oxford by Gustave Rudler. It was printed in *"Le Français,"* Oxford, 1912. The translation is by the author, edited, revised and re-translated in parts by the Editor.

I remember being years ago the recipient of a strange opinion confided in me by a foreign lady, not of this country, concerning Frenchwomen. She said they were charming and witty, but she could not understand how they could be sensible, serious, or even well-informed, for she thought them given to frivolity. Such outspokenness amused me more than it hurt me, and with equal candour I gently invited her to pack her trunks, take the train for France, and there resume her discovery of the Frenchwoman, who would prove to be a less rare phenomenon than she thought.

We have reason to believe that our literature is equally misunderstood. What an iniquitous thing is reputation! France passed in the minds of several nations for being the land that had deliberately adopted immorality. True, England enjoyed on the Continent the reputation of being the classic home of hypocrisy. Let us rise superior to prejudice and make an effort to understand each other. We are no more immoral than you are hypocritical. I should like an Englishman to tell us of the independence, the reverence, the self-respect and the respect for others, the modesty, the bashfulness, perhaps, but certainly the virtue that constitutes English "hypocrisy." I propose in my turn to set forth what I think about the charge of immorality brought against French literature, and I will go back to the tendencies of national temperament that may be responsible for having depicted it in a way as undeserved as it is regrettable.

On this delicate subject I am anxious to make my personal position perfectly clear. I unreservedly condemn every species of immorality. I do not claim for literature exemption from morality, still less any right to immorality; I leave it to artists to argue out such knotty points. On the other hand, I keep aloof from the stern attitude of an uncompromising Puritan, like the Prince de Conti, who condemns nature, stifles life, kills art, thought and genius, and will not take man as he is. I take up a position midway, one founded on facts which no well-informed and thoughtful man can escape from; and I begin by recommending to your consideration one which, in my opinion, is of special importance.

I have lately had the pleasure of reading the work of a young Englishman on Racine's *Phèdre*. The author, from first page to last, denounced what he called its "immorality."

And yet Racine flatters himself that he never put anything more "reasonable" on the stage. "Phèdre" he says, "is neither wholly guilty nor wholly innocent. By her destiny and through the anger of the gods she is involved in an unlawful passion, at which she is the first to be horrified. She makes all possible efforts to conquer it. She prefers to die rather than to confess it, and when she is compelled to reveal it she speaks of it with a shame that shows clearly that her crime is more a punishment from the gods than an impulse of her own will... What I can positively assert is that I have not written a single tragedy in which virtue is shown more conspicuously than in this one. The most trifling faults are severely punished. The mere thought of crime is regarded with as much horror as crime itself. The weaknesses of love count as real weaknesses; passions are presented to the eye only to show all the calamity they wreak, and vice is everywhere portrayed in colours which set off its hideousness and make it hateful."

Are we to no-suit Racine on his own pleading? Why, the instructors of his childhood a Nicole, an Arnauld, doctors of theology, doctors of the Sorbonne, serious, stern men, tried by persecution, Jansenists, necessarily experts in ethics endorsed his explanations and received his play with favour. "There is no fault to be found with the character of Phèdre," says Arnauld, "since in this character the author teaches us the great lesson that when, as a punishment for previous faults, God leaves us to ourselves and to the perversity of our own hearts, there are no excesses to which we cannot go, even whilst we detest them."

Here are three men of integrity, my young Englishman, Racine, Arnauld, Nicole—all Churchmen, or connected with the Church—who are scarcely of the same mind on this subject. The conflict of their opinions gives food for thought.

Well, then, *Phèdre* seems immoral if we consider only the plot, though it is a thousand years old, and the portrayal of the passions. But it loses all its virulence if we look at the scruples, the remorse, the crushing of the guilty woman and I am not speaking of a beauty that purifies. It seems supremely moral if we pass beyond them to study the intentions and the philosophy of the author.

Its underlying morality does not vary, yet it affects the reader variously, putting him into a condition of sensual excitement, or of romantic reverie, or of moral detestation, or of aesthetic enchantment, or of tender compassion for the misery of human nature, or of philosophical or theological meditation upon the conditions of liberty and the fatality of the passions.

To all appearances, indeed, every reader in the course of his life will pass through three or four at least of these conditions.

Immoral and depressing for one, the work will be a tonic and a moral lesson for another, or will leave him cold. The same individual will think it moral, immoral, indifferent, in succession.

What does this mean?

An undivided whole to begin with, morality separates into countless shades and degrees as it descends to men. It goes from baptismal ignorance to the wariest experience, from orthodoxy to heterodoxy, from narrowness to liberality, without ceasing to be vigorous and delicate. It coexists with and adapts itself to intellectual requirements and demands of varying extent and character.

With his single morality, the author should meet and satisfy countless moralities. His situation, if he were to think of it, would utterly freeze the exaltation out of which the work arises.

Now, amongst works admittedly moral, which are highly praised, however little they may be read, and works certainly immoral, which no one defends, though they may be more read, there are in all literatures certain powerful works on which unanimity of moral judgment is not forthcoming. Since the moral impression varies with the readers, and in each reader during the course of his life with experience, who shall we establish as a judge of morality? Imagine to what degree of insignificance literature will fall!

And who shall we condemn in this business? The author? But if he is an upright man; if his intentions are pure; if he respects his art; if he believes in his subject; if he does not speculate on the low instincts of a certain portion of the public; if his work is exalted; if it carries us to a loftier plane of art or thought? He might say to the reader: "Dear reader, you think me immoral. I might more justly make the reproach against you. It is you, from your lack of experience and courage, your suppressed eagerness, your indiscreet pruriency, who see immorality in my work. Don't wake the dormant animal in you. Read me as I have written, in a spirit of disinterested inquiry and fervent meditation. Can't you make this effort? Then go back, my friend, to the books that suit you, and leave me in peace."

A Flaubert would have spoken like this but with how much more vigour! Great was his outrage at having to appear, on January 31, 1857, before a magistrate, for an offence against morality and religion. Shut up in his *gueuloir*[1] at Croisset, he had laboured for four years on a subject *archicommun et archiplat*, extremely moral for all that—the ravages of a passion for luxury and of the romantic spirit in the mind of an outsider.

---

1 Flaubert called his *gueuloir* the pavilion at the bottom of his garden where he wrote and declaimed his periods to ensure he had the rhythm and tonality right.

But greatly he cared about his subject! What had tormented him to the point of frenzy were problems of aesthetics, almost as easy to solve as squaring the circle—"to write" the "real," to express without vulgarity the vulgar, to "distil" facts, disgusting though they might be, into form, to harmonize life in a poem, to give rhythm to prose while leaving it very much prose, to find the secret of "the colour of movement," to blend lyric exaltation with scientific precision, and, descending from the height of such transcendental verbal music, he found himself sitting in the dock of the police court, for an outrage against morality! The fall was a painful one. In the history of literature it would hardly be possible to quote a more complete misunderstanding. Who today would wish to eliminate *Madame Bovary* from French literature as immoral? "You would not allow your daughter to read it?" said Flaubert. "Very well; but I should strongly advise you to let your wife read it." Just glance at the ridiculous speech for the prosecution and the 'moral' doctrine expounded in it will seem peculiarly vapid and even replete with immorality; and you will not hesitate for a moment between the defendant and the magistrate. So change points of view.

Now this misunderstanding is constantly reproduced under forms less tragic. Disagreement between readers and authors is almost the rule, with its attendant train of accusations, reproofs, and anathemas.

What we need, then, is a solid moral education for the young and a watchful eye on their pruriency. We need syllabuses which do not set down too advanced works for courses of study and for examination. We need, at every age, a certain self-supervision, a certain reserve, holding the balance between reading and strength. For literature, like so many other things, may be nourishment or poison according to temperament and experience. It is a fact, to be regretted perhaps, but none the less a universal fact, due to human weakness and to the extreme dissociation of dispositions and characters, that the morality of a certain number of great works in all literatures is measured less, after all, by their intrinsic quality than by the very differing reactions of the intelligence and the feeling of the readers.

I come now to the reproaches brought against French literature on the score of immorality. They are all summed up in one word: materialism.

The reproach has only an apparent foundation.

Our literature, it is true, taken as a whole, is not spiritualistic. Still, we must not forget the powerful current of Christianity which, according to the period, penetrates it from top to bottom, or runs through it from end to end. But it remains true that many of our writers do not think from an accumulated store of inherited beliefs, regarded as sacrosanct, although they should receive not more than lip service.

Our literature is critical. It does not put faith before investigation. It does not allow the shadow of faith to extend over investigation and to limit it. It reserves faith until the investigation be completed.

It is lay, and this word conveys its own meaning.

It is rationalistic. The Frenchman has a mania for regulating the universe, humanity, society, and so forth, on the plan and according to the requirements of reason.

It is scientific, in attitude and in understanding.

It is realistic.

Ah! I know, these are sins, very great sins, the worst of sins. You see, I do not disguise them.

But that does not prevent our literature from being idealistic and moral in nature. Two ideas direct it, two passions uplift it, from the beginning of the ages.

Until the nineteenth century, great outbursts of imagination and feeling had hardly fallen to our lot. Our strictly defined climate, our limited horizons, our sedate landscapes have made us after their own image, one of clear mind and lucid understanding. Whilst others, through fantasy, poetry and philosophy escaped from the real, we have kept our eyes fixed upon it with extreme pleasure. Whilst others have lived in the lyric mood, listening to the songs or to the laments of their hearts, we have quietly explored our own; whence has arisen our great school of psychologists and moralists, with their precise descriptions, their "anatomies," or, as we say, their dissections, their science of the mechanisms of passion and mind. Man has long interested us more than Nature; we have gazed upon him, in ourselves and in others, with amused curiosity; we have noted his defects, his vices, his errors, his deceits, his follies; hence our rich satire and comic literature.

No humbug has imposed upon us for long, no hypocrisy, no mock grandeur, no usurped authority. We have promptly seen through the contradictions between the pettiness of men and the bombast of pretensions. From all idols we have torn away the veils; we have unmasked hypocrisies, upset forms, conventions, customs and traditions; from each idea we have demanded its proof, from each institution its title, from each individual his passport; and that is our great critical, political, and social literature.

Of the three joys that theologians distinguish—the joy of feeling, the joy of knowing, the joy of ruling—the second is the peculiarly French weakness. Frenchmen have a passion for seeing clearly, for knowing and for understanding. They are, above all things, an intellectual people. In no race does the instinct for life endue so large a role to the probings of the mind.

Psychologists, playwrights, philosophers—one single passion inspires all our writers. Just as the madman Captain Hatteras, in Jules Verne's *The Englishman at the North Pole*, turns invincibly to the north like the needle, so all French literature points from its origin towards Truth.

Let us add this: towards Justice also. Born of life, the image of the real, our literature irrevocably reflects its ugliness, its sorrows, its iniquities. Sometimes it laughs at them. More often it is annoyed and indignant. Where on this earth are we to find the good and the beautiful? Humanity is bad, society unjust and anarchical, power tyrannical and without conscience as it is without feeling, individuals are weak and wretched. Against iniquity, the conscience protests; against disorder, reason. Right raises its voice to heaven in the face of violation and cries for reparation. Innocence oppressed appeals to the future. Justice! It is the cry of the human race, and it is almost the national cry of France. Excess in certain of our books is only the revenge of wounded spirits and bruised hearts upon the horror of reality.

Truth, Justice: that is the instinct of our people, that is its mysticism, that its moral code. We think it exalted, and very lovely. We would not change it.

The French sceptics? There is not a people more passionate! Materialists? Since the beginning of time, since the *chansons de geste*, the Crusades, and the Gothic cathedrals, in a hundred forms their invincible idealism bursts forth.

You say "God." We say "Truth and Justice." Are they so different? Let us learn to perceive the sameness of things disguised by different terms. Justice and Truth are the best part of God, are the very essence of God. All humanity moves along apparently different paths towards the same lofty goals. And I say that it is a spectacle not only stirring, and tragic, but highly moral, religious and mystical, that of a people who, pursuing the ideal for ten centuries; marching perpetually to the assault of all Bastilles; who, by their own unaided abilities and without help from metaphysics, seek to wrest the solution of the enigma and decipher the smile of the Sphinx; who confront the Unknown; who persist in seizing a fugitive truth and in seeking the absolute and the eternal in the forms of the relative and the transitory; under the impulse of the lure of perfection.

Such is the point of view from which we must consider our literature, if we would feel the breath which animates every work in the sometimes unconscious harmony which unites it with all other works and with the deepest feeling of our race.

Let me now point out two or three consequences of our intellectualism, and a few precautions to be taken if you would read certain of our works aright.

Our passion for truth implies special nuances in the conception of morality. Our tendency is to associate, indeed to identify, the two things. Our writers consider themselves sufficiently moral if they are true. They think, and we think, that truth is its own justification. Our cardinal virtues are clearsightedness, sincerity, veracity, probity, moral courage. We have no other concepts of morality. Now, I ask you, what end do our virtues really serve, unless it be to make us appear vice-ridden? Clearsightedness, integrity and candour have evidently no other function than to denounce evils whose portrayal and presentation must seem immoral to others. We say aloud what we ought to keep silent about; sometimes we even exaggerate it. But it is not for want of morality; it is from excess of morality that we incur the suspicion of the "moralizers."

Secondly, our writers situate themselves, by their very intellectuality, on a plane of thought and art. To bring them down, when we read them, to the level of the practical is to misrepresent them and to wrong them. We, at all events, are thoroughly aware that it is literature. Our first impulse, when we open our books, is not to shoot out our moral prickles at them, but to give them a congenial welcome. A noble construction of thought and art, even made out of impure materials, attracts and delights us. Are we immoral for that reason? By no means. The fact of being raised to a level of disinterested contemplation by a literary work destroys or weakens for us the virus of immorality, supposing it to exist. We stare down the things that alarm and shock our "moralizers." Molière said long ago that moralizing creates the very shadows at which it takes offence. But we recover all the vigour of our moral sense when, from the transcendent play of thought and art, we come back to the practical. By "we," of course, I do not mean France as opposed to the rest of the world. The distinctions are made, not by whole peoples, but in each people by universally related families of hearts and minds

Certain excesses of our writers—philosophical, romantic, naturalist—are to be explained by their circumstances. Our literature is a combative literature. Of many of our books we must ask against whom and against what they are written, and we must make allowance for excesses inseparable from the conflict. We know how to situate them within the chain of tradition and explain them by their surroundings. But foreigners are liable to judge them abstractly and absolutely; they do not know what factors must be discounted; they have methods of judgement that are often inaccurate and an irrelevant scale of values. They run the risk of seeing mountains where there are only molehills.

One last reflection will throw some light upon our profoundest inclinations. By a significant abuse of terms we go so far as to declare these things immoral: insipid works, escapist books, and 'blue' books, novels dubbed idealistic and meant for the "chic," for women, young people and children. For the fact is they represent a false idea of life, with its realities and duties. We have an especial distrust of the romantic. Wrong judgment appears to us not merely a sure road to the corruption of the heart: it appears gravely immoral in itself.

Such, I think, are the natural tendencies from which arise the prevailing misconceptions about our literature. In spite of its reputation, partly justified, for clearness and universality, it is an ethnic creation no less original, no less subtle, no less difficult to interpret than your own. We must look at it in terms of race to understand it, and in its homely setting in order to feel its lyrical and moral resonance.

Concerning the general charge of materialism, I should like to consider two points.

Love certainly occupies in our literature an excessive place. In fact, we are sick and tired of it! We cry out for something else, at any cost. The mere fact that a book does not mention love makes it appear almost original. One of the hopes raised by social literature has been precisely that of ridding us of the affliction.

Unhappily, our schools teach the youngsters scarcely anything more than how to hold a pen. They can write long before they have anything to say. And then they confide to us the workings of their hearts, but especially the workings of the hearts of others, plagiarized and exaggerated. A happy thing it is if they stop at the heart! It is terrible in many ways to be a nation that can write. It should be forbidden by law to write novels or plays, as it is to enter the Senate, before one is forty!

On the other hand, not all portraiture of love is immoral.

I condemn all that nearly or distantly resembles pornography. However beautiful the setting, however graceful and artistic the exposition, literature abandons its functions, fails in its duty, sinks into degradation, when, cynically or hypocritically, it makes sensual excitement its aim and object. It then becomes nothing more than a low trade, a disgusting speculation—a stupid trade and speculation when the writer possesses talent. For a fleeting and dishonourable success he sacrifices his whole future. Wounded morality ever wreaks its vengeance on those who profane it. We have in the eighteenth century magnificent analysts whose very names we shrink from mentioning. A certain degree of corruption is equivalent to suicide.

But *gauloiserie*, the mocking spirit that pries into unsavoury things and romantic misadventures, are we to call that immoral? The word would be a clumsy one; suffice it to call it vulgarity. Nay, in the eighteenth century, permeated as it is with wit and fashionable elegance, it becomes a chartered wantonness, often exquisite, which delights us as does champagne. Let us keep intact our sense of proportion and sense of humour; for decency there would be no need to seek shelter from *gauloiserie*; all that it would require would be delicacy and taste.

Now we come to naturalism—naturalism in its broad sense, the naturalism of Rabelais, the lyrical enfranchisement of instinct, that joyous liberation of the whole being, that repudiation of every check and every limitation. Is it immoral? Let us cut out the coarseness, now spontaneous, now deliberate, with which it is occasionally accompanied. There remains a general view, incomplete perhaps, but perfectly philosophical and perfectly true, of human nature, a view which sufficed the centuries of antiquity, and so little immoral in itself that for three hundred years a host of dreamers and serious thinkers have sought in it the basis of different ethical codes, so that is quite impossible to foresee what if anything will remain of them in the moral standards of the future.

And Racine, are we to fling him overboard? Certainly not. His abstract psychology, disguised in artistic forms which serve as framework, might, like the ethics of Spinoza, be reduced to axioms, theorems, lemmas, and corollaries; it is a "geometry" of the soul far too deep, an intellectual creation far too precious for us to part with. We must be very young or very distrustful to be scared of Racine. His serious fatalistic concept of ruinous love offers nothing seductive; the emotion it inspires is far rather a frisson of fear and pity. A love bathed in tears and blood scarcely invites to love. No work, unless it be perhaps the *Princess of Cleves*, furnishes a nobler spectacle of dignity in passion than the painful sacrifice, the eternal farewell of Titus and Berenice. And no writer has left more exquisite models of womanly modesty.

Finally, romantic love takes on such strange and complex forms; and passion entails such serious social and moral disorders, that literature cannot remain indifferent to them. What works, for example, has not the subject of divorce produced that are beneficent, elevating, and affording food for reflection, without arousing unwholesome urgings or promoting the ills they describe?

In this way, then, I would draw the line between morality and immorality where love is concerned: everything that appeals to the senses, deliberately and solely, everything that corrupts the mind or the heart, I would condemn. But everything beyond the realm of sensuality that appeals to the loftier qualities of intellect and emotion, everything that exalts to the contemplation of life, everything that creates a passion for beauty, everything that opens the floodgates of merriment, no sympathetic or thinking being could possibly wish to eliminate from literature.

Note, moreover, that love occupies a very small place in our great works. You will find that at most it has been the triumphant theme of only three writers— Racine, Marivaux, Musset.

I come lastly to that abomination of desolation—Naturalism. Not, indeed, the naturalism of Rabelais, which is a philosophy, but the naturalism of Zola, which is an aesthetic school.

Here, again, let us make a clean cut. Let us put aside all that smacks of immorality, pornographic speculation, gratuitous coarseness, alluring mediocrity and vulgarity of expression. But if we take its principle— namely, the crude delineation of the lowly functions and elementary forms of life, of the miseries and blemishes of physiological and social origin—is that immoral? Not a bit of it!

Of course, it offends shallow minds, and people optimistic by nature or calculation. Those who find pleasure in Octave Feuillet, Jules Sandeau, or Maxime du Camp, cannot stand Flaubert or Zola.

But if some people are depressed by pessimism, there are others who are invigorated by it. A gloomy, violent view of life acts on certain natures like a counter-irritant: despair may become a very solid foundation for a moral code.

Does naturalism trouble consciences? Yes; but it awakens them, puts them on the alert. We have not forgotten the profound impression produced in this country, as in France, by Zola's *l'Assommoir*.

The most imperious duty of man is not to defend his ignorance, his separateness, his complacency—to put it bluntly, his selfishness. It is to fight against evil, and in order to fight against it he must know it.

Confined to my study and library, and bound by the demands of my profession—you and me alike—how are we to educate ourselves in the miseries of life? How are we to break down the walls that separate us from our fellow-men? By literature; by the literature of realism.

This literature, therefore, performs a function, fulfils a moral and social mission of the highest importance. It reveals to men of goodwill and upright heart the evils which it is their duty to correct. Its only law is to be faithful to the truth. And they who, bent on destroying Zola, knew it well too; for they levelled their accusation less against the immorality of his work than against its falseness. But to all appearances its truth is not uniform. So long as it keeps within the bounds of truth I am not shocked by its tragic sordidness.

No doubt it does no honour to human kind that life is really so ugly; but the only reasonable conclusion to be drawn from it is that human kind must reform.

I admire people who treasure their indifference to or indulgence for life and their indignation against literature. What does evil matter? If you don't speak of it, it will be as if it did not exist. Are they horrified, then, only by words?

Let us not waste our time lopping off branches: they grow again. Let us pluck up the roots. Let us reserve our seething anger and our energies for the struggle against life. After all, if we improve life, we will at the same time be elevating literature, which is its representation. If we maintain it in all its ugliness, we will prevent neither sham artists from deriving scandal from it, nor right-minded and good-hearted writers from being shocked at it and depicting it in all its horror, in order to stimulate readers of integrity and good judgment.

Let us bring to bear uncompromising morality; we shall thereby derive from them only a more powerful love for good, a more ardent energy, a deeper pity, a loftier conception of human brotherhood. To the pure and to the strong shall be added an increase of strength and nobility.

By virtue of its realism, French literature has for ten centuries been crying *Peccavi!*—not for France alone or for Europe, but for all Humanity. It is a thankless role to play, one that calls for no gratitude. But, let there be no mistake: France is proud of the share that has come to her among the nations; she has no intention of allowing herself to be hauled before the tribunal of mankind and find herself accused, like Flaubert, of mischief.

12
French Thought and Art

by

Paul Valéry

"*Pensée et art français*" was a lecture given at the Institut de France on October 25, 1939, and published in its bulletin the same year. Republished in *Regards sur le monde actuel* (Paris: Gallimard, 1945) and in *Oeuvres II* (Pléiade ed., 1960). English translation from Paul Valéry: *History and Politics* (New York: Pantheon Books, 1962), Bollingen Series XLV.10, translated by Denise Folliot and Jackson Mathews. All attempts to locate the copyright holder of this text have failed.

*T*he circumstances in which we are now involved,[1] the pressure of events, the corresponding tension of our minds, have, among many other effects, that of making us more and more strongly aware of our intimate participation in a life greater than our own, which is the life of France. In calm and peaceful times, to be French in France is taken for granted, an almost unnoticed condition: in short, one is in a neutral equilibrium with one's native and natal surroundings. Being French is as natural as breathing. One comes to believe it impossible to be anything but French—Montesquieu remarked on it.

Of course, there have been Frenchmen who went abroad and soon felt their national difference. But in comparison to our total population, the number of those who have crossed the frontier—and, coming into contact with foreigners, discovered France—has been almost negligible.

But now our principal frontier is called the Maginot Line, and our contacts with foreigners—whether friend, enemy, or neutral—tend to make us more aware of our French personality. We are more and more sensitive to what we are. What is happening to us is what happens to any living thing compelled by circumstances to get ready to act or react. His thought can no longer ignore his body; he co-ordinates all his faculties; he turns the whole of himself into a single system of forces, and is finally aware of himself in his deep unity and essential individuality.

Can this feeling of nationality be clarified by a definition of ourselves simple enough, in the end, to be contained in a few ideas? I shall attempt one, with little hope of succeeding, limiting myself to the intellectual part of the question.

I shall assume, then, that we wish to form an idea of what France has created in the realm of the mind since France first came into being; that we must try to sum up the volume, the value, the particular nature, and the universality of her production; must melt down centuries, genres, schools, modes and persons, making a sort of compound so concentrated that it can be contained in a few pages. . . . I wonder how to set about this task and what can be hoped from it. In short, it is a question of defining or creating a Being, an Author, to be called France, who, in the course of a career of a thousand years, could have turned out so many monuments, priceless works of all kinds, expressions of intelligence or knowledge, which we look on as our capital of pride and tradition.

This is the problem as I see it. I know it is insoluble, if not absurd. But on either hypothesis it can at least be attempted. The mind can work,

---

1 Valéry is referring to the outbreak of the Second World War in September 1939.

even with profit, on the insoluble and the absurd; these are the subjects of most of our thoughts.

Here, then, is how one could perhaps begin. It would be vain, and moreover endless, to treat this problem by enumeration, by a chronological table of works and persons whose names form the catalogue of the works of France. I think that a list of names and titles, even when accompanied by dates, references, and a few notes, can teach us nothing substantial. Besides, such a list would alone fill my few pages. And, if I were to make a selection, I should have either to question or to justify my own preferences.

My plan is to imagine our total intellectual and artistic treasure at such a great remove that the whole composition of so many accumulated beauties and values is alone to be perceived, without separating them into distinct works, famous persons, and unusual events that may be isolated from the system of which they are parts: in short, to envisage France, the role or function of France in building up the capital of the human mind, but to include only what belongs to France alone, leaving aside both what is so plain as to be obvious and what is apparent only on close inspection.

* * * * * *

The first intellectual product of a people is its language, which is therefore the first thing to examine if we wish to appreciate the life of the mind among that people and the evolution of that life in connection with the dramatic development of its history. Language is formed statistically, and would be quite variable—very rapidly so, at times—if its instability and anonymous local differences could develop in unhindered anarchy, altering the sound and sense of words as well as their syntax. But this constant process is more or less hampered by certain wills or sensibilities above the average and dominating the many, whether such influence be that of individuals or institutions or even cities in which the exchange of ideas is particularly intense. Here, as in economic matters, the more active the exchanges, the more important it is that the conventions—the weights, measures, and currencies—should be stable and well defined.

* * * * * *

Our syntax is one of the most rigid. In the strictness of its conventions it equals our classic prosody. It is remarkable that a people whose mind is considered extremely liberal and logical should have conformed in speech to all sorts of constraints, many of which are inexplicable. Perhaps the French have felt that there is a freedom of a higher order, which is both revealed and attained by constraints, even useless ones.

However that may be, our language, not being given to forming compound words, nor to easy syntactical agreement, nor to the arbitrary disposition of words in a sentence, and being content with a somewhat limited vocabulary, is justly famous for the clarity of its structure, which, together with a frequent taste for abstract definitions and distinctions, has made possible the conception and realization of so many masterpieces of verbal construction—pages of such architectural perfection that they seem to exist and to have their effect independently of their meaning, of the images or ideas they embody, and even of their qualities of sound. In this respect, they are comparable to those pieces of cerebral music whose theme is slight and the immediate pleasure they give to the ear almost negligible, compared to the intellectual sensation we get from them and the superior enjoyment of understanding that sensation.

Since I have mentioned the name of architecture, I shall here introduce a reflection directly related to it. I have just been considering the specifically French qualities in our literature as if they formed a single work derived from that great collective work which is our language. In fact, any literature (and I do not except what is called philosophy) is and can be no more than the exploitation of some of the properties of a language. A Frenchman who is a writer will find in our language both resources and gaps, facilities and restrictions (the latter especially) which will be more or less clearly perceived in his work. Our language very often hinders an immediate expression of thought and compels us to a doubtless more difficult and more inward elaboration of our intentions or impulses than is necessary with other peoples. But the resulting constructions, which have been successfully carried out only through a conjunction of warring conditions, and which require as much skill, lucidity, and sustained will as invention, very often give the impression of a wonderful agreement between life and time, light and matter, "form" and "content."

Is it not true that very similar qualities place French architecture of the great epochs, together with the Greek of the best period, in the front rank of all that the art of building has produced?

* * * * * *

Whether it be a question of architecture or literature, it must be noted that in France there is a tradition, a need for fine work. We must admit that the conditions of modern life, the change from handicraft to manufacture, from individual workmanship to the mechanical mass production of objects on the assembly line, time saving, competition to give us "bargains," fashion and advertising giving rise to imitation at the expense of personal taste—these and other circumstances are not the most favorable for creating precious objects. Neither the inimitable nor the lasting is suited to our time.

I said one day to an architect who wanted to convince me of the superior beauty of very modern buildings rearing prodigious beehives of cement a thousand feet in the air, that these concrete masses certainly astonished the eye, presenting it with a marvellous setting of geometrical cliffs, exposed to all the higher variations of light throughout the day, and that I admired these superhuman structures. . . . But, although I could not help admiring them, that was not the same as loving them. A drawing, I continued, a blueprint tells all that can be known about them, but I do not see anyone looking at them with growing tenderness, lingering over a point, taking a notebook from his pocket to sketch some detail, some unusual solution of a problem that had arisen unexpectedly and forced the builder to combine function, material, and his own genius in an invention that would answer the purpose, with an effect of inspired discovery—the work of a living mind. . . . And yet that is what is often suggested by an old house or a little church in France. Some cottage, some fragment of a ruin have their own flavor, which is theirs alone.

There are still to be seen in the old quarters of Paris hundreds of little wrought-iron balconies, not one of which resembles any other, and each of which is a charming invention, a kind of idea, as simple as a theme of but a few notes. It was made by putting together a few pieces of iron with a great deal of taste. Nothing sums up for me more clearly what is most French in France.

Here I shall insert an observation that applies to a whole class of our works of art in every genre, but especially to writing.

From the sixteenth century onward, we developed a certain critical spirit in matters of form, which kept a strict "watch" over our literature during the so-called "classical" period, and has never ceased to exert a direct or indirect influence on judgments of value and, hence, on production. France is the country where considerations of pure form—care for form in itself—have dominated and persisted up to our own time. A "writer" in France is something more than a man who writes and publishes. An author, even one of very great talent who achieves very great success, is not necessarily a "writer." All the intellect, all the culture in the world cannot give him a "style."

Style is the result of a special sensitivity to language. This cannot be acquired, but it can be developed. With us this development has come not only from the artist's communion with his own thought, his solitary ambitions, and his own verbal resources, but also from the stimulus of competition and example in those restricted circles formed at different periods by the Court, the salons, the cafés, the cliques, or by the habitués of certain theatres. . . . These were so many courts of jurisdiction, hotbeds of the critical spirit. The demands they made, with their conservative or revolutionary traditions, have had the greatest possible effect on our literature and, indeed, on all our arts. All this would require prolonged demonstration and detailed examples, which I have no time to give in these few pages. I shall confine myself to stressing the importance of this entirely French manner of organizing literary activity, by the following remark: With us, the intellectual personality can scarcely develop in isolation, as a phenomenon unrelated to prevailing opinion, fashion, and taste. It must side with these or against them. For four centuries the evolution of our arts has proceeded through successive schools, actions and reactions, manifestos and pamphlets. We like innovations to explain themselves and traditions to defend themselves; a whole library of prefaces, proclamations, and theories, with their various arguments have accompanied the successive re-creation of value. In this way our literature resembles our politics. Finally, in the last half century or more, the former has become, oddly enough, a kind of experimental field in which all the possibilities (and consequently all the impossibilities) of language and prosody have been tried—highly daring experiments, with varying success, some proceeding from a profound analysis of thought and its means of expression, others purely adventurous and inspired merely by a burning desire to do something different from what had already been done. The present state of our literary production is remarkable for the coexistence of completely different ways of writing. All the gods are honored at once, without any great dispute among their worshippers. The age of battles, anathemas, and mutual contempt is past.

* * * * * *

My present attempt to perceive, isolate, and expound in a few words what is most purely French in the immense production of France becomes, by the very nature of things, more difficult and uncertain (if not entirely illusory) when we turn to the speculative and the scientific. It is clear that philosophic meditation, as well as scientific research, seeks universal results, results essentially transmissible to all men—an effort that tends to free the products of the mind from the hidden influences of race, local habits, and milieu. Abstract or "pure" thought, like scientific thought, endeavours to obliterate what comes to the thinker from his race or his nation, its aim being to create values independent of place and person. It is doubtless not impossible to discern, or think we discern, in a system of metaphysics or morals, the part that properly belongs to one race or nation: sometimes, indeed, nothing seems to define a certain race or nation better than the philosophy it has produced. It is claimed that certain ideas, though expressed in all universality, are almost unthinkable outside the climate of their origin. In a foreign land they wither away like uprooted plants, or else they look preposterous. That may well be.

In order to isolate what is specifically French in the abstract work of our philosophers, taking care (as far as possible in such matters) to avoid the vague and the arbitrary, we must rely on the simplest observations, but in addition we must allow ourselves a certain postulate, which is not an obvious one and which few will allow.

In my view (and I apologize for it), philosophy is a matter of form. It is not in the least a science, and it should free itself from any unconditional link with science. To be *ancilla scientiae* is no better for philosophy than to be *ancilla theologiae*.[2] In saying that it is a matter of form, I mean that if I seek an order and an expression that will sum up and compose for me the whole of my personal experience, the inner and the

---

2 "The servant of knowledge or science, ... of theology." The meaning of these expressions is made clear in this statement by Prof. Christos Evangeliou: "it seems that mainstream European philosophy has failed to follow the example of science and to liberate itself too. As in the Middle Ages, so in modern and post-modern times, "European philosophy" has continued to play the undignified and servile role of handmaiden of something. In addition to the medieval role of "handmaiden of theology" (*ancilla theologiae*), since the seventeenth century philosophy in Europe assumed the role of "handmaiden of science" (*ancilla scientiae*) and, with the coming of Marxist "scientific socialism", the extra role of "handmaiden of ideology" (*ancilla ideologiae*).

outer, then that is my philosophy and to do that is to seek a form. I do not say that I am right, which in any case would be meaningless. I say that in my present undertaking, this formula, however rash, enables me to consider that the form under discussion is one of those which a certain language is capable of, and that anyone who speaks this language, to others and to himself, can neither go beyond its means nor escape the suggestions and associations which the said language has insidiously implanted in him.

If I am French, there at the very point of my thought where thought takes shape and talks to itself, it takes shape in French, according to the possibilities and within the framework of French. This language has its (relative) virtues and vices: it has no license to compound words; it abounds in restrictions; it has a rather limited psychological vocabulary. Now, whoever thinks in a certain language pursues, from phrase to phrase, a kind of perfection, an inner satisfaction that he expects to find in one of those phrases. But the one he chooses, be what it may, will conform with the requirements of the language, will be modified by its peculiarities, suborned by its attractions. The thinker will be satisfied or his thought fix itself at such a critical point in such and such a language, and in this state it will become for him his definitive thought, to be written and exteriorized. Language, the common and undifferentiated work of a whole people, will thus finally have imposed conditions of expression and of meaning on a particular thought—conditions of which that thought is unaware. Suppose that our language did not allow us French to accept from ourselves any but finished and clearly articulated expressions, to tolerate any but those constructions whose framework can be seen—then our metaphysics would be completely governed by this. The passage from obscurity to clarity, which, for metaphysics, is the great hidden task, would be more laborious for us; our conceptions would be more restrained, and doubt would here play the greatest part metaphysics can allow without perishing. What we call profundity (without exactly knowing the abysses that lurk beneath this imposing word) would not be held, in France, to be a positive virtue. . . .

Here arises a great debate that can never be settled. Profundity and clarity, consciousness and the unconscious, introspection and objectivity, logic and . . . whatever it is that defies it, these are classic antitheses in all philosophies, yet with us they have been developed to the point of becoming national characteristics.

I shall sum up in a few words my general impression of this part of my subject. It seems to me that the French mind tends to mistrust and to shun every conception that does not allow the hope that it may in the end be reduced to a clear and unequivocal formula. In France, that is the price of success for any philosophy. I do not mean that systems of ideas not conforming to this principle cannot be produced here. What I mean is that they are never truly and, as it were, organically assimilated. Incidentally, I find analogous French reactions in politics and the arts.

Among the special products of our intellect, I must not forget that admirable array of studies, essays, novels, and plays whose object is the analysis of manners and character. We have in France more psychologists and moralists than metaphysicians. I do not hesitate to classify among such generally "acid" authors a few cartoonists whose captions and "sayings" are sometimes as good as their drawings.

It is perhaps a people's idea of man that is the best gauge of its national sensibility: its legislation, politics, literature, and manners are always directly inspired by this unexpressed idea. The French have more faith in men than illusions about men. The result is a rather striking contrast between the principles we admire, which express our confidence in human nature, and the cruel observations and dour maxims that so many great writers among us have so elegantly and forcefully struck off. Here I leave the domain of letters to cast a glance at our many tangible riches: painting, sculpture, the decorative arts, music. . . . The abundance and variety of these may discourage a mind wishing to extract the stuff of ideas from them, as though that were not an effort to destroy works of art intended for the sensibility, by claiming to exhaust them in a few "judgments."

French art has been practised with superior skill in every genre: from stained glass to engraving, from the cathedral to the "whatnot," from high-warp tapestry to enamels, from ceramics to typography; and this simple enumeration shows a variety of talents, throughout the ages, as rich as the variety we observed just now in terrain, climates, and the human constituents of France.[3] To grasp this richness we must picture it as made up of a considerable number of inventions, models, combinations, and procedures, to which we must add all the talent and skill required to imagine and bring into being so many possible forms.

The French hand has done wonders, whether in shaping stone or illuminating parchment. Of this abundance of research and discovery in the pursuit and practice of art I find a recent and shining example in the body of French painting from 1800 to the present day. I shall not

---

3 Discussed earlier, in a section not included here. Ed.

mention any names, and confine myself to this remark. Names are made only to send us back to things, yet they too often save us the journey.

What I should like to do here would be to show the astonishing diversity of solutions to the problem of painting which were proposed during these one hundred and thirty years: form, light, color, liveliness, or restraint, or urgency, or pure harmony, all, in turn, were taken as the aim of the artist's effort and a stimulus to his powers. All this is closely linked with the many literary experiments made during the same period, particularly in poetry.

How much I pass over in silence! Our sculpture, for the past two centuries, has been the finest in the world. Our music, the most subtle of all, seems to me (if I may allow my incompetence to speak) to have sought by way of intelligence to outflank the formidably fortified positions of a great symphonic power which until recently dominated the world of music. . . .

But the subject is vast and the conditions of the problem far too rigorous. You have no doubt noticed—with some surprise—that I have spoken no name, quoted no title, mentioned no date. If I had not kept to this rule, I should have had to offer you a huge book, a catalogue of persons and works. That would have been to show you multiplicity and individual differences, instead of composite unity and national harmony.

I will end by summarizing for you in two words my personal impression of France: our special quality (sometimes our foible, but often our finest claim) is to believe and to feel that we are universal—by which I mean, men of universality. . . . Notice the paradox: to specialize in the sense of the universal.

13
Reflections on the French Genius

by

Marcel Raymond

From: Marcel Raymond, *Génies de la France* (Neuchâtel, *Editions de la Baconnière*, 'Cahiers du Rhône' no. 4, 1942), chapter 1, "*Réflexions sur le génie de la France*". Translation by William T. Gairdner commissioned for this book, with advice from Carol J. Harvey. © J.E.G. Dixon.

I. The Problem

The Aim Defined

*I*n this article[1] I offer nothing but a few reflections, together with a glance at our history. I am not in search of a magic formula with which to sum up and define the genius of the French nation. I have no desire to imitate the good pyrotechnician, devising some final, dazzling rocket to outshine all the others that have gone before. Rather I propose to limit myself to recalling certain ideas propounded by others which I believe to be true, and others which I consider false. Nor do I propose to approach the problem from a single angle, presenting France as the land of liberty, or the French as the chosen people of Christendom. If the latter were true, their role would be to become the perfect example of the Christian faith, to offer this faith to the world, or to make the supreme sacrifice of themselves to God. (It is true that France has filled both these roles in the past, and may do so again.) Finally, I will resist the temptation to see the genius of the nation as wholly personified in some single author, a Ronsard, a Racine, or a Voltaire, or as totally expressed in a single painting, a Poussin, a Corot or a Cézanne, or in the harmonies of Debussy.

The Dangers of Subjectivity

As we set foot in this land of mirages and contemplate an object which is difficult to describe and delimit, it is important to define the terms we use, and then mentally substitute the definition for the thing defined, as Pascal would have us do. For those who write about the genius of nations, or their soul, their spirit, their psyche, their character or their temperament, do so ordinarily in the most happy-go-lucky way. When in the autumn of 1939 the "Nouvelles Littéraires" interviewed a number of foreign writers and scientists, and asked them what France 'represented' to them, it became perfectly clear that each of them had manufactured a France of his own, according to his personal predilections. For some she was the land of reason, for others of imagination, and so on. However, it remains true that the very diversity of their answers, and their incompatibility, is interesting, and we may well ask our-

---

1 I have attempted here to develop a theme which I treated in a lecture delivered in February 1941 before the Société de Sociologie of Geneva. The revue "*Suisse Contemporaine*" published an outline of it in June 1941.

selves whether so many contradictory statements could conceivably be made about any other nation in the world!

Our present situation is particularly favourable to these mirages. We are living in the thick of mighty events. The times are out of joint. All history, we feel, is at a crossroads, and we, too, are like the animal that sniffs the wind before deciding which way to go. Now at such moments one sees, with stupefied amazement, the role that chance plays in history, and how the accidental and the unpredictable influence the course of events. And yet, in a hundred years' time, perhaps in ten, historians will look back on our present age, or on the events on whose threshold we stand today, and will prove that the history of our time was the product of cast-iron law, in which chance played no part. And they will enjoy the intellectual pleasure of . . . predicting the past! We ourselves, with the defeat of 1940 fresh in our minds, list certain carefully chosen facts which we believe made that defeat inevitable. But might not those same facts observed in another context have served to explain something quite different—a victory, even? We have, indeed, already used some of them to explain our victory in 1918. The truth is that, taking incontrovertible facts as our starting point, or facts which we deem to be so, and then setting out on a search for their cause, we invest the past with a form, an interpretation, and with features which we then present as inevitable,—it could not have been otherwise. So was my allusion to the epoch-making events we are living through irrelevant? Perhaps so. For whatever the time or the circumstances, we are almost always prone to believe that what happened had to happen. (In Time and Movement Bergson has made several profound observations on this very point.) In particular, we are fatally inclined to regard the nation's history as a homogeneous whole; we see it as the product of immutable law. In all its corporate acts, as well as in the works of its creative artists, we are convinced that we can detect infallible marks of a national soul, manifestations of a hidden essence.

What is a "national genius"?

I wish to suggest, in the first place, that we make a distinction between the genius of a nation, and the mental and emotional traits which make up the character and temperament of the various peoples of which it is composed. The genius of a nation is the totality of all the creative forces at work in a given nation. Two philosophical systems here confront one another, the one realist, the other nominalist, in the mediaeval sense of those terms. The realist conceives of a national genius as a metaphysical entity; it exists by the grace of God, or as an aspect of the Incarnate Word, or as modes of a substance. (The least one can say about a belief of this kind is that we are not bound to believe it; and it is perhaps significant that it is to the genius of our own nation that we are most ready to attribute this ontological existence.) For the hard-bitten nominalist on the other hand, only individuals, and individual works of art, possess a genius. M. Louis Dimier, for instance, in his book *Le Nationalisme littéraire*, agrees that any given people have common ways of action, reacting, and feeling, but for him the individual genius is alone creative. The literature of France is nothing more nor less than the works of Frenchmen, or more precisely, of men who express themselves in French; it is the sum of "literary compositions"—in other words, of those that have artistic value—written in French; and its unity consists of nothing more than the common language.

Corporate Creations

How does one accept either of these extreme positions? First of all, it must be conceded that history has thrown up numerous and varied "corporate creations," original achievements which were, incontestably, not the work of individuals, but of the French people as a whole. The mediaeval commune was one, although it may well be true that certain individuals played a leading part in the organization when rioting broke out, as did, at various stages, individual lawyers and the authors of legal texts. The conception of the *honnête homme* in the seventeenth century was another; yet another was the idea of 'good taste'—one of the attributes of *honnêteté*. And finally, there is the language, a corporate creation if ever there was one, the most complex and the most important of them all in view of the extreme discipline it imposes on thought. If it is suggested that the unity of a literature is nothing more than the common medium in which the writers have expressed themselves, is this not tantamount to saying that the literary output of an author, its essential originality and all its innovations, can only come into existence within the body of a corporate creation?

Now, if we compare the corporate creations of the French people with the literary productions of French-speaking writers, certain affinities and common characteristics begin to appear; and, what is more, the similarities we detect are precisely those characteristics which we commonly attribute to the French people as a whole. Even if we invite Chance to the party, and attribute great importance to circumstances, we feel that we are witnessing the emergence of a fairly consistent spiritual world which obeys something like laws.

The Question of Perspectives

True, we must always take into account our own personal whims and imaginings; they are all liable to affect our conclusions. Is it not perhaps we ourselves, as I have already suggested, who "inform" the past, who read into it a form and an interpretation of our own who, as this spiritual world develops in time, attribute to it laws, rhythm, and an intelligent rather than an unconscious will? In the history of a nation Nature tirelessly pours forth her riches, at first sight without plan or purpose. But we cannot help asking: are her creations mere things, individuals, indeterminate and without relation to one another? Do they compose a lawless chaos in which we ourselves imagine a non-existent order, or a series of complementary orders? An unacceptable conclusion! The various attempts of historians to define the national character of peoples cannot have been pure fantasies, creations *ex nihilo*. For it is Nature herself who supplies pointers and signposts of different kinds. What we do is to choose between them. Most often, of course, we adopt, all unwittingly, the choice which our masters, "the authorities," have made before us. Racinian tragedy, we say, perfectly expresses the French genius. And there is no denying that it is an incomparable creation, which it is quite legitimate to prefer above all others; and so we decide (or consent) to see in it the inevitable and perfect consummation towards which the national genius had been moving in the seventeenth century.

But considered from another point of view, Racine's work has every appearance of an accident, a sublime exception, the supreme excellence of which was only perceived later, and the true meaning of which we are still debating today. The choice of symbols is always to some extent arbitrary. Some modern novel or poem which, relative to the accepted masterpieces I know so well, I place out on the periphery, may, in the eyes of a future generation, take on a significance which still remains partly hidden, or even wholly so, and for a lengthy period at that. And then perhaps, after one or several "transmutations of values," the historians will place it in the centre of our contemporary literary scene. Sainte-Beuve christened *Les Fleurs du Mal* the "Baudelairean folly," as though he were writing about some pavilion for light entertainment, standing, with its barbarous ornaments, alone on a remote forest path. And round about 1895, the "deadening hand" of Mallarmé appeared to have brought poetry to a full stop, while he himself seemed to be tiptoeing away into the wilderness, a poet without a following.

The Genius of a Nation: Part Corporate Creation, Part Myth

When the French of today think of France's lot, do they know who they really are? How could they? The image in their minds is what they think they are, or what they would like to be. If they reflect on the past, they recreate it in their imagination; they suppress details here and there, concentrating their attention on others—on pleasant ones—or on certain "values" which seem to them to have been realised in the history of their race, or on some work of art,—and here too, what they see is coloured by their sensual appetites or their emotions. If the idea of France as a nation has gradually come to be personified, both this idea and that of the genius of France belong to the class of corporate creations, in which a growing number of men have collaborated. Jacques Maritain had published a volume with the title, *A travers le désastre*, in which the following words are to be found: "Today more than ever one thinks of France as a living person, with a body and a soul, both infinitely precious; precious to ourselves and to the world at large, a child of promise endowed with manifold gifts, beauty . . . gentleness, . . . and now stricken, laid low, unspeakably humiliated." There could be nothing more natural than this heartfelt cry, nor the love that inspired it. And yet, Maritain's image partakes in some degree of the nature of a myth. This need not alarm us. A myth may be something very real, very beautiful, and—inevitable. I use the word here in this sense: a myth is a means to self-knowledge acquired by some nations through the medium of image, fable, or symbol, all of which become objects of faith, and which enlighten them on their conflicts and their destiny. The idea of France as a complete and mature person can exist only for those who love and serve her with body, mind, and spirit. This being so, we might say that a myth is a product of Nature fertilised by the spirit; however, the formula is unsatisfactory, for it leads straight to the question: "But what is Nature? Is she not herself of the spirit?" It has the merit, however, of expressing the idea that this semi-mythical being was not created out of nothing. I have spoken of pointers and signposts supplied by Nature. We cannot deny the existence of certain basic characteristics, a national temperament, a bundle of tendencies, habits created by a physical and social environment but now become a "second nature."

The Physical Environment

There can be no disputing its importance. We live in a land suited to certain types of farming—pasture, wheat, vines; a land with a well defined river system and prevailing winds, beneath a sky, or rather several skies, which produce their own effects of light and shade. Who could deny the subtle influence of these physical phenomena on the population that lives among them? The French were once indistinguishable from other men, but they have long since ceased to be so. A national character has evolved with the passing of the centuries, Nature and human nature each playing its part in its formation. Nature has supplied the fundamental and unchanging pressures, but in France they are so diverse and complex that the human spirit has not been crushed under their weight. So far from limiting the play of other forces,—those which are not rigorously predetermined, namely the spiritual forces,—they have offered them the widest scope for creative action. And that is what really matters.

II. Creation of a People

Ethnic Origins

In our search for the genius of the French people the clues which the physical environment provides are elusive and ambiguous. With our ethnic origins the situation is different. We are a nation of mixed blood, in which peoples of different races, converging from different points of the compass—Celts, Romans, Franks, Scandinavians or Normans—have, to quote Claudel, melted over the centuries into "*une très noire confiture*"—a dark, rich brew. But the French would be foolish to disavow their "turbid" origins. It partly explains, I believe, why their creative gifts are so varied. A wide keyboard makes possible rich and unexpected chords. Imagine an amorphous mass, quite heterogeneous at the outset, and destined to be almost continuously enriched by other newcomers. These people will be changed, but changed in different ways, by the physical environment in which they settle. (There is a world of difference between the natives of Lorraine, Brittany, and Provence; so much so that it is possible to speak of the genius of Brittany or of Lorraine.) This living mass is slowly moulded into a political entity, and the French people set forth on a particular historic destiny. Now consider France under Saint Louis, Louis XIV, and the Jacobins. At first sight it would be difficult to believe they are the same nation, but as soon as we begin to examine these three manifestations of the French spirit, we find an undeniable family resemblance between them.

The French: Revolutionaries or Conservatives?

France is a land in which political, intellectual, or moral revolutions are normal occurrences—a way of life; a land whose people periodically indulge in orgies of self-criticism, when they condemn their own past, more or less unjustly, and seem ready almost to destroy the nation in order to recreate it. (The Renaissance, the French Revolution, and our own times, offer all too many examples.) Each time, a new crystallization emerges, and a call to order is sounded. The new structure and the new principles seem well established, but, after a certain period, a new crisis and a new crystallization occur. For every successive revolution has left some element of the population dissatisfied and frustrated, and has failed to integrate others. The existence of these malcontents and their silent disaffection remain unnoticed, but they are the groups which will be responsible for the next upheaval. It seems that from time to time France needs to simplify herself at whatever cost, though the impulse does not become starkly visible before the Renaissance, with its passion for clear ideas and tyrannical formulas.

The "Conflict of Forces"

But if the history of France is a story of new beginnings, it is at the same time a picture of unbroken continuity. Indeed, France is the land *par excellence* of conservatism; she has more than once invented a system whose sole purpose was to conserve, even at the cost of strangling the life of the nation. In his stimulating book, *Paris, dernier modèle de l'Occident*, Leo Ferrero half playfully depicts Paris as the synthesis of the Athenian type of civilization, with its spirit of invention, and of a civilization of the Roman type, dominated by the spirit of conservatism. We can leave Athens and Rome out of the argument, for in his main contention Leo Ferrero is right: the idea of two conflicting forces, normally living in equilibrium, explains the history of Paris marvellously well, and even that of France herself, and not only modern France. At times of crisis, this conflict contains great dangers: we have recently witnessed the two forces vying with each other in the uncompromising tone of their ideologies and their slogans, the revolutionary element working itself to a frenzy, the conservatives becoming ever more obstinate and unyielding. And all to no purpose. To no purpose, that is, in the public domain. And we must add that, even in the periods of exhaustion, such as the one which began with the Armistice of 1918, and still more during the periods of great vitality, writers, artists, and scientists—the truly creative spirits—strive for dialogue, and in the first place a dialogue of thought with itself, as the natural and fruitful condition of the human spirit.

However, even in the twelfth and thirteenth centuries, which Auguste Comte called organic because, in his view, the French of this period were an embodiment of one great unifying principle, even then France had several traditions; she also had her rebels and her heretics. The crystallizations I referred to, splendid and solid though some were, never incorporated more than part of the body politic; the others would have their say later. In short, the history of France appears to consist of tendencies, some of major, others of secondary importance, some not mutually irreconcilable, others essentially so. At a given moment, one of them dominates the rest, and something like an equilibrium is achieved, which, as often as not, is more apparent than real. The latest structure may survive long after all vital force has died within it; it continues to subsist by obstructing the emergence of new life. Meanwhile, a new combination is forming beneath the surface.

The Language

There is no better evidence of these metamorphoses than the historic development of the language. But, in reality, there are two French languages, the ancient and the modern, the latter usually being considered the authentic one, and which at first was believed to have been "fixed" for all time by the work of the great "classical" authors. Now the virtues of clarity and purity belong to modern French only. Old French, with its semantically ill-defined vocabulary, was less precise but extremely colourful; it appealed to the senses and the imagination rather than to the intelligence, and had very little in common with the black-and-white idiom which became standard French after the time of Descartes and Vaugelas. Is it sufficient to argue that it had not been intellectualised by a people who had not yet discovered what they truly were? It would be more accurate to say, what a few future generations, imbued with humanist culture, were indeed going to become. The fact remains that the difference between English and German, as they were in the thirteenth century and what they are today, is less than the difference between old and modern French. This transformation measures the distance the French have travelled—as a result of specialisation. Could it be true that, here again, new habits have brought into existence a second nature?

France and Rome

How was civilization born in France, and with it that elusive genius we are trying to track down? In his *Essai sur la France*, E.-R. Curtius[2] invites us to consider the impoverished soil which the Roman Empire had become at its decline. This civilization, he assures us, was "second hand to the second degree"; in other words, it was an imitation of an imitation of an imitation, since the golden age of Rome was a mere derivative of the civilization of Greece. The living seeds which enabled a meagre culture to drag on through the twilight of the Roman Empire were laboriously collected by the "clerks"—Black Books and papyri, from which these men pieced together Latin sentences in prose or Latin verses, centos made up from various authors, and wisdom condensed into formulas for the benefit of the schoolboys of the Middle Ages. E.-R. Curtius considers that the principal beneficiary of all this was France, to whom he awards, by letters patent duly signed and sealed, the succession of Greece and Rome. He thus justifies the office which France is all too ready to attribute to herself: that of the guardian of civilization and culture.

The strange thing is that many Frenchmen agree with him, with this difference: that most of them are of the opinion that France had already been latinised in the Middle Ages, so that in the sixteenth and seventeenth centuries there was nothing left for her to do but to enter into the small part of the heritage which remained unsettled. According to this theory, France is the daughter, or rather the granddaughter,—but in either case predestined—of an ancient civilization, the only one that has ever been, that of Greece and Rome; born a fully grown adult, capable of making use of another people's experience, of rethinking the "ideas of antiquity," and created to be "reasonable," to live sheltered from the fury of the instincts and from life in the raw.

Here we must protest again, and come to the defence of France against the French. To consider France as nothing more than the heir of Rome, to exalt a single channel of communication with the past, and

---

2 See page 42.

to repudiate anything which does not pass through this channel, is to misread the facts; it is also to feel terribly far away from our youth! And yet it is precisely our professors of nationalism who, tirelessly rehashing the dreams of the Rhetoricians, offer us this theory, polishing and repolishing it, even though they thereby diminish the genius of their country and its creative originality.

For the picture of the mediaeval clerk with his earthenware pot in which he religiously conserves the ashes of Greece and Rome, let us substitute the image of grafting. Now, "one can only graft on a wild stock" (Ramuz). France is not a "second-hand civilization to the second degree," all Latin or post-Latin. Must we forget the inhabitants of this land before the Romanisation of Gaul? Or the peoples who were assimilated later—Nordic, Germanic, Arab—and all their creative energy? And can we forget Christianity? The conversion of Gaul to the Faith, which occurred originally in opposition to Rome at a time when Christians were being persecuted throughout the Empire, was not, as the professors seek so hard to persuade us, a second Romanisation, a second and more total enslavement to Rome. The watchword of the new faith was Liberty, the liberation of souls. (Daniel Halévy[3] pointed this out to E.-R. Curtius.) No doubt the religion of the Druids, with its rites to ensure the survival and happiness of the soul beyond the grave, had prepared the way by first canalising this very human aspiration. But it is no accident that the first great heresy in the West, which spread first throughout Gaul, should bear the name of the Breton, Pelagius, defender of the principle of the liberty of the soul, and even of the freedom of the will, against the official doctrine of efficacious grace.

Furthermore, this "primitive" Christianity remained faithful to its origins, which were Jewish. The conversion of Gaul to Christianity coincided with the arrival of the St. Marys on the Mediterranean sea coast—a sort of invasion from the East of Hebrews, Greeks, and Arabs. This mixed humanity provoked in France a grand renewal, a veritable regeneration. In his fine book, *L' Art des Sculpteurs Romans*, Henri Focillon makes the following observation: "The importance which Oriental studies has assumed in the analysis of Mediaeval art now makes it impossible to consider the East and the West as two separate worlds. Innumerable Asiatic influences have been discovered in our own time. The old controversy grows keener every day with the discovery of fresh evidence. It is now impossible to deny that the influence of Christians from the East, of Muslims, and of more ancient civilizations still, was of

3 D. Halévy: *La France jugée*, in issue 3 of the revue "*Esprit*".

considerable importance in the history of Romanesque art." On a later page, Henri Focillon defines the spirit of the great art works of the thirteenth century: "The Romanesque period was dominated by visionaries. The artists caught their transcendental aspirations, their mystical longings, and their search for hidden truths. They lost interest in the everyday world, its priorities and standards, its faith in reason and common sense. The raptures of St. John the Divine came to live in their work. But they were not content merely to illustrate his fiery epic; it became in their hands the substance of a dream which was wholly original and their own."

French Civilization and the 12th Century

Thus it was that, long after the Roman conquest of Gaul, and after the barbarian invasions, an entirely original civilization sprang up in France. A positivist historian, Charles Seignobos, not naturally disposed to praise the mediaeval spirit, wrote some fifteen years ago: "An unprecedented flowering, comparable to what has been called 'the Greek miracle,' marked the birth of French civilization in the twelfth century. It was radically different from all the ancient civilizations of the Mediterranean and the East."[4]

Of course, there is no such thing as an absolute beginning. Historians have insisted on the importance of the Latin writers and polygraphs at the height of the Middle Ages, of the humanism of the pre-Renaissance humanists, and of the work of the philosophers. A saying of Bernard de Chartres on the Greek and Roman authors has recently been widely quoted: "We are like dwarfs standing on the shoulders of giants, and thanks to them we see farther than they saw." But perhaps it is not in the schools and universities that are to be found the most original products and the true portrait of this radiant young civilization.

Romanesque art was of southern inspiration. It was during this period that "a white robe of churches spread over the land." The great tympana of the cathedrals are theologies and theophanies in stone; or again, they depict "divine apparitions." The frescoes portray God the Father, or St. Michel-du-Péril-de-la-Mer. The art we know as Gothic developed elsewhere, in the provinces adjoining the Ile-de-France and Normandy. While Romanesque iconography is epic in spirit, and based on the Apocalypse, Gothic iconography depicts a human Christ whose

---

4 Ch. Seignobos: *Histoire sincère de la nation française*

greatness has melted into the gentleness of the Gospel portrait, a Christ among men subdued by his spirituality. Their world is one at peace with itself; existence is neither a punishment nor a fall from grace; it has the innocence of a child. The mediaeval sculptors, according to Emile Mâle, "do not seek to read in the budding flowers of May the mystery of the Fall and the Redemption. In the first days of spring they would go out to the forests. The bracken is still covered with downy fluff, but along the streams the wild arum lilies are about to flower. They would pick the leaves and buds now ready to open, and gaze at them with the passionate, tender curiosity we only feel in early childhood, but which true artists feel all their lives long."[5]

That spring is still there, smiling in stone for all time. And if this primitive art keeps its freshness it is because men were inspired by a mystical love of nature rather than the desire to imitate the models of antiquity, or to improve on "what has already been transformed" by the artists of a great civilization of the past.

And so, during the two great centuries of the Middle Ages in France, incomparable masterpieces accumulated, monumental in character, which deserve to be called "classical," since they bear the hallmark of maturity, combining as they do technical mastery with imaginative daring. The humanism incarnate in the stones of Rheims or Notre-Dame de Paris, and other masterpieces of the "Praxitelian" age of Gothic sculpture,[6] is "classical" too, although part and parcel of the spontaneous flowering described by Seignobos.

The Cultural Supremacy of France in the 12th Century

During this period, Pérotin and Pierre de la Croix invented polyphony. This first-born art, *ars antiqua*, was soon followed by *ars nova*, initiated by the poet-musician Guillaume de Machaut. "In Paris," writes Henri Prunières, "there occurred the great revolution which was to give France an unquestioned supremacy for two centuries among the nations of Europe, in music as in the other arts."[7] In this same century, the *chanson de geste* appeared in southern France, "an offspring without a mother," while the first notes of lyric poetry were heard in the land of

---

5 E. Mâle: *L'art religieux au XIIIe siècle en France.*

6 Henri Focillon's expression, in *Histoire du moyen âge* (vol. VIII), published by G. Glotz, with the collaboration of H. Pirenne and C. Cohen (Presses Universitaires de France).

7 Henri Prunières: *Histoire de la musique* (vol. I).

Oc, in Limousin. Then the *trouvères* in the North appeared as a counterpart to the troubadors in the South. Poets from Italy, the predecessors of Dante, from Germany and Great Britain came to sit at their feet. It is doubtful whether, in any country in Europe, poetry aspiring to be a serious art was being written which did not derive from this Languedoc stock.

Where did the lyricism of the troubadors come from? Theories and hypotheses are endless, but no one really knows. In its highest manifestations this civilization represents a synthesis which is essentially oecumenical and universal, and the arts which flourished first are precisely those whose medium is "universal"—architecture, statuary, and music. A few masterpieces excepted, the literature in the vulgar tongue strikes us as less perfect; but at the time it was admired no less. In Great Britain at the end of the twelfth century, French had ousted English as the literary language in almost every part of the kingdom; and in 1260, Brunetto Latini, Dante's master, wrote his *Trésor* in French,—the most delectable of languages, and the most commonly spoken among peoples.

We have heard these things before, but we do not know them. Our schools and universities seem too unconcerned to remind us of them. Something in us persists in repeating that France did not know herself at this time, an age when the arts practically ignored the wars of princes, and when frontiers were still unsettled. It is true that the peoples of Europe had not yet learnt to assert who they were by vigorously protesting who they were not. But must we despise works of art *a priori* just because they are *naïve*? Mediaeval France gave a human form and face to the artistic aspirations of a whole continent, and by assimilating influences coming from afar, often from the East, she became the accepted authority in artistic matters in the whole of the West. All this has nothing dishonourable about it, unless the supreme honours are to be awarded exclusively to the man who stands apart, spending his time in the contemplation of his own image. Whether one likes it or not, this extraordinary cultural awakening had its roots in the soil of France, among this centrally placed conglomeration of ethnic bits and pieces, with its easy access to the North and East, Flanders and the Rhine Provinces, partially dependent in its western provinces on the kings of Great Britain, and communicating by sea and land with Spain, Italy, and the Levant. We do not know when the idea of *la patrie* began to emerge in France. Professors quote the *Chanson de Roland*, for in this famous poem Roland frequently speaks of *la douce France*. A vague patriotic feeling, according to Michelet, was widespread in "the wan hills and plains of central France," and he believes that the idea of nationality was born there. But we who are groping for a clear conception of the genius of France will not forget that the first in date of modern civilizations was born in France in the twelfth century, and that this flame of art and Christian culture shed its light over the whole of Europe. The Florentine Renaissance, which did indeed develop, as one might expect, out of the Italian Middle Ages, came later.

III. Her Literature

The Renaissance and its Consequences

After this, France fell a prey to armies, brigands, and epidemics. The civilization of the region of the *langue d'oc* was irretrievably undermined by the Albigensian Crusade. In the land of the *langue d'oïl* the kings of France and England fought a hundred years' war. I will not summarize the whole history of France . . . The age of the Renaissance—the idea and the word date from the eighteenth and nineteenth centuries, from Voltaire, Michelet and Jacob Burckhardt[8]—the age of humanism and of Italianism, was also the age when the religious unity of Christendom was finally shattered. Modern states were established, their rulers, guided solely by the very ancient "ideal" of state interest, finding that it was fully vindicated by its success in practice. A new language emerged, and a new literature. The latter was gradually to become "classical" after its potentialities had been revealed, rather suddenly, round about 1660, by the work of several geniuses. The preparation had lasted a hundred and fifty years. France had finally achieved self-knowledge and was showing her true face to the world. At least, that is what we have been taught; and we nearly all swallow it without a murmur.

The Great Repudiation

Never, perhaps, in the history of a great nation has there been a more complete repudiation of its past than that which took place in France between the sixteenth and seventeenth centuries. I wonder whether we have realised all the consequences. Everything before Malherbe, Simon Vouet, and Pierre Lescot's Louvre, was consigned to the outer darkness of "Gothic" ignorance,—they meant "barbarous." An ad-

---

8 *Renaissance*, p.11.

mirable genius like Ronsard, a man of the Middle Ages and a country-man born and bred, who asserted that he had himself already broken with the past, was proscribed in his turn,—written off as a pedant with an impure vocabulary and deplorably lacking in "urbanity."

What has not been alleged to explain or glorify this rejection? In the first place one may, and must, distinguish the theories of the human-ists and of the university professors from the works of the creative art-ists. La Fontaine, a passionate reader of the Greek and Roman authors, seems to distil a quintessential worldly wisdom, humour, and poetry from the *fabliaux* and from Boccaccio. The Cornelian heroes, "gener-ous" to a fault, and who express themselves with all the pomp of a Ro-man orator, are nonetheless chivalrous and courteous to the marrow. And it is easy to see what makes Molière "Gallic" and a "bourgeois" (in the mediaeval sense).

The plea of "vital necessity" is sure to make its appearance, as though a repudiation of the past were a necessary precondition of the renovation which, at the time, was generally felt to be necessary.

And in conclusion, whatever arguments the critics use, the tree is judged by its fruits, and suitable eulogies are bestowed on the produc-tions of their renovated France, who, they contend, "knows herself" for the first time.

All very well. But let us not forget that a comparison of what pre-ceded the Renaissance and what came after only results in a triumph for the "Classical" era on the condition that we exclude everything except the two literatures. All recent studies, and even the new discoveries,—I am thinking of all the old paintings which have been brought to light by modern cleaning methods—bear witness to the vitality of the spontane-ous renewal which had occurred in the fifteenth century in Burgundy and Flanders, in architecture, painting, and sculpture. It must be ad-mitted that Louis Courajod was not exactly tilting at windmills when, in his lectures in the Louvre[9] at the end of the nineteenth century, he denounced "the Machiavellian alliance between Italian art and the arts of the pagan civilizations" which resulted in the enslavement of artists to models of the past. Meanwhile musical inspiration was drying up. Is it sufficiently realised that Renaissance poetry was sung as often as it was read?—that it soared to heaven on the wings of music? Before repeating that the French are not musical, and that in France music is a sophisticated art—the refined pastime of an elite—one should take note

---

9 Louis Courajod: *Leçons professées à l'École du Louvre* (1887-1896), 3 vols.

that this is true of the last few centuries only. It is a fact that from the Renaissance onwards the French have left singing to the working classes and the soldiers: the cultural classes prefer to spend their time learning how to reason.

The largely Latin culture issuing directly from humanism presupposes an aristocracy of writers and readers. Such a class did in fact come into being, an aristocracy of the intelligence, confident in its rights and proud of its knowledge. For knowledge, it was contended, confers nobility on a man; evil is ignorance. Its motto was: *odi profanum vulgus,* "I hate the common herd" (Du Bellay paraphrases it in his manifesto); its besetting sin: *libido sciendi,* "the lust for knowledge." Do I exaggerate? The formation of this class which held itself apart from the rest of the nation was an immensely important event. One may regret it or approve of it, or one may regard it as having been inevitable. But one must realise what was involved, and further, we should recognise at what historical turning point this aristocracy claimed its rights and titles. It was precisely when the foundations of an all-European and Christian community were collapsing; when the individual was conscious of his supreme dignity and of everything that distinguishes him from other men; and when nations—the divinities of modern times—were recruiting their first converts. How many irresistible and often invisible influences there were, making for the separation of man from man! In the Middle Ages, in spite of the weight of the social hierarchy, in spite of all the miseries, human contacts were possible. A treasure-house of legends was at everyone's disposal, and symbols fraught with emotion, and images understood by all. Woe to the nations without legends; they are in danger of freezing to death, said Patrice de la Tour du Pin in his *Quête de joie.* You may answer that the artists and the poets now have another treasure-house of magnificent myths, Greek in origin, some of which have long been familiar to us and have been integrated into the Christian world, or are in the course of being integrated. True, no doubt, though many will use them as mere stylistic decorations. Henceforward, society will be divided into two classes: the cultured class—those who know, and who recognize each other at the first word spoken; and those who do not know.

'Rhetoric' as an Educational System

During the Renaissance and the period of academic classicism, philological questions were of the first importance. A scholastic discipline known as 'Rhetoric' was worked out at this time, and finally became established throughout the land. "One of the consequences (of this development)," writes Daniel Mornet, "was to imprison thought within a closed, highly defined, and artificial system of well-worn truths."[10] What was thus reduced to a system was the matter and methodology of thinking. The moment had come for a call to order, and for the most rigorous dragooning of the mind that has ever been attempted in the history of France. A mould was offered to writers and students, or rather was imposed upon them, which, they were promised, would give their compositions coherence and consistency. And this lasted for a long time, thanks to the work of the Jesuit fathers and their successors, the diligent professors of the Université de France, whether its sympathies at the time were Imperial or Republican. This highly specialised education, founded on the teaching of 'rhetoric', logic, and later, mathematics, brought to birth a superior expression of the French psyche. The system was extremely productive. Teachers deliberately economised and directed their pupils' natural endowments, in which policy they could count on the support of the parents, all of them, nobles or bourgeois, members of an intellectual élite, who had themselves been through the schools. But along with its undoubted merits, it had the defect of providing a diet which was too rich in second-hand truths, too poor in first-hand experience, or too rich in first-hand experience predigested and already "transformed"[11] by others. Too remote from life itself, as it was from the pupils' personal concerns and reactions, it was liable to clothe the mind without ever penetrating to its core and centre, without "turning it over" like a piece of arable land. This is the danger of all humanist education (in the narrow sense of the word), as Montaigne noted—the danger that it will be insufficiently Socratic: it will touch the pupil's personal responses too little, aim to form him too soon, and, by inculcating the cult of models, impose limits upon his development.

It is incontrovertible that the Frenchman's inborn taste for argument, combined with the programme of studies he had followed at school (including the use and abuse of syllogism, which was a feature of the system), explains, in part at least, why the latter succeeded so well and lasted so long. The Jesuits' "programme of studies" came into force in other countries besides France, but only in France were the results so widespread and so deep. It was the spectacle of generations of success-

---

10 Daniel Mornet: *Histoire de la clarté française.*

11 I am thinking of C.-F. Ramuz's recent observations on poetry in vol. XIV of his *Oeuvres complètes.*

fully indoctrinated students which inspired Hippolyte Taine, that arch-rhetorician who imagined himself to be breaking with orthodoxy, to paint an absurdly oversimplified picture of the history of French literature, with its emphasis on the importance of the "race" and the "milieu."[12] Before him, Nisard, who published his *Histoire de la Littérature* in 1844, had proclaimed that art can produce nothing but general truths, that literature begins with the Renaissance, and that this literature is "the idealised picture of human life in all places and at all times"; or better, he went on, "it is reality cleansed of its coarse and incidental features in order to render its study both useful and harmless." The theoreticians of the seventeenth century, brought up on Horace, asserted that literature should at once give "instruction and pleasure"—and that, surely, should have been harmless enough for Monsieur Nisard!

If I linger over this issue it is because some of our contemporaries who lack any real understanding of art would still have us believe that the study of human nature, suitably emasculated, suffices for the training of a man's intelligence and the formation of his character.

'Rhetoric' and the Cult of Reason

The consequence of all this has been that a great deal of French literature since the sixteenth century, and more particularly since the seventeenth, has developed in a watertight compartment, and that the working class finds it meaningless. Poetry, often exquisite poetry, is offered to lovers of poetry like a hothouse plant, a literary quintessence, unrelated to the hard facts of life—passionless, a laborious pattern-making with words. I am not myself impervious to this kind of beauty, still less am I indifferent to the insights of the seventeenth and eighteenth century moralists, or despise France's intellectual tradition, or that marvellous instrument of analysis and persuasion which we know as the *prose d'idées*, the French prose *par excellence*. So let us, in the first place, agree to put beyond criticism the profound intellectual effort of those writers who seek to establish a vital contact with reality (psychological and metaphysical), and then to let it find its way, directly or indirectly, into the reader's mind. But in an ancient nation, where the reasoning powers are highly developed and the taste for argument is widespread, the point may be reached where reason (which is, after all, but a mode and tool of the spirit) becomes an end in itself. The starting point is the ideas and words of others, matter which has already been digested and

12 See the Introduction to his *Histoire de la littérature anglaise*, his essay on Racine, etc.

intellectualized. There result formal thought patterns, along with formal logic and a formal language. The social consequences of such a development are real and long-lasting, but in the end reason is found to have lost contact with reality.

'Rhetoric' and the Creative Artists

In a situation of this kind great artists must choose between two alternatives. Either they will try to break through the "spiritual web" which threatens to imprison them, or they will adopt a subtler approach. This latter consists in bending and adapting the shackles of literary convention to their purposes, in order to return to the truly creative work of the spirit, which is purely personal. For their aim is not to explicate another man's thought, but to grasp something in its essential reality, and to express it. It is to "comprehend" the universe and human nature, which is to "take them together" in their mutual interactions, to carry about with them the burden of their vision like a pregnant woman. Or again, it is to transform states of being into states of consciousness. Is this not what the great Classical writers did, each in his own way— Montaigne and Pascal, Racine in *Phèdre*, Rousseau, even, in the *Confessions* and the *Rêveries*, a poet like Baudelaire, and poet-novelists like Flaubert and Proust? Of the two attitudes, the first was that of the Romantic and Baroque type—violent or impatient temperaments; the second, that of the "Classics." The first attitude is revolutionary, and in that is its strength; but it opens the door to every kind of extravagance. What is more, the writer who rejects 'rhetoric' and the rules of the game out of hand, may find himself lacking in the means to express himself. The reputation of the artists who choose the second type takes time to ripen, for they are rarely recognised immediately as innovators.

So it was that the work of the great Classics came to fruition in spite of the doctrines of the Academy—those doctrines which came, by way of Italy, directly from Latin orators and rhetoricians, or from Aristotle. In spite of their apparent submission to the "rules" of the professors, Racine, La Fontaine and Molière were "temperaments" nourished at the fountainhead of the Greco-Roman and national traditions. The justification of their art, together with its immanent law, came from within themselves, and from the demands of the subject they were treating.

The Tyranny of 'Rhetoric' in the Classical Period

But even so, society held them in its clutches; they were dependent on it—more than they would have liked perhaps—on its habits, and on the men and women of fashion, the grammarians and the purists, all leagued together for the 'right use' of reason (which was the use commonly approved of at that period), and for the expression of 'general truths'. Their great works, exceptional as they were in many respects, were conditioned by a culture, by its logic, and by the academic 'rhetoric'. However, this had one advantage: it gave the poet strength, leading him gently on till he reached the point where his genius could take wing. An enterprise as complex as was the Classical Movement owes its strength to the multiplicity of the elements which compose it, all holding together and each making its indispensable contribution. But its strength was bought at a price, just as in Nature every gain in one direction invariably entails loss in some other. It is like the law of choice and accepted sacrifice. The writer must play the game, and not hazard effects which run counter to the spirit of the age. Classical and post-Classical works, including those masterpieces which could never be widely popular, were accepted and enjoyed by the contemporary public precisely because their authors played the game according to the rules. But writing as they did for an extremely restricted public—though one which was being constantly reinforced with new recruits,—they only succeeded in performing their function in society at the price of what I, personally, feel was a cruel renunciation. I know it is foolish to waste time agonizing over might-have-beens. A creative writer can only make direct contact with the universe or with the human soul on condition that society has no objection to his mind being invaded from time to time by thoughts and images which seem, at first sight, signally to fail to pass Monsieur Nisard's test of "usefulness"; and further, he will not complain if those thoughts and images erupt unexpectedly in his style,—though the writer will of course control the flood, passing it through a filter of his own devising. There are innumerable examples of all this in Shakespeare. But to have expected such tolerance in seventeenth century France would have been crying for the moon. And yet this is precisely what I sometimes catch myself longing for,—that we too might have had a Shakespeare—a French Shakespeare, (who would, of course, have been very different from the English one). No, it could not be. "And then came Malherbe..." Oh, the pitiful, heart-breaking anticlimax! Everything in life and art has its price, as I have said; and I might have added: Everything wears out in time. Conventions which have dominated the artistic scene for one or two centuries or longer will finally cease to satisfy. Their limitations begin to outweigh their merits. Whence the revolt of so many artists during the last hundred and fifty years. Rousseau was the first, pitting himself against the whole of contemporary literature and philosophy, and society itself. After him and right down to our own time, artists have mostly been rebels. They have lived, and continue to live, with a terrible and exhausting companion—solitude. It would be comforting if one could reassure oneself with the thought that their strength had grown in proportion to the resistance they have met. But it is disturbing to observe that their non-conformism seems so often to be a sort of vocation, or a habit, or, for some even, an excuse for laziness.

* * * * * *

What apparently had been lost forever keeps reappearing in a new guise. The tyranny of the Academy could not check or restructure all the talents nature has bestowed on the French. The Frenchman has not been, at all times and exclusively, "the man of thought," the intellectual, as Madariaga claims.[13] He has become this, after centuries devoted to a variety of enterprises. Twice over, pre-Rousseau France had had a period of the most intense creative energy in her spiritual and artistic life, once at the height of the Middle Ages, and then again in the Classical era, though artistic creations have poured out in an almost unbroken stream between these two peaks. The man who cannot accept these obvious facts will be unable to appreciate many modern works of art, or the greatness of the nineteenth century, with its frequent fresh starts and recurrent rebirths, or the significance, for the French and for humanity in general, of several important historical events. All these will appear to him atypical and with no future, because, as he thinks, they lack roots.

He will reject, in the first instance, everything that can be classed under the vague heading of Romanticism, dismissing all such phenomena as foreign imports. Now the Romantic movement was, first and foremost, an upsurge of the irrational—that is, of the unconscious drives of the instincts, but also of the spirit—against both an aging society and the eighteenth century philosophers' too superficial conception of man. And this revolt was not the first of its kind in our history; it would have

---

13 S. de Madariaga: *Englishmen, Frenchmen, Spaniards.* French translation published by Gallimard. (See page 107. Ed.)

resembled the "mystical conquest"[14] of the years 1615-1650 more than it does, if the Church had been able to exercise its authority, as it did in the seventeenth century movement. And a host of common features link Romanticism to mediaeval Chivalry, which, like its nineteenth century counterpart, was rooted in Christianity, or at least deeply coloured by it. And both movements had heretical tendencies: both, for instance, flaunted the flower of the forbidden fruit—the longing for death.

Then there is the spirit of the French Revolution, rationalist and anti-Christian as it was by an accident of history, but with a rationalism indissolubly bound up with a somewhat vague article of faith. One senses in the Jacobins an emotional compulsion which has a very ancient historical precedent—the wild enthusiasm of the Crusades. Indeed, their creed is a secular version of the *Gesta Dei per Francos*. But such ideas he finds difficult to accept, or even to imagine, in a French context.

Or again, his first reaction will be to call the police, or to make sure that the locks of his doors are in order, when he thinks of the grand adventure of the poets from the Romantics to the Surrealists—that literary, but also metaphysical, revolt against rational arguments and a mechanistic universe; an attempt, also, to make poetry a law unto itself, so as to enable its sacred fire to burn undiminished; and meanwhile, to return to the first principles of the language, and to use words disallowed by the Classics, but full of meaning and suggestive power. So it is that sometimes we find poets protesting at one and the same time in favour of poetry and of the language of the common people; while the idiom of the modern poet borrows from this non-academic language, so sturdy and expressive, so full of picturesque metaphors, a language which, for long now, has been threatening the citadel of *le style élevé*.

Mallarmé and a New Religion

Early in the year 1866, Villiers de l'Isle-Adam wrote to Mallarmé thus: "I know that you care as little about happiness as I do myself. We are two cavemen, you and I. It's terrible!" A new human type was coming into existence, a man wholly shut in on himself, and wholly cut off from the everyday world. But the further a man penetrates into himself, the less individual substance he finds;—his consciousness of self becomes a form or reflection of his idea of the universe. At the end of a long period of concentration and asceticism, our poet had risen above

14 The title of vol. III of Henri Brémond's *Histoire littéraire du sentiment religieux*, which deals with this movement.

himself. He had dedicated himself to the creation of an object which was to be the Absolute of Beauty or Perfection, in which the world would be recapitulated, and which alone would justify the existence of the world. For him happiness *was* possible, but in this way and no other. "I was lucky enough last night to see my poem in its nudity, and I mean to attack the Great Work this evening," (letter from Mallarmé, March 3, 1866.)[15] The god had descended on the creature of flesh and blood who had given him birth, and had flooded him with light.

Unless I am much mistaken, the new religion, with its own imperatives, and with its devotees worshipping at the shrine of Absolute Perfection, could only have been born in France. In England, none of the most refined aesthetes were as scrupulously obedient to the new commandment: "Thou shalt create." "We are cavemen," Villiers de l'Isle-Adam had said. Perhaps, but he and Mallarmé were the progeny of two ancient French ancestries. Villiers was a Breton noble, while Mallarmé, George Moore tells us, looked strangely like a Parisian workingman. The quarry these two huntsmen were pursuing was very different from that which obsessed the soul of St. Julian the Hospitaler; it was a spiritual quarry. And Mallarmé's poetry, emerging from Romanticism like a spire from its cathedral, with lightning flashes flickering about it, was the "masterpiece" of a builder of days long gone by.

IV. *Conclusions*

If I were to attempt a broad and somewhat abstract definition of the conditions prevalent in French society which have deeply influenced the work of her artists during the last thousand years, I would shun the word 'rationalism'—a concept at once too rigid and too modern for my purpose; and I would play down the famous virtues of 'precision' and 'clarity'—virtues indeed, but effects rather than causes. I would, rather, enumerate a few mental and moral traits which have been fostered and diffused among the whole population by the accidents of history. I can claim at least that these national traits are not mutually incompatible.

1. *The Gift of Assimilation*

A biological and spiritual impulse to assimilate heterogeneous and

---

15 This and the preceding quotation are taken from the *Vie de Mallarmé*, by Henri Mondor, vol. I

dissimilar elements and to integrate them into a whole,—an impulse which has been at work from the Middle Ages down to our own day. The French have always welcomed men of different origins from their own. The newcomers, for their part, have found here a milieu favourable to thought and art, and a common life pulsating with a rapid but stable rhythm. And France has made them her own. How describe the Classical Movement without reference to Lully, a Florentine, jabbering broken French? The Neo-Classics of our own time have as their master Jean Moréas, whose real name was Papadiamantopoulos, an Athenian educated in German universities, and who as a young man was a specialist in Romance language and literature, and wrote pastiches of Guillaume de Machaut. The most moving paintings of the Ile-de-France countryside are signed by Sisley and Pissarro;—but Sisley was an Englishman, and Pissarro a Jew from the Caribbean, of Portuguese extraction. None of the Symbolists were at heart closer to French folklore than Francis Viélé-Griffin; his poetry reflects the sunlight of Touraine;—but Viélé-Griffin's family had emigrated to France from the United States. In recent anthologies, of whatever tendency, several pages are always reserved for Guillaume Apollinaire, whose real name was Wilhelm Apollinaris Kostrowitzki. It is beginning to be considered scandalous to ignore O. V. de L. Milosz, a Lithuanian, nationalised French. And France has just lost Bergson.

2. A Sense of Balance and Proportion

A feeling for balance and proportion, in thought and its expression. We must be careful not to confuse this with a timid preference for the *juste milieu*, the happy mean. A sense of balance may be present, or at least the search for it, in life's most extreme situations,—in Nerval's madness, for instance, or at least in the account of it he has left behind. It is the result of a victory in the spiritual domain; it is ground conquered which may always be lost again. It is due less to chance or to grace from on high than to sustained effort and extreme concentration. In the work of an artist, the result is the elimination of all vagueness, all confusion, and all unassimilable inconsistencies. The creators of the masterpieces in sculpture and architecture which were produced in France from the Middle Ages onwards had this instinct, and their works, which owe nothing, or very little, to the Greeks and the Romans, yet possess some of the features we think of as essentially "classical." The sense of balance is born of a special concentration of the faculties, and is expressed in many ways, some of rare subtlety. It proceeds from an instinct which lies deep in the French psyche. Historians who have searched for its origins and the influences which nurtured it have nothing to show but guess-work—pure conjectures. It is a national trait whose origin remains a mystery.

3. *A Talent for Self-Expression*

This ability is noticeable at every degree of the social scale, in the man in the street as much as in the artist. It would appear that these two share the belief that happiness consists in giving expression to thought, in forms both subtle and precise, and always with grace and style. The language which has evolved in the course of centuries reflects this talent in its structure and in its basic characteristics, and especially in its syntax, which defines the relations of the parts to each other, and especially to the sentence as a whole. A French sentence unfolds like a painting or a piece of music, but the similarity to painting is the closer; its musical flow seems to be drawn or painted,—with an arabesque-like movement. "The first things," said Corot in his old age, "is the drawing; then come the values; colour comes last." It is true of course that France has had great colourists, and great impressionists,—another instance of the diversity of her traditions. She stands at the meeting of the ways, and it is from the North, from the Flemish provinces, that the magical enchantment of colour comes.

This passion for form and beauty in style is not without its dangers. It may obstruct communication with what Goethe called "the Mothers."[16] An artist captivated by the beauty of the material world, a thinker intoxicated by the pleasure of organising ideas, may gradually lose touch with the essential, which in both cases is spiritual. Then, each of them may come to mistake for his true self the relatively superficial layers of his consciousness, where the intellect, clear and cold, and *Animus,* the spirit of controversy, hold sway. But this sort of distraction, in which the deepest and noblest faculties are allowed to sleep, is never found in the genuine artist, though occasionally one meets it in a painter of the second rank, or an intellectual, or a man of limited culture. For authentic French realism never stops short at mere appearances: it would be a mistake to look for it among the writers who chose the Realist label. The constant, unremitting attention to things as they are is a graver and more exacting state of mind than can be imagined by a hurried and

---

16 Goethe's "*Mères*"

superficial observer who, armed with an "idealist" philosophy, disdains appearances. It is the result of a desire to find presences in things, and these ineffable presences are what he seeks to clothe in material forms possessing a magical power of communication. This is a mystical aspiration on the part of the French artist, who is, notwithstanding, an eminently self-controlled and well-integrated human being. His mysticism goes hand in hand with self-mastery; he remains at all times calm and in control. His creations reflect his purpose and his goal. He pursues his tireless contemplation of men and things until he glimpses a unity which embraces them all,—the *ténébreuse et profonde unité* of Charles Baudelaire. He is not the man to imagine that the spirit can reside elsewhere than in what exists, lives and moves before his eyes.

* * * * * *

These three traits—a genius for assimilation, a sense of proportion, and a passion for self-expression—work together with the maximum effect in a man who has learnt the art of living, and can discern and appreciate fine nuances. Or rather, these same gifts are the condition of a wisdom, hammered out and constantly modified in contact with life, the supreme example of which is that of the philosopher eternally to be revered who bore the name: Michel de Montaigne. A practical wisdom such as this, with a style all its own, could not exist elsewhere than in a society with a passionate interest in the human condition. It must be conceded that France has become in the course of time,—but the tendency was manifest even before the Renaissance,—the most fully human of nations. I am not suggesting that the Frenchman feels closer to his fellow men than men of other races do, nor that charity towards the whole human race, the *caritas humani generis*, is more widespread in France than elsewhere. The simple fact is that the French have lived in close contact with other men and have studied them intently. In France, more completely than elsewhere, man has attained a knowledge of himself. All our literature bears witness to the fact: it is indeed "a long discourse on man," as Jacques Rivière said. In the old French tongue, before the invasion of Greek and Latin words, there was an exceptional number of verbs defining the different shades of feeling and judgment. The Christian mystics were also good psychologists;[17] for them as much as for others the art of living was important. And from the twelfth century onwards, before ever the sculptors started to grace their works with

17 See the anthology, *Mystiques de France*, published by Daniel-Rops (1958).

"urbanity" and "elegance," one senses the concern of their creators with human nature in all its variety and complexity.

The French and the Classical Renaissance

I am convinced that the close contact with other men, and the knowledge of them that they had acquired, is the reason why the French assimilated so easily and so successfully the writings of the Greeks and the Romans. Sometimes mistaking their original meaning, as they did with Plato and Aristotle, but taking them to their hearts, they "gallicised" them, as someone has said. It was their way of humanising them. From the time of Rabelais and Ronsard, these truths, this rediscovered learning, this timeless beauty of universal import, excited them as if it had been a memory long forgotten and suddenly rediscovered. In Homer and Plutarch, Virgil and Seneca, they discovered, as in a mirror, their own portrait, but also the portrait of all mankind. We have not sufficiently reflected on the conditions which made possible the revival of part of the Greco-Roman heritage in Western Europe. There had to be a people capable of taking it to their hearts, of transmitting it to others, and of becoming a crucible from which new forms might emerge.

French Humanism: the Instinct for the Universal

For the French have an instinct for the universal. This people of mixed race and blood has accepted and integrated the potentialities of their own nature, and those of human nature in general. This product of the most extreme ethnic diversity has been slowly composing from their experience the universal image of man. The French mind has never been shut in on itself, confined within its own particularities. Whether it be the rationalism of the eighteenth century *philosophes*, who hoped to prove that human reason is always and everywhere the same, or the humanism of the Classical authors, who sought to include in their works the largest possible number of human types, or again the humanism of the Christian thinkers, for whom humanism is first and foremost an ideal, to be realised in a communion established between persons of different colour, race, or creed, one always finds the individual transcended, and writers groping for the general, the universal.

Now the idea of the universal is an abstraction. It is a generalisation which the intellect deduces from what is shared in common by a number of concrete examples, and which the thinker tries to make as wide and inclusive as possible. The temptation to which French thinkers are exposed is to imagine that there are forms and formulas which exhaust all possibilities, and that one can define and describe human nature in a series of equations. If they have sometimes succumbed to this temptation, the fault is in part that of the Classical theorists with their optimistic belief in common sense as "the most widely shared quality there is." But in its most authentic form, faith in a common essence shared by all mankind never strays far from concrete man; man as he is in time and space. This idea is not a category of thought but the disposition of a mind capable of a sympathetic understanding of the dissimilar, heterogeneous, particular elements of which mankind is made. That is as much as to say that it exists in man simply as desire, as aspiration,—the desire to participate in the universal, and, by a privilege which belongs to art—for by its nature philosophy is confined to abstractions—to express it in its permanence and truth.

Ramuz was one day contrasting the poet Mistral with Cézanne,—the former too preoccupied, as he thought, with *farandoles*, while the genius of the latter, he contended, consisted in the ability to convey the universal in every thing envisioned. And he drew a moral from this contrast. "The Regional school," he said, "looks for the shock of surprise in the accident, while I prefer to find it in the essence. The Regionalists are obsessed with differences; I am interested in resemblances."[18]

Barrès on the French Genius

I will now quote a passage by Barrès:

> For a long time I had been exploring the idea of myself by introspection, the method of the poets and mystics; so once again I started on my way through the soft unresisting sands; but this time, at the end of my descent I came to rest in the collectivity of the French nation . . . Something eternal lives in us. We have nothing even that is conditioned by the dead. All the great teachers of the past whom I loved so much . . . believed in an independent reason, existing in each one of us and enabling us to discern the truth. A strange idea indeed, that the individual with his puny intelligence should be capable of grasping the laws governing the universe! We must be more modest! We do not pick and choose our thoughts; they

18 C.-F. Ramuz: *L'exemple de Cézanne* (vol. XI of his *Oeuvres complètes*)

are reactions conditioned by ancient physiological patterns. Our convictions, together with the arguments with which we buttress them, are dictated by the milieu into which we have been born. There is no such thing as a "personal" idea. On the contrary, all our ideas, including the most original, all our opinions, including those on the most abstract questions, together with the sophisms of the most grotesque metaphysical systems, are corporate reactions; they come ineluctably to all those who are endowed with a similar physical constitution and are bombarded with the same sights and sounds. Our reason is a queen, but a queen in chains; she is *bound* to set our feet in the footsteps of our ancestors.

But as we realise the extremity of our humiliation, a wonderful peace descends upon us, and we joyfully accept our slavery,—the slavery of being the prolongation of our fathers and mothers.

It is not enough to say that the dead think and speak in us; we must add that untold generations constitute a single living soul . . . . We are like a house in which the furniture has been rearranged; the foundations remain unchanged, the original masonry is intact; it is still the same house. The man who lets these incontrovertible facts sink deep into his mind will never again claim that his thoughts, his feelings, and his resolves are better than his father's and his mother's. No; he will whisper softly to himself: 'I am them.'

Immense consequences in every sphere of his life will follow from this realisation. Blessed resignation! Delicious ecstasy! The individual he thought he was melts away, to be reconstituted in the race and the nation, as they stretch back through the centuries, death-defying![19]

Raymond on Barrès: Man not a Prisoner of the Past

A fine page—and a decadent conclusion!

It is indeed true that our reason is something quite different from an omnipotent queen; also, that a man is never as alone as he likes to think. The presence of the dead within us, the inhabitants of this Celtic land of the West, is a certainty more than twice a thousand years old: the age-old reactions of the typical peasant can only be explained by

---

19 M. Barrès: *Le deux novembre en Lorraine.*

the ceaseless pressure of the generations past on the living. But Barrès is quite wrong to assert that we are captives in our own land,—the
prisoners of our forebears. If we return far enough back into the mists
of time, national and family structures melt away; their countless roots
plunge far beyond Lorraine, indeed far beyond the frontiers of France,
out among the teeming hordes of *"pagani,"* to disappear finally among
our anonymous ancestors, migrants from the North, the South, and the
West of Asia. What is more, though a collectivity develops biological
characteristics which become ever more accentuated with the passing of
the centuries, it is never shut in on itself; or, if it is, the barriers are easily
broken through.

I will never believe that a nation develops like a zoological species, producing nothing but creatures of a fixed type, wholly subject to
the law of their inheritance. The genius of a nation is not an essence,
a mysterious something, incapable of communicating with any but its
own progeny. Let us boldly assert, against the adherents of a romantic
faith in a national essence, that at the heart of a national literature there
is no house with doors and windows barred, as Barrès claims; no sacred
wood where lies a beautiful sleeping princess whom no foreigner can
ever wake. And for that matter, we must allow that among the children
brought up to believe that only members of the same race can understand one another, some will themselves remain forever unmoved by
the beautiful princess, whose charms, it is claimed, leave foreigners cold.

It will be said that I, like the Romantics, am making an unprovable
assumption. I do not deny it. But it is a matter of faith for me that the
magic of art, the appeal of human sympathy, the stirrings of the unconscious (which are collective, and perhaps in some cases universal), and
the bonds of love, which are nobler than all these, make it possible for a
man to escape from his self. And further, I believe that at any time the
collectivity can renounce the exclusive cult of its ancestors and the fas-
cination they exert upon their descendants. At any moment, they may
open their hearts to others, and play their part in the destiny of the human universe, of humanity as a whole. As Montaigne said: "Every man
bears within himself the entire form of the human condition."[20] Now for
philosophers, form is that which is opposed to matter; it is the principle
and pattern of all the possibles. The unique experiences, aptitudes, and
customs of every nation have determined its structures, and brought to
birth an unrepeatable "nature." All this is reflected in its language, the
mirror which reflects and the crucible which forms the national mind.

---

20 Montaigne, *Essays*, III, 2, "On Repentance" - Ed.

All this is indisputable; but even so, it may be that all the peoples of humanity have a common source, and also a common "form."

Epilogue

The Twentieth Century

Preface

What will be the verdict of History when it comes to judge the twentieth century? If attempted today, the answers might be as varied as the spheres of interest of the hypothetical respondents. The matter of history may be concerned with economics and trade, with scientific discoveries and technological advances, with social change and the migration of peoples, with educational practices and intellectual climate, or with any other field of human activity—such is the fragmentation into compartments of the discipline of history, and of all human learning

The question posed above, by the very use of the word 'history', might incline one to ponder an answer exclusively or chiefly in terms of political events. We are concerned here, however, with a *vue d'ensemble*. Let us, in this regard, cite the opinion of one writer, a distinguished English journalist, an admirer and commentator of Pascal:

> The half-century in which I have been consciously alive seems to me to have been quite exceptionally destructive, murderous and brutal. More people have been killed and terrorized, more driven from their homes and native places; more of the past's heritage has been destroyed, more lies propagated and base persuasion engaged in, with less compensatory achievement in art, literature and imaginative understanding, than

in any comparable period of history.[1]

The man-made crises and calamities we have passed through since those words were written, in our eyes unexampled in the history of mankind and of civilization, have been provoked, enflamed and aggravated by power-seeking factions of all stripes to the point at which people, and peoples, no longer trust governments today to do what is right and have largely given up any hope of their doing so.

It is tempting to think that it was not always thus.

In the 1920s the Great War was held to be, for a time, 'the war to end wars', and hope was high. One writer, who emerged from the war a household name, expressed the hopes of the time in Europe and the Western World in these moving terms:

> The morning freshness of the world-to-be intoxicated us. We were wrought up with ideas inexpressible and vaporous, but to be fought for. We lived many lives in those whirling campaigns, never sparing ourselves: yet when we achieved and the new world dawned, the old men came out again and took our victory to re-make in the likeness of the former world they knew.[2]

Even twenty years later, after France had been subjugated and was in no state even to conceive such dreams, at the height of the German bombing attacks against Great Britain in that, for Britain, 'glorious summer' of 1940, hope had not been killed. An English social philosopher looked forward to the founding of a new, and juster, social order.

> We're not fighting to restore the past (he said in a radio broadcast); it was the past that brought us to this heavy hour; but we are fighting to rid ourselves and the world of the evil encumbrance of these Nazis so that we can plan and create a noble future for all our species.[3]

The 'world-to-be' and the 'noble future' fought for did not come to pass. And there is far less prospect today of their realization even in the

---

1 Malcolm Muggeridge, "What I Believe," *The Observer*, 26 June 1966

2 T.E. Lawrence, *Oriental Assembly*, IV. The Suppressed Introductory Chapter for *Seven Pillars of Wisdom* (London, Williams and Norgate, 1939), p. 142.

3 J.B. Priestley, *Postscripts* (London, Heinemann, 1940), p.33.

near or distant future.

The manner in which this historical question has up to now been discussed has focused attention only on the substance of history. The question has another facet: it is meant to have more important implications. By 'the verdict of History' we mean not only the judgements to be made and the conclusions to be drawn, but also the manner in which history is conceived and written.

For over 2,000 years, from Thucydides to the present time, History has been regarded, in the abstract, as a detached and veracious judge of past events and the men and women whose actions brought them about; and the historian as a researcher and writer who, despite his errors and frailties, has conscientiously tried, in the light of the facts known and discoverable, to arrive at the Truth. That concept of History and of the historian is still, today, very much honoured and observed in the practice. But it is not the sole practice: the verdict of some historians, as opposed to that of History, may well be distorted by political or other biases.

Every observer of tyrannical régimes, both past and present, is familiar with the 'philosophy' of history practised by their 'official' historians. The nature of totalitarian systems of government cannot be other: for the rulers, far from pretending to believe that they possess the 'truth', are concerned only to justify their policies and practices—if indeed they go so far—and to sanction the dissemination of ideas consistent with them, and forbid, under pain of torture and death, all other publications. (Criticism of orthodoxy is a challenge to their authority, which can be maintained only by the threat or use of massive physical coercion. Conflicting ideas stimulate people to think for themselves, who would come to see that the official 'line' is falsehood and deception.)

Intellectual repression is anathema to free peoples, and inimical to the traditions of western civilization, which has always regarded the witness to Truth as the noblest calling of man.

The search for Truth, and the fearless declaration of Truth, are only made possible by the protection and the cultivation of the spirit of free inquiry. It is to the moral credit of all in free societies—of individuals as of groups and institutions, no matter how much they may disagree at times with the results—that they not only tolerate free inquiry, if it is responsible, but actively foster the spirit that nourishes it; for they know that it is a calling dedicated to the interest of all.

A free people exercise their freedom not only for themselves but for others. "*Remonstrez à vostre roy les erreurs que congnoistrez, et ja-*

mais ne le conseillez ayant esgard à vostre profit particulier, car avecques le commun est aussy le propre perdu."[4]

There are two classes of people—or perhaps two branches of one class—for whom the pursuit of truth is their especial vocation and prerogative: the Artist and the Intellectual. In our day, the intellectual is predominantly the university teacher. He knows the indissoluble bond that weds truth and morality eternally. For him—the professor, the scholar, the teacher—all learning, all teaching, all scholarship and research, are founded and repose, not distantly or incidentally, but directly and immediately upon moral principle. "*Le premier trait de la corruption des moeurs c'est le bannissement de la vérité.*"[5]

It may seem that we have been concerned with ideals, and have wandered far from the practical business of daily life or from the matters of history. Yes, ideals indeed; but wander, not in the least: for the ideal and the individual's life, the ideal and national life, are intimately related in every society of free men. The more honoured the ideal, the freer the society, and the better, and juster, that society is. The ideal is the very foundation-stone of the edifice of western civilization, and must remain so if civilization is to endure, if men would remain or become free.

The consciousness of their relatedness is one of the especial distinctions of French literature, remarked upon by nearly all the writers in this volume; it is a marked characteristic of all great French writers in whose works the ideal is seen as rooted in the reality of the human condition. In no particular is this characteristic more in evidence than

---

4 "Point out to your king [or: ruler, government] whatever errors you see, and never advise him with a mind to your personal profit, for with the common good will your own be ruined." (Rabelais, *Gargantua*, ch. 46.)

5 "The first stage in the corruption of morals is the banishing of truth." (Montaigne, *Essais*, II, 18.) No human group, no men or women, understand this truth more lucidly that the dissident writers and intellectuals of the former Soviet Union and Eastern Europe. Or of present-day China, North Korea, Burma, Iran, Syria, Cuba, Venezuela... the list goes on. We in the West do not risk the same dangers if we dissent publicly. Yet the citizenry are so uninformed and complacent, especially in the English-speaking countries, that they do not see the menace lurking behind the concept and practice of 'political correctness', and even of 'human rights', movements espoused by minorities, promoted and funded by governments, to advance their interests at the expense of the majority—and of intellectual freedom. We today, however, who are the heirs and beneficiaries of the standard-bearers of the Truth of the past, bear for that reason a responsibility not to be shirked—yet which is shirked constantly. Some universities are hotbeds of agitation by minorities. Scandals against intellectual freedom, supported by administrations, occur while professors and whole faculties either side with the administrations or cower in silence.

in their concept of man. It is when the concept of man becomes debased and corrupted that the atrocities that have been perpetrated in this century become possible. A personal witness has written:

> I became acquainted with the last stage of that corruption in my second concentration camp, Auschwitz. The gas chambers of Auschwitz were the ultimate consequence of the theory that man is nothing but the product of heredity and environment—or, as the Nazis liked to say, of 'Blood and Soil.' I am absolutely convinced that the gas chambers of Auschwitz, Treblinka, and Maidanek were ultimately prepared not in some Ministry or other in Berlin, but rather at the desks and in the lecture halls of nihilistic scientists and philosophers.[6]

What an infinite moral distance separates such academic abstractions, with their evil consequences, from the tradition and spirit of French literature, as from the beliefs of the persecuted dissidents of the former Soviet Union and other, all too real, repressive régimes. The traditional credo of the French writer and intellectual may be summed up in the words of Albert Schweitzer: "Wherever there is lost the consciousness that every man is an object of concern for us just because he is a man, civilization and morals are shaken, and the advance to fully developed inhumanity is only a question of time."[7]

If a special epilogue to this volume has been deemed necessary, it is because the twentieth century has witnessed a progressive degeneration of intellectual integrity. Julien Benda was one of the first writers of Western Europe to declaim against it, in his landmark essay, *La Trahison des clercs*. Benda attributes this degeneration to the practice by many artists and intellectuals of prostituting their talents in the interest of a political or national passion. What has made this prostitution unique to the twentieth century is the fact that it has been carried on consciously and with self-justification, and elevated to a status equal to, or higher

---

6 Viktor E. Frankl, *The Doctor and the Soul* (New York, Knopf, 1966), p. xxi. There was nothing new in this conviction of Frankl's. As far back as 1680 Thomas Hobbes stated his belief that the ultimate cause of the Civil Wars in England was to be found in the teaching in the universities of political theory derived from Aristotle, Plato, Seneca and the Greek and Latin historians.

7 Albert Schweitzer, *The Philosophy of Civilization*: I. "The Decay and the Restoration of Civilization" (London, A. & C. Black, 1950), p.24.

than, the cause of Truth. It has sought to substitute the Temporal for the Spiritual, and to endow the Temporal with the same transcendent value.[8]

By what they did, the artists and intellectuals castigated by Benda helped to prepare the Second World War and the social and political evils that followed upon it. Benda wrote before the war, but he could not have been surprised by what it produced.[9] Simone Weil, that tormented and unhappy genius, wrote during the war the two articles included here; and in them she blamed French writers and intellectuals for the disasters that befell France. We who have lived in the aftermath of that war have had to contend with the existence of a vast and powerful State which threatened the continuity of Western Civilization and with it the freedoms, the virtues and the principles which created and sustained it. With the collapse, and then the radical transformation of the Soviet Union into numerous independent nation-states, it is not clear whether the struggle endured by the West was also too much for it and saw the gradual erosion of the very qualities and principles it sought to defend and protect.

The collapse of the Soviet Union changes nothing in terms of the thesis propounded here. What we can state with some degree of certainty is that man's nature seems to contain more than mere seeds of a force which can only thrive at the cost of others' suffering. Oppression— political, social, moral and intellectual oppression—would seem to be more the norm of human existence in many regions of the world than freedom, tolerance, justice, kindness and good humour.

We have only to recall the Rushdie outrage to convince ourselves of that. Oppression in the old Soviet Union was carried out in the name of the State. The proclamation of the death sentence by the late Ayatollah Khomeini, ruler of Iran, a fundamentalist Islamic state, upon Salman Rushdie for a supposed slur against Islam in a book—and Rushdie is the

---

8 The English-speaking world is not exempt from this taint. During the past quarter-century we have witnessed numerous efforts by some academic historians to deliberately distort historical events in order to present an interpretation in conformity to a 'truth' pre-determined by the writer's political ideology. See, for example, R.J. Maddox, *The New Left and the Origins of the Cold War* (Princeton, Princeton University Press, 1973) and reviews in various journals.

9 A relatively recent book, *French Literary Fascism*, by David Carroll (Princeton University Press, 1995) studies the emergence in France of a group of writers—among whom Brasillach, Drieu la Rochelle, Drumont and Céline (who was 'excused' by Gide)—who preached a xenophobic idea of France in which anti-semitism played an important role.

citizen of another country at that—was made in the name of an offended militant religious extremism. If such conduct on the part of nations is to become the norm in a world running amok, the intellectual and moral virtues of French Literature will be more than ever necessary, and the integrity of the writer, artist and intellectual must be defended with an uncompromising and inflexible resolve.

If the French writer was in no spiritual state in 1940 to express hope for the future political and social landscape, he redeemed himself later in the war and in the post-war generation by forging a new image and philosophy of man which, by virtue of its reversion to its humanistic roots and traditions, had a profound influence on the West's resistance to evil and its support of dissident writers and intellectuals throughout the world.[10]

The creed of the artist of integrity in such a world as we have depicted has been well expressed by many a writer. But the statement which seems most faithfully to incarnate these traditional ideals of France and French literature, in the political sphere, is that given by Albert Camus in his eloquent Nobel Prize speech. Camus it was who, in a direct national context, gave his definition of love of country, which has a lesson for those who are tempted to subscribe to the idea of 'My country, right or wrong!', or to any form of nationalism, despite the manifest evils which this perverse dogma has always brought about. Camus is replying to a former friend, a German, who had accused him of not loving his country.

> No, I do not love my country, if not loving means denouncing what is unjust in the thing we love, if it means insisting that what we love should come up to the noblest conception we have of it.[11]

Equally, many French literary figures might be quoted to refute religious fanaticism and all the evils perpetrated in its service. Of the moderns I could find inspiration and hope in Mauriac. However, the writer we have chosen to conclude this Preface is Montesquieu. Here he expounds a principle which, in our pragmatic and materialistic age, seems impossibly idealistic. All the more reason, then, to ponder it care-

---

10 We think, for example, and especially, of Mauriac, St. Exupéry, Malraux, and Camus.

11 Albert Camus, *Lettres à un ami allemand* (Paris, Gallimard, 1948), p.20. (Editor's translation.)

fully.

> If I knew something that was useful to me and harmful to my family, I would cast it from my mind. If I knew something that was useful to my family, but not to my country, I would strive to forget it. If I knew something useful to my country and which was harmful to Europe and to the human race, I would consider it a crime.[12]

If this principle seems to us today unattainably idealistic we have only to remind ourselves of the decision made by Aung San Suu Kyi to leave home and family in England to serve her people in Burma. Suu Kyi herself has written of the goal she is devoting her life to in these terms:

> Of the four Buddhist virtues conducive to the happiness of laymen, *saddha*, confidence in moral, spiritual and intellectual values, is the first. To instil such confidence, not by an appeal to the passions but through intellectual conviction, into society which has long been wracked by distrust and uncertainty is the essence of the Burmese revolution for democracy. It is a revolution which moves for changes endorsed by universal norms of ethics. The quest for democracy in Burma is the struggle of a people to live whole, meaningful lives as free and equal members of the world community. It is part of the unceasing human endeavour to prove that the spirit of man can transcend the flaws of his own nature.[13]

Only people who have been forced to digest the bitter fruits of tyranny in their daily lives for years can write of the freedoms promised by democracy in such accents that keep alive the spirit of resistance and of hope. We in the West are grown smug and complacent in our relatively free lives, and have little notion how easily the subtle agents of a conformity imposed in the name of the citizens' well-being or security can effect their insidious schemes.

---

12 Montesquieu, *Cahiers* (Paris, Editions Grasset, 1941), pp. 9-10. (Editor's translation.)

13 Aung San Suu Kyi, *Freedom from Fear*, p.178-79.

14
The Treason of the Intellectuals

by

Julien Benda

Excerpts from Julien Benda: *La Trahison des clercs* (Paris: Grasset, 1927), published in English translation as *The Great Betrayal* by Richard Aldington (London, Routledge, 1928). Routledge is owned by Taylor and Francis Books UK. They could not trace the owner of the copyright. This text is excerpted and edited by the Editor.

Author's Foreword

*T*olstoi relates that when he was in the Army he saw one of his brother officers strike a man who fell out from the ranks during a march. Tolstoi said to him:-

"Are you not ashamed to treat a fellow human being in this way? Have you not read the Gospels?"

The other officer replied: "And have you not read Army Orders?"

This retort will always be thrown back at the spiritual man who tries to take the direction of the material. To me it seems a very wise one. Those who lead men to the conquest of material things have no need of justice and charity.

Nevertheless I think it important that there should be men—even if they are scorned—who urge their fellow beings to other religions than the religion of the material. Now, those who should play this part (to whom I have given the name of "clerks" in the medieval sense of the word) have not only ceased to do so, but are playing an exactly contrary part. Most of the influential moralists of the past fifty years in Europe, particularly the men of letters in France, call upon mankind to sneer at the Gospel and to read Army Orders.

This new teaching seems to me all the more deserving of serious attention because it is addressed to a humanity which of its own volition is now established in materialism with a decisiveness hitherto unknown.

I

We are to consider those passions termed political, owing to which men rise up against other men, the chief of which are racial passions, class passions and national passions. Those persons who are most determined to believe in the inevitable progress of the human species, especially in its indispensable movement towards more peace and love, cannot deny that during the past century these passions have attained—and day by day increasingly so—in several most important directions, a degree of perfection hitherto unknown in history.

In the first place they affect a large number of men they never before affected. When, for example, we study the civil wars which convulsed France in the sixteenth century, and even those at the end of the eighteenth century, we are struck by the small number of persons whose minds were really disturbed by these events. While history, up to the nineteenth century, is filled with long European wars which left the great majority of people completely indifferent, apart from the material losses they themselves suffered, it may be said that to-day there is scarcely a mind in Europe which is not affected—or thinks itself affected—by a racial or class or national passion, and most often by all three. The same progress seems to have taken place in the New World, while immense bodies of men in the Far East, who seemed to be free from these impulses, are awakening to social hatred, the party system, and the national spirit insofar as it implies the will to humiliate other men. To-day political passions have attained a *universality* never before known.

They have also attained *coherence*. Thanks to the progress of communication and, still more, to the group spirit, it is clear that the holders of the same political hatred now form a compact impassioned mass, every individual of which feels himself in touch with the infinite numbers of others, whereas a century ago such people were comparatively out of touch with each other and hated in a "scattered" way. This is singularly striking with respect to the working classes who, even in the middle of the nineteenth century, felt only a scattered hostility for the opposing class, attempted only dispersed efforts at war (such as striking in one town, or one union), whereas today they form a closely-woven fabric of hatred from one end of Europe to the other. It may be asserted that these coherences will tend to develop still further, for the will to group is one of the most profound characteristics of the modern world, which even in the most unexpected domains (for instance, the domain of thought) is more and more becoming the world of leagues, of "unions" and of "groups." Is it necessary to say that the passion of the individual is strengthened by feeling itself in proximity to these thousands of similar passions? Let me add that the individual bestows a mystic personality on the association of which he feels himself a member, and gives it a religious adoration, which is simply the deification of his own passion, and no small stimulus to its intensity.

The coherence just described might be called a surface coherence, but there is added to it a coherence of essence. For the very reason that the holders of the same political passion form a more compact, impassioned group, they also form a more *homogeneous*, impassioned group, in which individual ways of feeling disappear and the zeal of each member more and more takes on the colour of the others. In France, for instance, one cannot but be struck by the fact that the enemies of the democratic system (I am speaking of the mass, not the highest points) display a passion which has little variety, shows very slight differences in different persons. How little this mass of hatred is weakened by personal and original manners of hating—one might almost say that this passion itself is obedient to "democratic levelling down"! How much more uniformity is shown now than a hundred years ago by the emotions known as anti-semitism, anti-clericalism, and socialism, in spite of the immense number of varieties in the last-named! And do not those who are subject to these emotions now all tend *to say the same thing*? Political passions, as passions, seem to have attained the habit of discipline; they seem to obey a word of command even in the manner they are felt. It is easy to see what increase of strength they acquire thereby.

With some of these passions the increase in homogeneousness is accompanied by an increased *precision*. For instance, we all know that a hundred years ago socialism was a strong but vague passion with the great mass of its supporters. But to-day socialism has more closely defined the object it wishes to attain, has determined the exact point where it means to strike its adversary and the movement it intends to create in order to succeed. The same progress may be observed in the antidemocratic movement. And we all know that hatred becomes stronger by becoming more precise.

There is another sort of perfecting of political passions. Throughout history until our own days I see these passions acting intermittently, blazing up and then subsiding. I see that the undoubtedly terrible and numerous explosions of class and race hatred were followed by long periods of calm, or at least of somnolence. Wars between nations lasted for years, but not hatred—even if we may say that it existed. Today we have only to look every morning at any daily paper and we shall see that political hatreds do not cease for a single day. At best some of them are silent a moment for the benefit of one among them which suddenly claims all the subject's strength. This is the period of "national unions," which do not in the very least herald in the reign of love, but merely of a general hatred which for the moment dominates partial hatreds. Today political passions have acquired *continuity*, which is so rare a quality in all feelings.

* * * * * *

I created him to be spiritual in his flesh; and now he has become carnal even in the spirit. (Bossuet, *Elévations*, VII, 3.)

In all that I have said hitherto I have been considering only masses, whether bourgeois or proletarian, kings, ministers, political leaders, all that portion of the human species which I shall call "the laymen," whose whole function consists essentially in the pursuit of material interests, and who, by becoming more and more solely and systematically realist, have in fact only done what might be expected of them.

Side by side with this humanity whom the poet has described in a phrase—*O curvae in terram animae et celestium inanes*[1]—there existed until the last half century another, essentially distinct humanity, which to a certain extent acted as a check upon the former. I mean that class of man whom I shall designate "the clerks," by which term I mean all those whose activity essentially is *not* the pursuit of practical aims, all those who seek their joy in the practice of an art or a science or meta-physical speculation, in short in the possession of non-material advan-tages, and hence in a certain manner say: "My kingdom is not of this world." Indeed, throughout history, for more than two thousand years until modern times, I see an uninterrupted series of philosophers, men of religion, men of literature, artists, men of learning (one might say al-most all during this period), whose influence, whose lives, were in direct opposition to the realism of the multitudes. To come down specifically to the political passions—the "clerks" were in opposition to them in two ways. They were either entirely indifferent to these passions, and, like Leonardo da Vinci, Malebranche, Goethe, set an example of attachment to the purely disinterested activity of the mind and created a belief in the supreme value of this form of existence; or, gazing as moralists upon the conflict of human egotisms, like Erasmus, Kant, Renan, they preached, in the name of humanity or justice, the adoption of an abstract prin-ciple superior to and directly opposed to these passions. Although these "clerks" founded the modern State to the extent that it dominates indi-vidual egotism, their activity undoubtedly was chiefly theoretical, and they were unable to prevent the laymen from filling all history with the noise of their hatreds and their slaughters; but *the "clerks" did prevent the laymen from setting up their actions as a religion, they did prevent them from thinking themselves great men as they carried out these activi-ties.* It may be said that, thanks to the "clerks," humanity did evil for two thousand years, but honoured good. This contradiction was an honour to the human species, and formed the rift whereby civilization slipped

---

1 "O grovelling souls! And void of things divine!" (Gifford). Persius, *Satires*, II, 61.Ed.

into the world.

Now at the end of the nineteenth century a fundamental change occurred: *the "clerks" began to play the game of political passions.* The men who had acted as a check on the realism of the people began to act as its stimulators. This upheaval in the moral behaviour of humanity operated in several ways.

First: the "clerks" have adopted political passions.

First of all the "clerks" have adopted political passions. No one will deny that throughout Europe today the immense majority of men of letters and artists, a considerable number of scholars, philosophers, and "ministers" of the divine, share in the chorus of hatreds among races and political factions. Still less will it be denied that they adopt national passions. Doubtless, the names of Dante, Petrarch, d'Aubigné, certain apologists of Caboche or preachers of the Ligue will suffice to show that certain "clerks" did not wait for our era to indulge in these passions with all the strength of their souls. But, upon the whole, these "clerks" of the forum were exceptions, at least among the great ones. If, in addition to the great masters named above, I evoke the phalanx of Thomas Aquinas, Roger Bacon, Galilei, Rabelais, Montaigne, Descartes, Racine, Pascal, Leibniz, Kepler, Huyghens, Newton, and even Voltaire, Buffon and Montesquieu (to mention only a few), I think I may repeat that until our own days the men of thought or the honest men remained strangers to political passions, and said with Goethe: "Let us leave politics to the diplomats and the soldiers." Or if, like Voltaire, they took these passions into account, they adopted a critical attitude towards them, did not espouse them as passions. Or if, like Rousseau, Maistre, Chateaubriand, Lamartine, even Michelet, they did take these passions to heart, they did so with a generalizing of feeling, a disdain for immediate results, which in fact make the word "passions" incorrect. Today, . . . we have to admit that the "clerks" now exercise political passions with all the characteristics of passion—the tendency to action, the thirst for immediate results, the exclusive preoccupation with the desired end, the scorn for argument, the excess, the hatred, the fixed ideas. The modern "clerk" has entirely ceased to let the layman alone descend to the market place. The modern "clerk" is determined to have the soul of a citizen and to make vigorous use of it; he is proud of that soul; his literature is filled with his contempt for the man who shuts himself up with art or science and takes no interest in the passions of the State. He is violently on the side of Michelangelo crying shame upon Leonardo da Vinci for his indifference to the misfortunes of Florence, and against the master of the Last Supper when he replied that indeed the study of beauty occupied his whole heart. The time has long past by since Plato demanded that the philosopher should be bound in chains in order to compel him to take an interest in the State. To have as his function the pursuit of eternal things and yet to believe that he becomes greater by concerning himself with the State—that is the view of the modern "clerk." It is as natural as it is evident that this adhesion of the "clerks" to the passions of the layman fortifies these passions in the hearts of the latter. In the first place, it abolishes the suggestive spectacle (which I mentioned above) of a race of men whose interests are set outside the practical world. And then especially, the "clerk," by adopting political passions, brings them the tremendous influence of his sensibility if he is an artist, of his persuasive power if he is a thinker, and in either case his moral prestige.

Before proceeding any further, I feel I ought to make myself clear on certain points:

(a) I have been talking of the *whole* of the men of thought anterior to our own age. When I say that the "clerks" in the past opposed the realism of the laymen and that the "clerks" of today are in its service, I am considering each of these groups as a whole; I am contrasting one general characteristic with another. This means that I shall not feel myself contradicted by a reader who takes the pains to point out to me that so-and-so in the former group was a realist, and that so-and-so in the second is not, so long as this reader is obliged to admit that as a whole each of these groups does manifest the characteristic I have indicated. And also, when I speak of a single "clerk," I am thinking of his work in its chief characteristic, *i.e.* in that part of his teaching which dominates all the rest, even if the remainder sometimes contradicts this dominant teaching. This means that I do not consider that I ought to refrain from looking upon Malebranche as a master of liberal thought because a few lines of his *Morale* seem to be a justification of slavery, or upon Nietzsche as a moralist of war because the end of *Zarathustra* is a manifesto of fraternity which outdoes the Gospels. And I see the less reason for doing so, since Malebranche as a defender of slavery and Nietzsche as a humanitarian have had no influence at all, and my subject is the influence which the "clerks" have had in the world, and not what they were in themselves.

(b) Some will object to me: "How can you treat men like Barrès and Péguy as "clerks" and blame them for lacking the true spirit of "clerks" when they are so openly men of action, with whom political thought is obviously occupied solely with the needs of the present hour, solely spurred on by the events of the day, while the former scarcely ever gave expression to his political thought except in newspaper articles?" I reply, that this thought, which in truth is practically nothing but a form of immediate action, is given out by its authors as the fruits of the highest speculative intellectual activity, the result of the most truly philosophical meditation. Barrès and Péguy would never have consented to be looked upon as mere polemical writers, even in their polemical works. These men, who indeed are not "clerks," gave themselves out to be "clerks" and were considered as such. (Barrès gave himself out to be a thinker who condescended to the arena.) And it is precisely as such that they enjoy a particular prestige among men of action. In this study my subject is not the "clerk" such as he is, but the "clerk" such as he is considered to be and as he acts upon the world in that capacity.

I shall make the same answer with regard to M. Maurras and the other instructors of the Action Française, of whom it will be said even more truly that they are men of action and that it is indefensible to cite them as "clerks." These men claim to carry out their action by virtue of a doctrine derived from a wholly objective study of history, from the exercise of the most purely scientific spirit. And they owe the special attention with which they are listened to by men of action entirely to this claim that they are *men of learning*, men who are fighting for a truth discovered in the austerity of the laboratory. They owe it to their pose as combative "clerks," but essentially as "clerks."

(c) Finally I should like to define my views on another point and to say that when the "clerk" descends to the market place I only consider that he is failing to perform his functions when he does so, like those I have mentioned, for the purpose of securing the triumph of a real-ist passion, whether of class, race or nation. When Gerson entered the pulpit of Notre-Dame to denounce the murderers of Louis d'Orléans; when Spinoza, at the peril of his life, went and wrote the words *Ultimi barbarorum* on the gate of those who had murdered the de Witts; when Voltaire fought for the Calas family; when Zola and Duclaux came for-ward to take part in a celebrated lawsuit (the Dreyfus affair); all these "clerks" were carrying out their functions as "clerks" in the fullest and noblest manner. They were the officiants of abstract justice and were sul-lied with no passion for a worldly object. Moreover, there exists a certain criterion by which we may know whether the "clerk" who takes public action does so in conformity with his true functions: it is that he is immediately reviled by the laymen, whose interests he thwarts (Socrates, Jesus). We may say beforehand that the "clerk" who is praised by the laymen is a traitor to his office.

Second: They bring their political passions into their activities as "clerks."

The "clerks" have not been content simply to adopt political passions, if by this one means that they have made a place for these passions side by side with the activities they are bound to carry on as "clerks." They have introduced these passions into those activities. They permit, they desire them to be mingled with their work as artists, as men of learning, as philosophers, to colour the essence of their work and to mark all its productions. And indeed never were there so many political works among those which ought to be the mirror of the disinterested intelligence.

You may refuse to be surprised by this in the case of poetry. We must not ask the poets to separate their works from their passions. The latter are the substance of the former, and the only question to ask is whether they write poems to express their passions or whether they hunt for passions in order to write poems. In either case one does not see why they should exclude national passion or the spirit of party from their vibrant material. Our political poets, who are not numerous however, have only followed the example of Virgil, Claudian, Lucan, Dante, d'Aubigné, Ronsard, and Hugo. Yet we cannot deny that political passion, as it is expressed by Claudel or d'Annunzio, a conscious and organized passion *lacking all simplicity*, coldly scornful of its adversary, a passion which in the second of these poets displays itself as so precisely political, so cunningly adapted to the profound cupidity of his compatriots and the exact point of weakness in the foreigner—we cannot deny, I say, that this political passion is something different from the eloquent generalities of the *Tragiques* of the *Année Terrible*. A work like *La Nave*, with its national plan as exact and practical as that of a Bismarck wherein the lyric gift is used to extol this practical character, seems to me something new in the history of poetry, even of political poetry. The result of this new departure on the minds of laymen may be judged by the present state of mind of the Italian people. But in our day the most remarkable example of the poets' applying their art to the service of political passions is that literary form which may be called "lyrical philosophy," the most brilliant symbol of which is the work of Barrès.

It begins by taking as its centres of vibration certain truly philosophical states of mind, such as pantheism, a loftily sceptical intellectualism, and then entirely devotes itself to serving racial passion and national feeling. Here the action of the lyric spirit is doubled by the prestige of the spirit of abstract thought. (Barrès admirably caught the appearance of that spirit—he stole the tool, a philosopher has said to him.) In France as elsewhere the "clerks" have thereby stimulated political passions among the laymen, at least in that very important section of them who read and believe that they think. Moreover, in regard to poets and especially the poet I have just named, it is difficult to know whether the lyrical impulse lends its aid to a genuine and preexisting political passion, or whether on the contrary this passion puts itself at the service of a lyrical impulse which is seeking inspiration. *Alius judex erit.* (Let another judge.)

But there are other "clerks" who introduce political passion into their works with a remarkable consciousness of what they are doing, in whom this derogation seems more worthy of notice than in the poets. I mean the novelists and dramatists, *i.e.* "clerks" whose function it is to portray in as objective a manner as possible the emotions of the human soul and their conflicts—a function which, as Shakespeare, Molière, and Balzac have proved, may be carried out with all the purity I have here assigned to it. One may show how this function has been more than ever perverted by its subjection to political ends by the example of many contemporary novelists, not because they scatter "tendentious" reflections throughout their narratives (Balzac constantly does so), but because instead of making their heroes feel and act in conformity with a true observation of human nature, they make them do so as the passion of the authors require. Shall I cite those novels where the traditionalist, whatever his errors, always finally displays a noble soul, whereas the character without religion inevitably, and in spite of all his efforts, is capable of none but vile actions? Or other novels in which the man of the people possesses every virtue, and vileness is the exclusive portion of the bourgeois? Or the novels where the author displays his compatriots in contact with foreigners and, more or less frankly, gives all moral superiority to his own people?

There is a two-fold evil in this proceeding. Not only does it considerably inflame political passion in the breast of the reader, but it deprives him of one of the most eminently civilizing effects of all works of art, *i.e.* that self-examination to which every spectator is impelled by a representation of human beings which he feels to be true and solely preoccupied with truth. From the point of view of the artist and of the value of his activity alone, this partiality indicates a great degradation. The value of the artist, the thing which makes him the world's high ornament, is that he *plays* human passions instead of living them, and that he discovers in this "play" emotion the same source of desires, joys and sufferings as ordinary men find in the pursuit of real things. Now, if this accomplished type of exuberant activity places itself at the service of the nation or of a class, if this fine flower of disinterestedness becomes utilitarian, then I say with the poet of the "*Vierge aux Rochers*" when the author of *Siegfried* exhales his last sigh: "The world has lost its import."

I have pointed out that certain "clerks" have put their activities as "clerks" at the service of political passions. These are the poets, the novelists, the dramatists, the artists, *i.e.* they are men who may be permitted to give passion, even wilful passion, a predominant place in their works. But there are other "clerks" in whom this derogation from the disinterested activity of the mind is far more shocking, "clerks" whose influence on the laymen is much more profound by reason of the prestige attached to their functions. I mean the historians. Here, as with the poets, the phenomenon is a new one on account of the point of perfection it has reached. Assuredly, humanity did not await our age to see History putting itself at the service of the spirit of party or of national passion. But I think I may assert that it has never seen this done with the same methodical spirit, the same intensity of consciousness which may be observed in German historians of the past half century and in the French Monarchists of the past twenty years. The case of the latter is the more remarkable since they belong to a nation which has acquired eternal honour in the history of human intelligence by explicitly condemning pragmatic history, and formulating, as it were, the charter of disinterested history through the works of Beaufort, Fréret, Voltaire, Thierry, Renan, Fustel de Coulanges. Yet the true novelty here is the admission of this spirit of partiality, the expressed intention to employ it as a legitimate method. "A true German historian," declares a German master, "should especially tell those facts which conduce to the grandeur of Germany." The same scholar praises Mommsen (who himself boasted of it) for having written a Roman history "which becomes a history of Germany with Roman names." Another (Treitschke) prided himself on his lack of "that anaemic objectivity which is contrary to the historical sense." Another (Guisebrecht) teaches that "Science must not soar beyond the frontiers, but be national, be German." Our Monarchists do not lag behind. Recently one of them, the author of a *History of France*, which tried to show that the French kings since Clovis were occupied in trying to prevent the war of 1914, defended the historian who presents the past from the point of view of the passions of his own time. By his determination in bringing this partiality to historical narrative the modern "clerk" most seriously derogates from his true function, if I am right in saying that his function is to restrain the passions of the laymen. Not only does he inflame the laymen's passions more cunningly than ever, not only does he deprive them of the suggestive spectacle of a man solely occupied by the thirst for truth, but he prevents the laymen from hearing speech different from that of the market place, speech (Renan's is perhaps the finest example) which, coming from the heights, shows that the most opposite passions are equally justified, equally necessary to the earthly State, and thereby incites every reader who has any capacity for getting outside himself to relax the severity of his passions, at least for a moment.

Let me say, however, that indeed men like Treitschke and his French equivalents are not historians; they are men of politics who make use of history to support a cause whose triumph they desire. Hence, it is natural that the master of their method should not be Lenain de Tillemont but Louis XIV, who threatened to withdraw Mezeray's pension if the historian persisted in pointing out the abuses of the old monarchy; or Napoleon, who ordered the chief of police to take measures for the history of France to be written in a manner favourable to his own throne. Nevertheless, the really cunning ones assume the mask of disinterestedness.

I believe that many of those whom I am here accusing of betraying their spiritual ministry, that disinterested activity which should be theirs by the mere fact of their being historians, psychologists, moralists, would reply to me as follows, if such a confession did not destroy their influence: "We are not in the least the servants of spiritual things; we are the servants of material things, of a political party, of a nation. Only, instead of serving it with the sword, we serve it with the pen. We are the *spiritual militia of the material.*"

Among those who ought to show the world an example of disinterested intellectual activity and who nevertheless turn their function to practical ends, I shall also mention the critics. Every one knows that innumerable critics today consider that a book is only good insofar as it serves the party which is dear to them, or as it manifests "the genius of the nation," or as it illustrates a political doctrine in harmony with their own political system, or for other reasons of the like purity. The modern "clerks," I said before, insist that the just shall be determined by the useful. They also want the useful to determine the beautiful, which is not one of their least originalities in history. Nevertheless, here again those who adopt such a form of criticism are not truly critics, but men of politics, who make criticism serve their practical designs. Here is a perfecting of political passion, the whole honour of which must be given to the moderns. Neither Pius XIV nor Napoleon apparently thought of using literary criticism in support of the social system in which they believed. This new departure has brought forth its fruits. For instance, if you assert with the French Monarchists that the democratic ideal is inevitably bound up with bad literature, you are dealing that ideal a real blow in a country like France, which has a real devotion to literature, at least among those who will consent to believe that Victor Hugo and Lamartine were mere scribblers.

But the most remarkable thing about the modern "clerk" in his desire to bring political passion into his work, is that he has done so in philosophy, more precisely, in metaphysics. It may be said that until the nineteenth century metaphysics remained the inviolate citadel of disinterested speculation. Among all forms of spiritual labour metaphysics best deserved the admirable tribute which a mathematician rendered the theory of numbers above all branches of mathematics, when he said: "This is the really pure branch of our science, by which I mean that it is unsullied by any contact with practical application." In fact thinkers free from any sort of earthly preference, like Plotinus, Thomas Aquinas, Descartes, Kant, and even thinkers strongly imbued with the superiority of their class or nation (like Plato and Aristotle), never thought of directing their transcendental speculations towards a demonstration of this superiority or the necessity of this adoption by the whole world. It has been said that the morality of the Greeks was national, but their metaphysics were universal. The Church itself, so often favourable to class or national interests in its morality, thinks only of God and Man in its metaphysics. It was reserved for our own age to see metaphysicians of the greatest eminence turning their speculations to the exaltation of their own countries and to the depreciation of other countries, fortifying the will to power of their compatriots with all the power of abstractive genius. Fichte and Hegel made the triumph of the German world the supreme and necessary end of the development of Being, and history has showed whether the action of these "clerks" had an effect on the hearts of their laymen. Let me hasten to add that this spectacle of patriotic metaphysics is provided by Germany alone. In France, even in this age of nationalist "clerks," we have not yet seen any philosopher (at least not one who is taken seriously) build up a metaphysical system to the glory of France. Neither August Comte nor Renouvier nor Bergson ever thought of making a French hegemony the necessary result of the world's development. Need I add what a degradation this has been for metaphysics, as it has been for art? It will be the eternal shame of the German philosophers to have transformed the patrician virgin who honoured the Gods into a harpy engaged in shrieking the glory of her children.

Third: The "clerks" have played the game of political passions by their doctrines.

But where the "clerks" have most violently broken with their tradition and resolutely played the game of the laymen in their eagerness to place themselves in the real, is by their doctrines, by the scale of values they have set up for the world. Those whose preaching for twenty centuries had been to humiliate the realist passions in favour of something transcendental, have set themselves (with a science and a consciousness which will stupefy history) to the task of making these passions and the impulses which ensure them, the highest of virtues, while they cannot show too much scorn for the existence which in any respect raises itself beyond the material. I shall now describe the principal aspects of this phenomenon.

A. The "clerks" praise attachment to the particular and denounce the feeling of the universal.

In the first place, the "clerks" have set out to exalt the will of men to feel conscious of themselves as distinct from others, and to proclaim as contemptible every tendency to establish oneself in a universal. With the exception of certain authors like Tolstoi and Anatole France, whose teaching moreover is now looked on with contempt by most of their colleagues, all the influential moralists of Europe during the past fifty years, Bourget, Barrès, Maurras, Péguy, d'Annunzio, Kipling,[2] the immense majority of German thinkers, have praised the efforts of men to feel conscious of themselves in their nation and race, to the extent that this distinguishes them from others and opposes them to others, and have made them ashamed of every aspiration to feel conscious of themselves as men in the general sense and in the sense of rising above ethnical aims. Those whose activity since the time of the Stoics had been devoted to preaching the extinction of national egotism in the interest of

2 A truer picture of Kipling and his ideas obtains today and would exclude his presence in this gallery. Ed.

an abstract and eternal entity, set out to denounce every feeling of this kind and to proclaim the lofty morality of that egotism. In our age the descendants of Erasmus, Montaigne, Voltaire, have denounced humanitarianism as a moral degeneration, nay, as an intellectual degeneration, in that it implies "a total absence of practical common sense"; for practical common sense has become the measure of intellectual values with these strange "clerks".

I should like to draw a distinction between humanitarianism as I mean it here—a sensitiveness to the abstract quality of what is human, to Montaigne's "whole form of (the) human condition"—and the feeling which is usually called humanitarianism, by which is meant the love for human beings existing in the concrete. The former impulse (which would more accurately be called humanism) is the attachment to a concept. It is a pure passion of the intelligence, implying no terrestrial love. It is quite easy to conceive of a person plunging into the concept of what is human without having the least desire even to see a man. This is the form assumed by love of humanity in the great patricians of the mind like Erasmus, Malebranche, Spinoza, Goethe, who all were men, it appears, not very anxious to throw themselves into the arms of their neighbours. The second humanitarianism is a state of the heart and therefore the portion of plebeian souls. It occurs among moralists in periods when lofty intellectual discipline disappears among them and gives way to sentimental exaltation, I mean in the eighteenth century (chiefly with Diderot) and above all in the nineteenth century, with Michelet, Quinet, Proudhon, Romain Rolland, Georges Duhamel. This sentimental form of humanitarianism and forgetfulness of its conceptual form explain the unpopularity of this doctrine with so many distinguished minds, who discover two equally repulsive commonplaces in the arsenal of political ideology. One of them is "the patriotic bore" and the other "the universal embrace."

The humanitarianism which holds in honor the abstract quality of what is human, is the only one which allows us to love *all* men. Obviously, as soon as we look at men in the concrete, we inevitably find that this quality is distributed in different quantities, and we have to say with Renan: "In reality one is *more or less* a man, *more or less* the son of God. . . I see no reason why a Papuan should be immortal." Modern equalitarians, by failing to understand that there can be no equality except in the abstract and that inequality is the essence of the concrete, have merely displayed the extraordinary vulgarity of their minds as well as their amazing political clumsiness.

Let me point out another and remarkable form of this extolling of particularism by the "clerks": the extolling of particular systems of morality and the scorn for universal morality. During the past half century a whole school, not only of men of action but of serious philosophers, has taught that a people should form a conception of its rights and duties from a study of its particular genius, its history, its geographical position, the particular circumstances in which it happens to be, and not from the commands of a so-called conscience of man in all times and places. Moreover, this same school teaches that a class should construct a scale of good and evil, determined by an inquiry into its particular needs, its particular aims, the particular conditions surrounding it, and should cease to encumber itself with such sensibilities as "justice in itself," "humanity in itself," and other "rags and tatters" of general morality. To-day with Barrès, Maurras, Sorel, even Durckheim, we are witnessing the complete bankruptcy among the "clerks" of that form of soul which, from Plato to Kant, looked for the notion of good in the heart of eternal and disinterested man. The example of Germany in 1914 shows the results of this teaching which exhorts a group of men to set themselves up as the sole judges of the morality of their actions, shows what deification of their appetites leads to, what codification of their violence, what tranquillity in carrying out their plans. One day perhaps we shall see the same thing throughout Europe exemplified by the bourgeois class, unless the doctrines of that class are turned against itself and we see it exemplified by the working classes.

I dare to say that the indignation of certain French moralists at the action of Germany in 1914 surprises me, when I reflect that some sixteen years earlier, during the famous "affair" which I have already mentioned, these moralists preached to their compatriots exactly the same doctrines, urging them to reject the concept of absolute justice, and to desire only a form of justice "adapted to France," to its particular genius, its particular history, its particular, eternal, and present needs. For the honour of these thinkers—I mean for the honour of their consistency—one likes to think that their indignation in 1914 was not the result of any moral conviction, but only of the desire to place the enemy of their nation in the wrong with a naïve universe.

This last-named activity of the "clerks" seems to me one of those which best display their determination and skill in serving the passions of the laymen. If a man exhorts his compatriots to recognize only a personal morality and to reject all universal morality, he is showing himself a master of the art of encouraging them to want to be distinct from all other men, *i.e.* of the art of perfecting national passion in them, at least in one of its aspects. The desire to take none but oneself as a judge of one's actions and to scorn every opinion of other people is undoubtedly a source of strength to a nation, as every exertion of pride is a source of strength to an institution, whose fundamental principle—whatever may be said to the contrary—is the assertion of an ego against a non-ego. What ruined Germany in the last war was not its "irritating arrogance," as is asserted by certain visionaries who have made up their minds that malevolence of soul must be an element of weakness in practical life, but the fact that its material strength was not equal to its arrogance. When arrogance finds an equivalent material power at its disposal, it is very far from ruining nations; witness Rome and the Prussia of Bismarck. The "clerks" who, thirty years ago, exhorted France to make herself the sole judge of her own actions and to despise eternal morality, showed that they possessed in the highest degree the perception of the national interest, insofar as that interest is wholly realist and has nothing to do with disinterested passion. It remains to be seen, once more, whether the function of the "clerks" is to serve this sort of interests.

But the modern "clerks" have held up universal truth to the scorn of mankind, as well as universal morality. Here the "clerks" have positively shown genius in their effort to serve the passions of the laymen. It is obvious that truth is a great impediment to those who wish to set themselves up as distinct; from the very moment when they accept truth, it condemns them to be conscious of themselves in a universal. What a joy for them to learn that this universal is a mere phantom, that there exist only particular truths, "Lorraine truths, Provençal truths, Brittany truths, the harmony of which in the course of centuries constitutes what is beneficial, respectable, *true in France*" (the neighbor similarly speaks of what is *true in Germany*), that in other words Pascal had the mind of a clown, and that what is true on one side of the Pyrenees may perfectly well be error on the other side! Humanity hears the same teaching about the classes and learns that there is a bourgeois truth and a working-class truth; better still, that the functioning of our minds should be different according to whether we are working men or bourgeois. The source of your troubles (Sorel teaches the working classes) is that you do not think in the mental way suited to your class. His disciple, Johannet, says the same thing to the capitalist class. Perhaps we shall soon see the results of this truly supreme art of the "clerks" in exasperating the feeling of their differences among the classes.

* * * * * *

(B) The "clerks" praise attachment to the practical, and denounce love of the spiritual.

But the "clerks" with their doctrines have inflamed the realism of the laymen in other ways besides praising the particular and denouncing the universal. At the very top of the scale of moral values they place the possession of concrete advantages, of material power and the means by which they are procured; and they hold up to scorn the pursuit of truly spiritual advantages, of non-practical or disinterested values.

This they have done, first of all, as regards the State. For twenty centuries the "clerks" preached to the world that the State should be just; now they proclaim that the State should be strong and should care nothing about being just. (Remember the attitude of the chief French teachers during the Dreyfus affair.) Convinced that the strength of the State depends upon authority, they defend autocratic systems, arbitrary government, the reason of State, the religions which teach blind submission to authority, and they cannot sufficiently denounce all institutions based on liberty and discussion. This denunciation of liberalism, notably by the vast majority of contemporary men of letters, will be one of the things in this age most astonishing to History, especially on the part of the French. With their eyes fixed on the powerful State, they have praised the State disciplined in the Prussian manner, where every one has his post, and under orders from above, labours for the greatness of the nation, without there being any place left for particular wills. Owing to their cult of the powerful State (and also for other reasons I shall mention later), they want the military element to preponderate in the State, they want it to have a right to privileges and they want the civil element to agree to this right. (See *L'Appel au Soldat*, and the declarations of numerous writers during the Dreyfus affair.) It is certainly something new to see men of thought preaching the abasement of the toga before the sword, especially in the country of Montesquieu and Renan. And then they preach that the State should be strong and contemptuous of justice, above all in its relations with other States. To this end they praise in the head of the State the will to aggrandisement, the desire for "strong frontiers," the effort to keep his neighbours under his domination. And they glorify those means which to them seem likely to attain these ends, *i.e.* sudden aggression, trickery, bad faith, contempt for treaties. This apology for Machiavellianism has inspired all the German historians for the past fifty years, and in France it is professed by very influential teachers, who exhort France to venerate her kings because they are supposed to have been models of the purely practical spirit, exempt from all respect for any silly justice in their relations with their neighbours.

The novelty of this attitude among the "clerks" can best be displayed by quoting the famous answer of Socrates to the realist in the *Gorgias*:

> In the persons of Themistocles, Cimon and Pericles, you praise men who made their fellow citizens good cheer, by serving them with everything they desired without caring to teach them what is good and right in food. They have enlarged the State, cry the Athenians, but they do not see that this enlargement is nothing but a swelling, a tumour filled with corruption. This is all that has been achieved by these former politicians by filling the city with ports, arsenals, walls, tributes, and the like follies, and by not adding Temperance and Justice.

* * * * * *

On their own showing, many modern "clerks" have adopted these realist doctrines because they want to have done with the moral disarray into which they are thrown by the spectacle of philosophies, "none of which bring certainty," and which all collapse upon each other as they cry to heaven their contradictory absolutes. There again the "clerk's" political attitude is the result of a great decline in his intellectual discipline, whether we consider that this decline is shown by his belief that any philosophy can bring certainty, or whether we think that it lies in his inability to stand upright on the ruins of the schools, devoting himself to reason, which is above all the schools, and is their judge.

I shall also admit as one other cause of realism in the modern "clerks" the irritation produced in them by the teaching of some of their predecessors—I mean certain masters of the year 1848, with their visionary idealism, their belief that justice and love were suddenly about to become the essence of the soul of nations, an irritation greatly increased by seeing the dreadful contrast between these idyllic prophecies and the events which followed them. Nevertheless, the point to remember is that the modern "clerks" replied to these errors by hurling anathemas at every sort of idealism, whether visionary or not, thereby showing an incapacity to distinguish between species, an inability to rise above passion to judgement. And this is but one other aspect of their loss of the good manners of the mind.

Let me recapitulate the causes for this change in the "clerks": The imposition of political interests on all men without any exception; the growth of consistency in matters apt to feed realist passions; the desire and the possibility for men of letters to play a political part; the need in the interests of their own fame for them to play the game of a class which is daily becoming more anxious; the increasing tendency of the "clerks" to become bourgeois and to take on the vanities of that class; the perfecting of their Romanticism; the decline of their knowledge of antiquity and of their intellectual discipline. It will be seen that these causes arise from certain phenomena which are most profoundly and generally characteristic of the present age. The political realism of the "clerks," far from being a superficial fact due to the caprice of an order of men, seems to me bound up with the very essence of the modern world.

15
Morality and Literature

by

Simone Weil

The two articles reprinted here are: I. *"Morale et Littérature"* (under the pseudonym Emile Novis), and II. *"Lettre sur les reponsabilités de la littérature"*, which appeared in *Cahiers du Sud*, No. 263, Jan. 1944, and No. 310, 1951, respectively. The translations are from *On Science, Necessity, and The Love of God* (London, Oxford University Press, 1968) by Richard Rees, and are reprinted by permission of Peters Fraser and Dunlop, London.

I

othing is so beautiful and wonderful, nothing is so continually fresh and surprising, so full of sweet and perpetual ecstasy, as the good. No desert is so dreary, monotonous, and boring as
evil. This is the truth about authentic good and evil. With fictional good
and evil it is the other way round. Fictional good is boring and flat, while
fictional evil is varied and intriguing, attractive, profound, and full of
charm.

This is because there are necessities and impossibilities in reality
which do not obtain in fiction, any more than the law of gravity to which
we are subject controls what is represented in a picture. In the space
that separates heaven from earth, things fall easily and indeed inevitably
whenever they are not supported; they never rise, or only a very little
and by painful contrivance. A man coming down a ladder, who misses
a step and falls, is either a sad or an uninteresting sight, even the first
time we see it. But if a man were walking in the sky as though it were a
ladder, going up into the clouds and coming down again, he could do it
every hour of every day and we would never be tired of watching. It is
the same with pure good; for a necessity as strong as gravity condemns
man to evil and forbids him any good, or only within the narrowest limits and laboriously obtained and soiled and adulterated with evil; except
when the supernatural appears on earth, which suspends the operation
of terrestrial necessity. But if I paint a picture of a man walking up into
the air it has no interest. That is a thing which is only interesting if it really happens. Unreality takes away all value from the good.

A man walking in the ordinary way is a sight of no interest, whereas men wildly jumping and leaping about would intrigue me for a few
minutes. But if I notice that both the one and the others are going bare-
foot on red-hot coals my reactions change. The jumping and leaping
become frightful and unbearable to watch and, at the same time, behind
the horror, tedious and monotonous, whereas my attention becomes
passionately fixed upon the man who is walking naturally. Thus it is that
evil, so long as it is fictional, acquires interest from the variety of forms
it can assume, which then seem to spring form pure fancy. But the necessity which is inseparable from reality completely cancels this interest.
The simplicity which makes the fictional good something insipid and
unable to hold the attention becomes, in the real good, an unfathomable
marvel.

It seems therefore, that immorality is inseparable from literature, which chiefly consists of the fictional. It is quite wrong to reproach writers for being immoral unless one reproaches them at the same time for being writers, as there were people in the seventeenth century with the courage to do. Writers with pretensions to high morality are no less immoral than the others, they are merely worse writers. In them as in the others, whatever they do and in spite of themselves, good is tedious and evil is more or less attractive. One might, therefore, on these grounds, condemn the whole of literature *en bloc*. And why not? Writers and devoted readers will cry out that immorality is not an aesthetic criterion. But they must prove, as they have never done, that aesthetic criteria are the only ones applicable to literature. Since readers are not a separate animal species and since the people who read are the same ones who perform a great many other functions, it is impossible for literature to be exempted from the categories of good and evil to which all human activities are referred. Every activity is related to good and evil twice over: by its performance and by its principle. Thus a book may on the one hand be well or badly written and on the other hand it may originate either from good or from evil.

But it is not only in literature that fiction generates immorality. It does it also in life itself. For the substance of our life is almost exclusively composed of fiction. We fictionalize our future; and, unless we are heroically devoted to the truth, we fictionalize our past, refashioning it to our taste. We do not study other people; we invent what they are thinking, saying and doing. Reality provides us with some raw material, just as novelists often take a theme from a news item, but we envelop it in a fog in which, as in all fiction, values are reversed, so that evil is attractive and good is tedious. If reality administers a hard enough shock to awaken us for an instant, by contact with a saint, for example, or by falling into the world of destitution or crime, or some other such experience, it is then and only then that we feel for a moment the horrible monotony of evil and the unfathomable marvel of good. But we soon relapse into the waking dream peopled by our fictions.

There is something else which has the power to awaken us to the truth. It is the works of writers of genius, or at least of those with genius of the very first order and when it has reached its full maturity. They are outside the realm of fiction and they release us from it. They give us, in the guise of fiction, something equivalent to the actual density of the real, that density which life offers us every day but which we are unable to grasp because we are amusing ourselves with lies.

Although the works of these men are made out of words there is present in them the force of gravity which governs our souls. It is present and manifest. In our souls, although this gravity is often felt, it is disguised by the very effects it produces; submission to evil is always accompanied by error and falsehood. The man falling down the slope of cruelty or error cannot discern what is the force that impels him nor the relations between it and all the other external conditions. In the words assembled by genius several slopes are simultaneously visible and perceptible, placed in their true relations, but the listener or reader does not descend any of them. He feels gravity in the way we feel it when we look over a precipice, if we are safe and not subject to vertigo. He perceives the unity and the diversity of its forms in this architecture of the abyss. It is in this way that in the *Iliad* the slope of victory and the slope of defeat are manifest and simultaneously perceptible, as they never are for a soldier occupied in fighting. This sense of gravity, which only genius can impart, is found in the drama of Aeschylus and Sophocles, in certain plays of Shakespeare, in Racine's *Phèdre* alone among French tragedies, in several comedies of Molière, in the *Grand Testament* of Villon. There, good and evil appear in their truth. Those poets had genius, and it was a genius oriented toward the good. There are also demoniacal geniuses; and they too have their maturity. But since the maturity of genius is conformity to the true relations of good and evil, the work which represents maturity of demoniacal genius is silence. Rimbaud is its example and symbol.

The sole *raison d'être* of all those writers who are not possessed by a genius of the very highest order in its full maturity is to constitute the milieu within which such a genius will one day appear. It is this function alone that justifies their existence, which ought otherwise to be prevented because of the immorality to which the nature of things condemns them. To reproach a writer for this immorality is to reproach him for having no genius, or only genius of the second order, if such an expression makes sense, or a still undeveloped genius. If he lacks genius it is not his fault, in a sense; but in another sense it is his one crime. It is completely vain to seek a remedy for the immorality of literature. The only remedy is genius, and the source of genius is beyond the scope of our efforts.

But what can and ought to be corrected, in view of this very fact of irremediable immorality, is the usurpation by writers of the function of spiritual guidance, for which they are totally unsuited. Only writers of the highest order of genius in their full maturity are fit to exercise those functions. As for all the other writers, unless they have a philosophic bent in addition to a literary one, which is rare, their conceptions about life and the world and their opinions on current problems can have no interest at all, and it is absurd that they should be called upon to express them. This abuse dates from the eighteenth century, and especially from romanticism, and it has introduced into literature a Messianic afflatus wholly detrimental to its artistic purity. Formerly, writers were domestics in great men's households, and although this position sometimes caused very painful situations it was much more favourable than the Messianic delusion, not only to the moral health of writer and public, but also to the art of literature itself.

It is only within the last fifty or twenty-five years that we have seen the gravest possible effects of this usurpation, because it is only since then that it has extended to the masses. No doubt there has always been a slight diffusion of bad literature, oral or written, among the people. But formerly it had an antidote in the things of pure beauty which impregnated popular life—religious ceremonies, prayer, song, story, and dance. And above all, it was without authority. But during the last quarter of a century all the authority associated with the function of spiritual guidance, usurped by men of letters, has seeped down into the lowest publications. Because from these publications up to the highest literary production there was continuity, and the public knew it. In the one milieu of literary men, in which no one ever refused to shake anyone else's hand,[1] were to be found those who occupied themselves exclusively with the lowest publications, and their occasional collaborators, and also our greatest names. Between a poem by Valéry and an advertisement for a beauty cream promising a rich marriage to anyone who uses it there was at no point a breach of continuity. So as a result of literature's spiritual usurpation a beauty cream advertisement possessed, in the eyes of village girls, the authority that was formerly attached to the words of priests. Is it surprising that we should have sunk to where we now are? To have permitted that state of affairs is a crime for which all who can hold a pen should bear the responsibility as a remorse.

For centuries the function of director of conscience had been exclusively in the hands of priests. They often performed it atrociously badly, as witness the fires of the Inquisition, but at least they had some title to it. In reality it is only the great saints who can perform it, as it is only the greatest geniuses among writers. But all priests, in virtue of

---

1 This may be a reminiscence of an occurrence related by Saint-Simon, *Mémoires* (Pléiade ed.), t.vi, p. 1062, and which Proust has Swann recount in *Swann's Way* (London, Chatto & Windus, 1992), p. 29.

their profession, speak in the name of the saints and look to them for inspiration and try to imitate and follow them, and principally the one veritable saint, who is Christ. Or if they do not, as in fact often happens, they are failing in their duty. But in so far as they do it they are able to communicate more good that they themselves possess. A writer, on the other hand, has only himself to fall back on; he may be influenced by a number of other writers, but he cannot draw his inspiration from them.

When, as a result of what was called the Enlightenment in the eighteenth century, the priests had in fact almost entirely lost this function of guidance, their place was taken by writers and scientists. In both cases it is equally absurd. Mathematics, physics, and biology are as remote from spiritual guidance as the art of arranging words. When that function is usurped by literature and science it proves that there is no longer any spiritual life. Numerous signs today seem to indicate that the usurpation by writers and scientists has come to an end, although the appearance of it still lingers. This should be a matter for rejoicing, were there not reason to fear that they will be replaced by something much worse than themselves.

But the works of authentic genius from past ages remain, and are available to us. Their contemplation is the ever-flowing source of an inspiration which may legitimately guide us. For this inspiration, if we know how to receive it, tends—as Plato said—to make us grow wings to overcome gravity.

II

The allusion by Gros to the controversy about the responsibility of writers[2] impels me to return to the subject, in defence of a point of view opposed to that of the review and of almost everyone I sympathize with, and seeming, unfortunately, to resemble the one held by people for whom I feel no sympathy at all.

I believe in the responsibility of the writers of recent years for the disaster of our time. By that I don't mean only the defeat of France; the disaster of our time extends much further. It extends to the whole world,

---

2 The controversy was whether the amorality of modern literature was a contributing factor in the disasters of 1940 and, more generally, in the demoralization of modern life. Simone Weil is referring to two articles by Léon-Gabriel Gros, "*La poésie demeure*" and "*Actualité de la poésie*" in *Cahiers du Sud*, October 1940 and March 1941 respectively. (This letter was probably written a year or so after the defeat of France. Simone Weil died in 1943.) Ed.

that is to say, to Europe, to America, and to the other continents in so far as Western influence has penetrated them.

It is true, as Mauriac has observed, that the best contemporary books are very little read. But the responsibility of writers cannot be measured by circulation figures. For literature has immense prestige. This was shown by the efforts which used to be made by certain political bodies to obtain the support of well-known writers' names for demagogic purposes. And even those who have never heard the celebrated writers' names feel the prestige of the literature which is unknown to them. People have never read so much as today. They don't read books but they read mediocre or bad periodicals. These periodicals penetrate everywhere, in village and suburb; and, thanks to the literary customs of our time, there is no break of continuity between the worst of these periodicals and the best of our writers. This fact, which is known or, rather, confusedly felt by the public, endows the basest publicity rackets in their eyes with all the prestige of high literature. In recent years there have been some unbelievable degradations; for example, advice on love affairs by well-known writers. Of course they didn't all degrade themselves in this way; far from it. But those who did so degrade themselves were not disowned or repulsed by the others; they continued to enjoy the esteem accorded to their profession. Such easy morals in literature, such tolerance of baseness, involve our most eminent writers in the responsibility for demoralizing little country girls who have never left their villages and have never heard the writers' names.

But writers have a more direct responsibility.

The essential characteristic of the first half of the twentieth century is the growing weakness, and almost the disappearance, of the idea of value. This is one of those rare phenomena which seem, as far as one can tell, to be really new in human history, though it may be, of course, that it has occurred before during periods which have since vanished in oblivion, as may also happen to our period. It has appeared in many domains outside literature, and even in all of them. In industry, the substitution of quantity for quality; among the workers, the discrediting of skilled workmanship; among students, the substitution of diplomas for culture as the aim of education. Even in science there is no longer any criterion of value since classical science was discarded.[3] But above all

---

3 The distinction drawn between 20th century science and classical science by Simone Weil in other writings of hers (see, for example, the volume in which these translations appeared), is that the former is directed to practical, utilitarian ends and concerned with control of the environment, whereas classical science was inspired by the desire to

it was the writers who were the guardians of the treasure that has been lost; and some of them now take pride in having lost it.

Dadaism and surrealism are extreme cases; they represented the intoxication of total licence, the intoxication in which the mind wallows when it has made a clean sweep of value and surrendered to the immediate. The good is the pole towards which the human spirit is necessarily oriented, not only in action but in every effort, including the effort of pure intelligence. The surrealists have set up non-oriented thought as a model; they have chosen the total absence of value as their supreme value. Men have always been intoxicated by licence, which is why, throughout history, towns have been sacked. But there has not always been a literary equivalent for the sacking of towns. Surrealism is such an equivalent.

The other writers of the same and the preceding period have gone less far, but almost all of them—with perhaps three or four exceptions—have been more or less affected by the same disease, the enfeeblement of the sense of value. Such words as spontaneity, sincerity, gratuitousness, richness, enrichment—words which imply an almost total indifference to contrasts of value—have come more often from their pens than words which contain a reference to good and evil. Moreover, this latter class of words has become degraded, especially those which refer to the good, as Valéry remarked some years ago. Words like virtue, nobility, honour, honesty, generosity, have become almost impossible to use or else they have acquired bastard meanings; language is no longer equipped for legitimately praising a man's character. It is slightly, but only slightly, better equipped for praising a mind; the very word mind, and the words intelligence, intelligent, and others like them, have also become degraded. The fate of words is a touchstone of the progressive weakening of the idea of value, and although the fate of words does not depend upon writers one cannot help attributing a special responsibility to them, since words are their business.

The work of Bergson has been much and rightly praised in our day, and a lot has been said about its influence on the thought and literature of the period. Now, at the centre of the philosophy on which his first three books are based there is a conception which is totally alien to any considerations of value, namely, the conception of Life. The attempt to make this philosophy a foundation for Catholicism was very ill-judged, and in any case it was unnecessary because Catholicism has

know and to understand the phenomena of the organic and inorganic worlds; namely, what we call, respectively, applied and pure science. Ed.

older foundations. And then there is the work of Proust, which makes many attempts to analyse non-oriented states of the soul; in his work the good only appears at those rare moments when, by the effect either of memory or of beauty, we are allowed a glimpse of eternity through the veil of time. One could make similar comments on many writers before and still more after 1914. In a general way, the literature of the twentieth century is essentially psychological; and psychology consists in describing states of the soul by displaying them all on the same plane without any discrimination of value, as though good and evil were external to them, as though the effort towards the good could be absent at any moment from the thought of any man.

Writers do not have to be professors of morals, but they do have to express the human condition. And nothing concerns human life so essentially, for every man at every moment, as good and evil. When literature becomes deliberately indifferent to the opposition of good and evil it betrays its function and forfeits all claim to excellence. Racine laughed at the Jansenists in his youth, but he was no longer laughing at them when he wrote *Phèdre*, and *Phèdre* is his masterpiece. From this point of view it is not true that French literature possesses continuity. It is not true that Rimbaud and those who have followed him (if we except certain passages of the *Saison en Enfer*) are a continuation of Villon. What if Villon did steal? In his case the act of stealing was perhaps the result of necessity or perhaps a sin; it was not a thrill or a gratuitous act. The sense of good and evil permeates all his verse, as it permeates all that is not irrelevant to man's destiny.

It is true that there is a certain kind of morality which is even more alien to good and evil than amorality is. Those who are now blaming the eminent writers are worth infinitely less than they, and the 'moral revival' which certain people wish to impose would be much worse than the condition it is meant to cure. If our present suffering ever leads to a revival, this will not be brought about through slogans but in silence and moral loneliness, through pain, misery, and terror, in the profoundest depths of each man's spirit.

16
An Artist's Creed

by

Albert Camus

From Albert Camus: *Discours de Suède*. Nobel Prize speech delivered at Stockholm City Hall on December 10, 1957. Translated by J.E.G. Dixon ©. The French text is used by the gracious permission of The Nobel Foundation 1957©.

*I*n accepting the distinction which your free Academy has been so good as to honour me with, my gratitude was the more deeply felt as I considered how far the award exceeded my personal merits. Every man, and *a fortiori* every artist, desires recognition. I too desire it. It was not possible for me to learn of your decision, however, without comparing the repercussion it caused with what I really am. How could a man, who is still relatively young,[1] and accustomed to living in the solitude of his study or the sanctuary of friendship, and whose only assets are his questionings and a work still in progress—how could such a man not feel a sort of panic on learning of a judgment which thrust him suddenly, alone and reduced to himself, into the centre of a harsh spotlight? And in what spirit could he accept that honour at a moment when other writers in Europe, including some of the greatest, are reduced to silence, and at the very time when his native land is passing through an endless calamity?[2]

I have known this disarray and inner turmoil. In order to find some peace, I have had, in short, to come to terms with an over-generous providence. And since I could not measure up to it on the strength of my unaided merits, I have found no other recourse than what has sustained me, in the most adverse circumstances, throughout my life: the idea I have of my art and the function of the writer. Permit me to tell you, in a spirit of gratitude and friendship, and as simply as I know how, what that idea is.

For myself, I cannot live without my art. But I have never set that art above all else. If it is necessary to me it is because it does not set itself apart from any man, and enables me to live, such as I am, on equal terms with all. Art is not, in my view, a thing to be enjoyed alone. It is a means of moving the greatest number of people by offering them a privileged portrayal of common sufferings and joys. It requires the artist not to isolate himself; it subjects him to the most elementary and universal truth. And, often, the man who has chosen to follow the artist's life because he felt he was different, very quickly learns that he may cultivate his art, and his difference, only by acknowledging what he has in common with others. The artist fashions himself in that constant give-and-take between himself and others, mid-way between the beauty he cannot live

---

1 Camus, born in 1913, was 44 at the time. Ed.

2 The Author is referring to the Algerian troubles. From 1939 to 1958 Camus wrote many articles on Algeria; they were published in *Actuelles III* (Paris, Gallimard). See also *Resistance, Rebellion and Death* (New York, Alfred A. Knopf, 1964), translated by Justin O'Brien, pp. 109-153, and note 1, p. 123.

without and the community from which he cannot detach himself. That is why true artists hold nothing in scorn; their task is to understand, not to judge. And, if they are to take sides in this world, it can only be that of a society in which, to borrow Nietzsche's fine saying, it will no longer be the judge who prevails, but the creator, whether he works with his hands or his mind.

The rôle of the writer, by the same token, cannot be divorced from onerous duties. By definition, he cannot today put himself in the service of those who make history: he is at the service of those caught in its moils. Failing that, he will be alone and cut off from his art. All the armies of tyranny, with their millions of men, will not tear him from his solitude, even if—especially if—he deigns to follow their way. But the silence of a prisoner, subjected to humiliations at the other end of the world, is enough to draw the writer from exile, whenever, at least, amidst the privileges of freedom, he manages not to forget that silence and gives it resounding expression through his art.

No one of us is big enough for such a calling. But the writer, in all the circumstances of his life—be he unknown or provisionally famous, whether enslaved in an iron tyranny or free for a time to make his voice heard—can rediscover the spirit of a living community which will justify him, on the sole condition that he take up, as far as possible, the twofold responsibility which constitutes the greatness of his craft: the service of Truth and of Freedom.

Since it is his vocation to unite the greatest possible number of men, he can have no truck with lies and servitude, which, wherever they prevail, proliferate the solitudes of men.

Whatever our personal shortcomings, the nobility of our craft will unfailingly be rooted in this twofold commitment, difficult as it is to sustain: the refusal to lie about what one knows, and resistance to oppression.

For over twenty years of a demented history, helplessly adrift, like all men of my age, in the convulsions of our times, I have been sustained in this way by the obscure feeling that today writing was an honour, because it was an act of obligation, and not an obligation merely to write. In particular it obligated me, such as I was and according to my strength, with all who lived the same history, to bear the misfortune and the hope that we shared. Those men who, being born at the beginning of the First World War, were twenty when Hitler's régime and the first revolutionary courts were being established, and whose education was completed by their then being faced with the Spanish Civil War, the Second World

War, the concentration camps, and a Europe of torture and imprisonment—those men are required today to bring up their sons and produce their works in a world threatened with nuclear destruction. No one, I suppose, can expect them to be optimists. It is even my opinion, in fact, that we must understand the error of those who, overwhelmed by despair, have claimed the right to dishonour and plunged into the nihilistic ideologies of our age—without ever ceasing to combat them. The fact remains, though, that most of us, in my country and in Europe, have rejected nihilism and set out in quest of a legitimate order. They have had to fashion for themselves an art of living in an age of catastrophe, in order to be born anew, and then to struggle fearlessly against the instinct of death which stalks our history.

Every generation believes, no doubt, that it has the mission to remake the world. Mine knows however that it will not remake it. The task it has, greater still perhaps, is to ensure that the world does not destroy itself. This generation—which has inherited a degenerate history compounded of discredited revolutions, technology gone mad, dead gods, and outworn ideologies; in which mediocre powers can today destroy everything but no longer convince; and in which intelligence has debased itself so low as to serve as lackey to hatred and oppression—this generation, starting from its negative values alone, has had to re-establish in and around itself a little of what makes it worth living and dying for. Faced with a world threatened with disintegration, in which our grand inquisitors would establish the kingdoms of death once and for all, this generation knows that it has the task, in a kind of hectic race against time, of restoring between nations a peace which is not the peace of slavery, of again reconciling labour and culture, and of building a new ark of the covenant with all men.

It is not certain whether it can ever accomplish this great task; but what is sure is that it has already taken up the twofold challenge of Truth and Freedom throughout the world, and has shown it can die for it without hatred. It is this generation which deserves to be saluted and encouraged wherever it is met with, and especially wherever it accepts sacrifice. It is to this generation in any event that, confident of your heartfelt approval, I would pass on the honour you have just bestowed on me.

By the same token, after asserting the nobility of the writer's craft, I would have restored the writer to his true place, since he has no other distinctions than those he shares with his comrades-in-arms, vulnerable yet unyielding, unjust yet with a passion for justice, constructing his work openly and without shame or pride, ever divided between pain and beauty, and dedicated to creating from his twofold being the works he tries obstinately to erect in the destructive path of history.

Who, after that, could expect pat solutions and high-sounding moral lessons from him? Truth is mysterious, and difficult to live by as it is exalting. We have to strive for those twin goals: the way will be arduous but we resolute, and mindful in advance of our shortcomings over so long a journey. What writer would thenceforth, in all conscience, dare to set himself up as a preacher of virtue? For myself, I must reiterate once more that I have no part in that. I have never been able to forego the light, the joy of being, the life of liberty in which I grew up. But while this nostalgia explains many of my failures and mistakes, it has doubtless helped me to a better understanding of my craft, it helps me still today to take my place, unsteadily, beside all those silent men who only bear with the life that is made for them in this world because of the memory or the return of free and fleeting joys.

Thus reminded of what I am in reality, of my limitations and my debts, as of my exacting credo, I feel the freer to point out to you, finally, the extent and the generosity of the distinction you have conferred upon me; freer also to tell you that I should like to accept it as an homage to all who, while having shared in the same struggle, have received no privilege for it, but who have on the contrary known grief and persecution.

It remains only for me to thank you with heartfelt sincerity, and to make publicly before you here, in personal acknowledgement of gratitude, the same time-honoured vow of fidelity that every true artist makes to himself, every day, in silence.

Index

Bernard, see Saint Bernard
Bernini 52, 156
Bismarck 241, 249
Bloy 116
Boccaccio 205
Boileau 52-3, 56, 58, 80, 91, 93, 153, 155-56
bon sens 45, 58
Bossuet 49, 53, 58, 61, 80, 85-87, 100, 115, 125, 139, 237
Bourdaloue 87, 100
Bourget 246
Boylesve 113, 116
Brandès 119
Brasillach 230
Brémond 57, 212
Britain 33, 203, 226 (see also England, Great Britain)
Brittany 32, 140, 196, 249
Buffon 61, 88, 165, 238
Burckhardt 204
Burgundians 32, 35, 141
Burgundy 53, 141, 205
Byron 110

C
Caboche 238
Calas (Jean) 27, 240
Caldéron 84
Calvin 105, 141
Camus, Albert 231
Caribbean 214
Carroll, David 230
Cartesianism 45, 53, 88, 129, 144, 165
Catalonia 72
Catherine (of Russia) 90
Catholicism 260
Catholics 147
Catullus 69

Céline 230
Celtic 32-33, 35-37, 164, 219
Celts 196
Cervantes 54, 84
Cézanne 191, 218
Chamfort 88, 98
chansons de geste 35, 39, 174, 202
Chanson de Roland 19-20, 35, 39, 203
Chanson de Saint Alexis 38
Characters 98
Charlemagne 20, 34
Charles II 90
Charles V 75
Charles VIII 24
Chartreuse de Parme 60
Chateaubriand 43, 64-5, 115, 238
Châtelet, Mme Du 61
Chaucer 39, 84
Chénier 55
Chesterfield 85
Chevalier 45
Chevalier au Lion 83
Childe Harold 74
chivalry 6, 67, 212
Chrétien de Troyes 83, 85, 142
Christ 25, 201, 202, 258 (see also Jesus)
Christendom 191, 204
Christian xv, 20-21, 23-24, 35, 41, 67, 69, 98, 143, 152, 157, 161, 191, 200, 204, 206. 216-17
Christianisme 65
Christianity 15, 20, 21, 23, 35, 41, 61, 65, 67, 69, 74, 87, 98, 143, 152, 157, 161, 172, 191, 200, 204, 206, 212, 216-17
Chrysostom 69, 74
Churchmen 170
Cicero 69

About the Author

Jack Dixon was born in England and following school joined the Royal Air Force to begin aircrew training in 1943. He gained his pilot's 'wings' too late for active combat and left the Service shortly after. He studied in France for a year before going to Merton College Oxford in 1949, graduating with an honours degree in Modern Languages. During his time at Oxford he flew with the University Air Squadron for 3 years. He emigrated to Canada in 1952, and after five years with the Royal Canadian Air Force, he took his PhD at Stanford, in 1963-65, and taught French Language and Literature at the University of Winnipeg for 31 years, retiring to Victoria, on Vancouver Island in 1991. He has published four previous books, of which may be mentioned *Concordance des Œuvres complètes de François Rabelais* (Genève, Droz, 1992) and *Dowding and Churchill. The Dark Side of the Battle of Britain* (Barnsley, Pen and Sword, 2008). In 1959 he married his wife, Rika who, was born in Arnhem, Holland. They have a daughter, Jacqueline, a water resource management officer in Manitoba. The author is currently finishing a Memoir of his wife's and her family's ordeals in Holland during the War; and is preparing a book on disobeying orders in war.